"博学而笃志,切问而近思。"
（《论语》）

博晓古今,可立一家之说；
学贯中西,或成经国之才。

复旦博学·复旦博学·复旦博学·复旦博学·复旦博学·复旦博学

主编简介

高凌云，复旦大学法学院教授，美国纽约州、俄勒冈州律师，美国纽约大学法学院Hauser Global Senior Fellow（海外高级研究员），美国圣约翰大学法学院国际法与比较法研究中心客座高级研究员，曾任美国凯斯西储大学、圣约翰大学和杜兰大学客座教授，为美国JD/LLM学生讲授国际商事交易法、中国商法和比较信托法等三门课程，并先后应邀在比利时根特大学法学院、美国哈佛法学院、加州大学尔湾分校、纽约大学、康奈尔大学、哥伦比亚法学院、福德姆大学以及国际信托协会与美国纽约律师公会等发表公开演讲或做有关信托法和商法的学术报告。出版 *Chinese Business Law*（合著，美国Thomson West法律出版公司）、《被误读的信托——信托法原论》《中华人民共和国民法总则（中英对照）》《金融创新与监管前沿文集》等专著、译著和教材，并在国内外法学期刊发表信托法与比较法内容相关论文。主要研究与授课领域为英美法、信托法、国际金融法、国际商法和法律英语。

博学 法学系列

英美法判例读写教程

高凌云　编著

内容提要

本书主要介绍学习英美法的方法,包括如何阅读英美法判例及如何撰写英文法律文件。第一部分介绍英美法律制度的基础知识,第二部分介绍判例法的遵循先例原则及其适用,第三部分详细介绍判例阅读与分析路径,以及撰写案情精要的方法,第四部分有关法律文件的撰写要点与格式。本书的特点之一是配有大量的判例与写作范例,以及写作材料,可供读者练习,实用性较强。二是采用原版判例,语言准确,并辅以适当的中文解释,减轻初学者的学习难度。三是本书的内容,对于英美法的任何学科都是敲门砖,因为本书的主题是学习方法,而不是只针对某一法律领域。四是本书适应的读者群比较广泛,既可以用作法科学生学习英美法或比较法全英文课程的教材,也可以用于法律英语课程的教学,还可以为其他对英美法感兴趣的读者提供全面的英美法的知识。对于计划到英美法系国家攻读法学位的读者而言,本书是一个很好的预备;而对于没有计划出国学习的读者而言,本书是可以据此一窥全豹的工具。

前　言

随着全球经济一体化的发展以及法律在我国地位的不断提升,法律英语的学习成为我国法科学生的必修课以及大多数综合大学学生的选修课。法律英语应包括两个层面:一是以英语表达的外国法,主要以英美普通法为主;二是以英语表达的中国法,主要包括中国法条英译以及中国法律概念、法律文献的英译等。而要做到能够准确将我国的法条与法律文献翻译成英语,首先必须了解在英美法系和其他英语国家是否有类似的法律概念以及这些概念是否有约定俗成的表达方式,否则即便把我国的法律概念翻译成英文也可能牛头不对马嘴。因此,学习英美法是将我国法律准确翻译成英语的基础。

一般而言,学习英语要同时注重听说读写,学习法律英语也是如此。

以前网络不发达,寻找原版听力材料比较困难,只能依靠国内的有声出版物或者电台。而有声出版物大多经过编辑,可能失去原汁原味;收听电台也有很多不便,诸如信号问题以及时间问题。现在我们处于网络时代,通过网络很容易找到各种音频和视频资料,英美国家的有些法院也把庭审资料放到官方网站。因此,我们有条件听到未经编删的原版资料,"听"的资源问题比较容易解决,只要我们坚持不懈地听就能够提高法律英语学习中的听力水平。另外,通过参加法律英语课或者其他全英语法律课的学习,在课堂上一直听老师和同学们用英语讨论法律问题,这本身也是提高听力的一个好办法。

"说"对于中国学生一直是个大问题,因为缺少说的环境,且通过上课来锻炼说的能力也很有限。由于上课时间较短,班上同学可能较多,不大可能轮到每个人发言。我建议有心练习口语的同学在课下自己组织类似"英语角"等活动,作为法科学生,也可以积极组织或参加英美法模拟法庭,用英语辩论。当然,在课堂上应该主动积极用英语发言。曾有学生告诉我,他们在连续上英语课或者全英语法律课之后,到食堂打饭时都不由自主对着打饭的阿姨说起英语来。这充分说明"说"的能力是完全可以培养的。

"读"和"写"对中国学生来说相对容易,尤其"读",我们同学的阅读能力一般都很强。可是法律英语的读和写与普通英语不同,因为面对的是英语法条、判例或法律文献,里面大量的法律词汇对英语是母语的学生而言也很难,何况我们的母语不是英语。因此,学习法律英语,一定要重视读和写。英美法的特点是以判例法为主,因而读案例就成为英美律师每天最重要的功课,而对于我们来说,也是学习英美法的基本功。能够读懂一般的英语并不一定能读懂案例。"写"也是如此,即便能够用英语写信,写短文,甚至写小说,却并不一定能够写法律文书,除了特殊的法律英语词汇外,法律文书的写作有其特殊的格式与要求。

因此,本书着重介绍如何阅读英美判例,如何撰写案例综述,如何用英语撰写一种最重要的法律文书——法律分析报告,又叫备忘录(memorandum)。本书的前身是《英美法:案例分析与法律写作》,曾在复旦大学法学院作为法律英语教材使用了6年多,且经过了超过1 000多名法科学生的验证,并于2006年荣获上海市优秀教材三等奖。2012年再版后,又经过了6年多的教学检验,成就了现在的版本。

感谢复旦大学出版社的张炼编辑对本书所做的贡献,她在本书稿的修订过程中认真细致,一丝不苟,提出了很多宝贵意见。另外,复旦大学法学院国际法专业2018级研究生管洁泉和丁伯韬同学在帮助审阅本书稿的同时还帮忙选定了一些较难的法律词汇并翻译成中文,复旦大学2015级本科生罗杰韬同学协助最后审稿,在此一并表示感谢。

限于篇幅,本书着重于案例分析,并不需要读者具备某一部门法的知识,因此适用性较强;然而这同时也是本书的短处,如果读者想要学习英美法中的部门法,例如英美合同法、侵权法等,仅仅看这本书是不够的。目前国内市场上有不少很好的法律英语教材,由浅入深地介绍英国或美国的各个部门法,并附有词语解释和翻译练习等,适合非法科学生或者对自己的英语程度不够自信的同学使用。另外国内还出版了不少原版法律书的影印本,大都是英美等国法学院的教材,适合英语程度较高,又对某一部门法有特殊兴趣的同学学习。另外,复旦大学出版社于2016年7月出版的《英美合同侵权法(第二版)》作为本书的姊妹篇,针对合同法和侵权法这两门部门法,可供有心者配套学习。

我建议有志于提高法律英语能力并希望学习英美法的同学在学习本书的同时还可以根据自己的英语程度购买一本或一套其他法律英语教材,不在多,而在于把书从头读到尾。

最后,由于能力与时间所限,错误在所难免,敬请指正。

高凌云

2019年4月于纽约大学曼哈顿校区

lygao@fudan.edu.cn

CONTENTS

PART I INTRODUCTION TO COMMON LAW SYSTEM

Chapter 1 COMMON LAW ········· 003
  1.1 Law ········· 003
  1.2 Common Law ········· 004
  1.3 Law *versus* Equity ········· 007
  1.4 Statutory Law *versus* Case Law ········· 008
  1.5 Summary ········· 010
  Review Questions ········· 011

Chapter 2 COMMON LAW COURT SYSTEM ········· 012
  2.1 The English Court System ········· 012
    2.1.1 Magistrates' Courts — For Both Civil and Criminal Cases ········· 013
    2.1.2 County Courts — For Civil Cases Only ········· 013
    2.1.3 Crown Court — For Criminal Cases Only ········· 014
    2.1.4 High Court — For Both Civil and Criminal Cases ········· 015
    2.1.5 Court of Appeal — For Both Civil and Criminal Cases ········· 017
    2.1.6 Final Court of Appeals ········· 017
    2.1.7 European Court of Justice ········· 019
  2.2 The American Court System ········· 019
    2.2.1 The Federal Courts ········· 019
    2.2.2 State Courts ········· 021
  Review Questions ········· 025

Chapter 3 SOURCES OF LAW ········· 026
  3.1 Sources of Law in England ········· 026
    3.1.1 The European Union Law ········· 026
    3.1.2 Statutory law ········· 026
    3.1.3 Case Law ········· 027
  3.2 Sources of Law in the United States ········· 027
    3.2.1 Constitutions ········· 028
    3.2.2 Statutes ········· 028
    3.2.3 Administrative Regulations ········· 029
    3.2.4 Case Law ········· 029
  Review Questions ········· 030

Chapter 4　LEGAL PROCEEDINGS ········· 031
4.1　Commencement of the Proceeding — Pretrial ········· 032
    4.1.1　Filing with the Court: Complaint ········· 032
    4.1.2　Service of Process ········· 033
    4.1.3　The Response: Motion, Answer, and Reply ········· 033
    4.1.4　Discovery ········· 034
4.2　Trial Date and Jury Selection ········· 034
    4.2.1　Trial Date Assignment ········· 034
    4.2.2　Jury Selection ········· 035
    4.2.3　Preliminary Instructions of Law ········· 036
4.3　Trial ········· 036
    4.3.1　Opening Statements ········· 037
    4.3.2　Plaintiff's Case in Chief ········· 037
    4.3.3　Defendant's Case in Chief ········· 039
    4.3.4　Closing Arguments ········· 039
    4.3.5　Jury Instructions ········· 039
    4.3.6　Verdict ········· 040
    4.3.7　Motions ········· 041
    4.3.8　Judgment ········· 043
4.4　Appeal ········· 044
4.5　Summary ········· 045
Review Questions ········· 048

PART II　CASE LAW

Chapter 5　DOCTRINE OF *STARE DECISIS* ········· 051
5.1　Rule of Precedent ········· 051
5.2　Doctrine of *Stare Decisis* ········· 051
5.3　The Function of *Stare Decisis* ········· 053
5.4　Courts Affected by *Stare Decisis* ········· 057
    5.4.1　The Courts in England ········· 057
    5.4.2　The Courts in the United States ········· 058
5.5　Components of a Judicial Decision ········· 059
5.6　Types of Judicial Decisions ········· 060
    5.6.1　Majority Opinion ········· 060
    5.6.2　Dissenting Opinion ········· 061
    5.6.3　Concurring Opinion ········· 061
5.7　Different Ways to Use Precedents ········· 062
    5.7.1　Following Prior Precedents ········· 062
    5.7.2　Distinguishing Prior Precedents ········· 063
    5.7.3　Overruling Prior Precedents ········· 063
Review Questions ········· 064

Chapter 6　COMMON LAW REASONING ········· 065
6.1　Typical Types of Common Law Reasoning ········· 066

	6.1.1	Deductive and Inductive Reasoning	066
	6.1.2	Analogy and Distinction	066
	6.1.3	Arguments in Common Law Reasoning	068
6.2	Techniques and Arguments Used with Case Authorities		069
	6.2.1	Favorable Authorities	069
	6.2.2	Adverse Authorities	070
6.3	Illustration of the Common Law Reasoning		070
	6.3.1	Fletcher v. Rylands — The Establishment of the Rule	071
	6.3.2	Rylands v. Fletcher — Modification of the Rule	079
	6.3.3	Rickards v. Lothian — Exceptions to the Rule	085
	6.3.4	Read v. Lyons — Interpretation and Application of the Rule	094
	6.3.5	Turner v. Big Lake Oil Co. — The Impact of the Rule on the U.S. Courts	109
	6.3.6	Foster v. Preston Mill Co. — A Later Case Decided By a U.S. Court	125
	6.3.7	Siegler v. Kuhlman — Adoption of the Rylands Rule	131
	6.3.8	Clay v. Missouri Highway & Transportation Commission — New Development	146
Review Questions			157

Chapter 7 CASE REPORTING SYSTEMS 158
7.1	Law Reports in England		158
	7.1.1	Law Reports	158
	7.1.2	Format of a Case in the Law Reports	159
7.2	Case Reporters in the United States		162
	7.2.1	Case Reporters	162
	7.2.2	Case Digests	164
	7.2.3	Format of a Case in the Case Reporters	165
7.3	Case Names and Citations		169
	7.3.1	Case Names	169
	7.3.2	Case Citations	170
Review Questions			172

PART III CASE ANALYSIS

Chapter 8 CASE ANALYSIS 175
8.1	Basic Structure of a Judicial Opinion		175
	8.1.1	Different Types of Opinions	176
	8.1.2	Common Actions of a Court	178
	8.1.3	Essential Elements of an Opinion	180
8.2	Procedural History		183
8.3	Statement of Facts		185
8.4	Issue		188
8.5	Holding		190
8.6	Reasons and Policies		194

8.7　Judgment ·· 195
8.8　Summary ·· 195
8.9　Case Brief Exercises ·· 196
　　8.9.1　Exercise 1：Katko *v*. Briney ··· 196
　　8.9.2　Exercise 2：Palsgraf *v*. Long Island Railroad Co. ························· 204
　　8.9.3　Exercise 3：Barnes *v*. Treece ··· 218
8.10　Summary ·· 225
Review Questions ·· 226

PART IV　LEGAL DOCUMENT DRAFTING

Chapter 9　Memoranda Drafting ·· 229
9.1　Common Law Analyses ·· 229
9.2　Principles of Drafting ·· 231
9.3　Writing Techniques ··· 233
9.4　Elements of a Memorandum ·· 234
9.5　Heading ··· 240
9.6　Questions Presented ··· 241
9.7　Brief Answers ·· 244
9.8　Statement of Facts ·· 245
9.9　Discussion ·· 247
9.10　Conclusion ·· 250
9.11　Summary ·· 251
9.12　Drafting Exercise ··· 253
Review Questions ·· 258

REFERENCES ·· 259

PART I
INTRODUCTION TO COMMON LAW SYSTEM

legal system 法系

civil law system 大陆法系，指包括欧洲大陆大部分国家从19世纪初以罗马法为基础建立起来的、以1804年《法国民法典》和1896年《德国民法典》为代表的法律制度以及其他国家或地区仿效这种制度而建立的法律制度。它是西方国家中与英美法系并列的渊源久远和影响较大的法系，以制定法为判案依据。

written statute 成文法

common law system 共同法系，国内普遍译为普通法系，是以英国共同法为基础发展起来的法律的总称，指英国从11世纪起主要以源于日耳曼习惯法的共同法为基础，逐渐形成的一种独特的法律制度以及仿效英国的其他一些国家和地区的法律制度，产生于英国，后扩大到曾经是英国殖民地、附属国的许多国家和地区，是西方国家中与大陆法系并列的历史悠久和影响较大的法系，注重法典的延续性，以传统、判例和习惯为判案依据。

case law 判例法，是指由一个个实际案件中的司法判决所确立的原则和规则集合的总称，是一种区别于制定法或其他形式法律的法律渊源；从学理意义上来说，是由判例所构成的一套法理。

sources of law 法律渊源，指法律的创制方式和外部表现形式。

THERE are two main legal systems in the world: one is civil law system under which written statutes play an important role, and the other is common law system whereby case law has been in a dominant position. Chinese legal system roughly belongs to the civil law system because written statutes are the main sources of law in China, although some scholars would name it as an independent "Chinese Legal System." The differences between civil law system and common law system are not only reflected in the forms of the law (written statutes or case law), but also reflected in the methodologies of teaching and studying the law. While a law student in China normally learns the general theories of law and the framework of the written statutes, a law student in a common law country would read cases from the day he enters law school. Therefore, understanding and analyzing cases is one of the most fundamental skills that a common law lawyer must possess. This book will focus on common law case analysis and legal writing, and Part I will introduce the basic features of common law.

Chapter 1
COMMON LAW

1.1 Law

What is the law? Even experienced judges, law professors, or lawyers may not be able to give an answer to it right away. Even if they may, the definitions given by different people are different. It is almost impossible to give an accurate definition of "law" that covers every aspect of it. There is simply not a unified or all-inclusive definition of law. It is probably wiser not to probe the exact meaning of law; instead, it is more important to understand what the law is mainly comprised of, who made the law, and what will happen if the law is not observed.

Among the various definitions and descriptions of law, one commonality is that they all agree laws are rules. There are many rules in our life but only the legal rules are laws. *Webster's New World Dictionary* defines a legal rule as

a) a regulation or guide established by a court governing court practice and procedure;
b) a declaration, order, etc. made by a judge or court in deciding a specific question or point of law;
c) a legal principle or maxim.

This description of legal rules is not complete because in common law system legal rules require the participation of government in their creation and enforcement and may be made by the legislature, the executive, and the judiciary. The laws made by the legislature are called statutes or acts; the laws made by the executive are named administrative regulations or administrative rules; and the laws made by the judiciary in the course of deciding cases are known as case law. The executive and the judicial courts have power to enforce the law. Any disputes will be

observe 遵守

rule 规则

regulation 规章,条例
guide 指南,指导
court 法院;法庭
procedure 程序
declaration 声明
order 命令,指示
legal principle 法律原则
maxim 法律准则,基本原理

enforcement 执行
the legislature 立法机关
the executive 行政机关
the judiciary 司法机关
statute 法规,法令
act 法案,法令

enforce 实施,执行
dispute 争端,纠纷

resolved and any person who fails to observe the law will be punished through the procedure provided by the legal rules.

Therefore, law can generally be understood as rules and the underlying policies for guiding or regulating people's behavior in society. It is the regime that orders human activities and relations through systematic application of the force of politically organized society, or through social pressure, backed by force, in such a society. BLACK'S LAW DICTIONARY (9th Ed.) 962 (West 2009). It tells people what is allowed to do and what is not allowed to do, what procedures must be followed, and what happens to those who do not follow them. Law defines relations among individuals and groups and helps people arrange or conduct their business with greater security.

1.2 Common Law

Common law is also called case law or judge-made law, which is the basis of law in countries that have been at some time under British influence, with England and the United States as the representative countries. This system had been well established since 1215 and it "originates from English law, consisting of the decisions given by English judges in tens of thousands of individual disputes, as set down in records and reports published over the past five hundred years." Michael H. Whincup, CONTRACT LAW AND PRACTICE, THE ENGLISH SYSTEM AND CONTINENTAL COMPARISONS 1-2 (3d Ed., Kluwer Law Int'l 1996).

Owing to the underdeveloped economy and the difficulties for people to travel around, the British communities in their early history were small and isolated. Justice was maintained by local courts through applying local customs and rules which were divergent and different from community to community. Since the Norman Conquest in 1066, the English had started to establish a stronger centralized legal system. They divided the whole country into circuits which judges would follow and administer justice. They decided not to write down all known laws on paper. "They won basic rights from their rulers, such as *Magna Carta* from King John in 1215. For the rest, they contented themselves with the developing courts and with trials by jury for contests between individual citizens over property, personal injuries and contracts." Zhongcheng Chen, A SELECTION FROM LEGAL LITERATURE IN ENGLISH 17 - 18

(Shanghai Translation Publishing Co. 1987). As the judges became more established in their traveling of circuits, the King created new legal rules for the whole country in order to unify the rules on the land, and gradually, local customs were replaced by these unified new rules. Since these legal rules were commonly applied throughout the whole country, they eventually became known as the common law.

In the beginning of common law, there were few statutes or written laws, and judges would look to prior similar cases for guidance. The prior cases are called precedents. Later on, the English Parliament started to enact acts to define specific crimes and to prescribe penalties. These acts were relied on by judges when resolving disputes; they gradually formed part of the common law. Judges and the members of Parliament made British law by bits and pieces. Therefore, the English common law is composed of custom, tradition, decisions by judges in specific cases, and acts of Parliament.

After the common law had been established in England, it started to spread and develop in the countries under the British influence. For example, it has become the most important single root of the American legal system. Now English law and American law constitute a legal family with a closer relation to each other than is the case of the civil law system. The following excerpt may help us better understand the development of American legal history:

> American legal history begins with the first English settlement in Jamestown, Virginia in 1607. Its phases comprise the history of the English colonial period, *the Declaration of Independence* by the then thirteen colonies in 1776, the period of state formation (1776-1788), and the period of independent statehood of the "United States" which began with the ratification of *the Federal Constitution* (1788) and the assumption of office by President Washington (1789). During the colonial period English law was in force, statutory law as well as case law. It was supplemented by colonial legislation tailored to local conditions and needs. The different colonies varied in their legal structure and, with it, in the legislative competences they possessed. Some of them were provinces of the Crown and were subject to

unify 统一

precedent 先例
the English Parliament 英国议会
enact 颁布
crime 罪行
prescribe 规定
penalty 处罚、惩罚
by bits and pieces 一点一滴地
custom 习惯

spread 传播

excerpt 摘录,节选

settlement (争端的)解决

colonial period 殖民时期
the Declaration of Independence《美国独立宣言》

ratification 批准
the Federal Constitution《联邦宪法》
assumption of office 担任职务

colonial legislation 殖民地立法
tailor to 使合适

competence 权限
Crown 王国政府

Royal Patent 王室特许
charter 特许

citation 援引
render 作出

constitution 宪法
breach 违反

codification 法典
Civil Code 民法典

family property law 家庭财产法

James Kent 詹姆斯·肯特,著名法学家,纽约州最高法院大法官
Joseph Story 约瑟夫·斯多利,美国律师、法学家,曾任美国最高法院大法官
Blackstone's Commentaries《英国法释义》,作者是威廉·布莱克斯通。该书论述了英国法的基本原理和英国民主政体的形成基础,对英国宪法的起源、历史及其合理性作了涵盖甚广的阐述。
facilitate 促进,推动
legal methodology 法学方法论
private law 私法
grow apart 往不同的方向发展
modify 修改

superimpose 附加,安装
American gloss 美国元素

a royal governor. Others were administered by private companies or groups on the basis of a Royal Patent, while a third group were independent legal entities chartered by Royal Patent and therefore possessed greater independence from the English Crown.

The revolution resulted in reactions against the application of English law. The legislation of some of the states prohibited the citation of English decisions which had been rendered after independence; alone the circumstance of the adoption of a written constitution appeared "as a breach with the English tradition." Louisiana, admitted to the Federation in 1812, continued to follow its French law tradition, adopted codifications modeled after the French example (among them a Civil Code) and adheres to this tradition into modern times. In Western and Southwestern States there is still today a remarkable influence of originally Spanish and French legal concepts, for instance, in the area of family property law. In general, however, the nineteenth century saw a return to English legal tradition to which the great works of James Kent and Joseph Story contributed decisively. Blackstone's Commentaries first appeared in America in 1803 and facilitated access to English law.

Legal methodology, legal language, and the basic concepts of private law in the United States thus are still "English" today and many State statutes provide expressly for the reception of English Common Law. Approximately at the time of the American Civil War (1861-1865) the English and American legal systems began to grow apart. American legislation increasingly modified and developed the case law of the common law and judicial decisions superimposed an "American gloss" on the received common law. American courts today rarely refer to English decisions. The legal literature seeks solutions for modern problems in the structure of its own law, at times under consideration of English developments in comparative perspective.

See Peter Hay, AN INTRODUCTION TO UNITED STATES LAW (American Elsevier Pub. Co. 1976).

1.3 Law *versus* Equity

Since the fourteenth century, common law had been recognized as the common customs of all Englishmen and applied throughout the English realm. All English courts applied the common law and they only tried the cases based on various types of "writs." These "writs" were actually causes of actions and each of them was very specific in nature so that the types of writs were quite limited. Basically, in order to bring a lawsuit in a common law court at that time, a plaintiff must first obtain a writ from a court. If one could not obtain such a writ that fits his particular case, then he would not be able to bring a lawsuit in a common law court seeking for remedies. The result of such a rigid common law system was that there were few remedies and people's rights and interests were not sufficiently protected. Accordingly, it was extremely difficult and expensive to get justice done. People who were not satisfied with the common law court rulings then complained to the King, and the King gave these petitions to his Lord Chancellor and asked the Chancellor to decide the case in the Court of Chancery. The Chancellor then decided the cases without being bound by the common law rules so that the aggrieved people would get remedies that they could not get from a common law court. At that time, damages were the most important legal remedy granted by common law courts. However, the Courts of Chancery were able to grant other forms of relief such as injunctions and specific performance decrees, which were the most important equitable remedies. As time went by, the Court of Chancery had also formed its procedures and rules, which were much more flexible than in the common law courts. Therefore, people who could not obtain a writ from the common law courts could turn to the Court of Chancery for relief. Later on, the Court of Chancery was referred to as court of equity.

In the beginning of the court of equity, the Chancellor decided the cases before it on a case-by-case basis so that each case could be decided on its own merits and most people could get relief from the Chancellor. Gradually, when there were more and more people petitioned to the court of equity, the Chancellor's practices developed into a system, and eventually into a system of courts with rules and precedents which became even more complicated and cumbersome than the common

---

equity 衡平法

writ 令状,书面命令
cause of action 案由,诉因

lawsuit 诉讼(主要指民事诉讼)
plaintiff 原告

remedy 救济
rigid 死板的

ruling 判决,裁定
petition 申诉
Lord Chancellor 御前大臣
the Court of Chancery 大法官法院或衡平法院
bound 受约束的,有义务的
aggrieved 权利受侵害的

damages 损害赔偿金

relief 救济措施
injunction 禁制令
specific performance 特定履行;实际履行
decree 判决,裁定
equitable remedy 衡平法上的救济

merits (案件的)是非曲直

cumbersome 难处理的

law. Equity, which was created in order to cure the rigidity of the common law rules, had itself become as rigid and overburdened in form as the common law. In order to address this issue, the English Parliament enacted the *Judicature Act 1873* to abolish the dual-court system and to establish a single court which could administer both common law and equity. The Court of Chancery then became one of the Divisions of the High Court in England. From then on, legal remedies and equitable remedies were both available in all law courts in England. This tradition has been kept by the U.S. courts.

Since the equity rules have been developed independently from the common law rules, it is not uncommon that they may be contradictory. Back in 1615, the court in the *Earl of Oxford's Case* (Mich. 13 Jac. 1 [1615] 1, Chan. Rep. 5-16 in English Reports, vol. 21. pp. 485-9) held that if the common law system and the equity system were contradictory, equity would prevail. Later in 1873, the English Parliament adopted this decision and incorporated it into the *Judicature Act*. Although rules of common law and rules of equity are now administered by the same courts, the distinction between the two concepts remains important. Today, when a common law court judge invokes equitable rules, it means that the judge has first considered the relevant common law rules and found them insufficient to remedy the aggrieved party for one reason or another, and would prefer the different solution to the problem available to him or her under the rules of equity. To some extent, equity represents an alternative source of case law, whose principles are generally more flexible and adaptable than those of the common law.

1.4 Statutory Law *versus* Case Law

With the modern development of common law, legislature has played an increasingly important role in law making process. In the modern sense, a common law country usually has both case law and statutory law. Judges in common law countries apply not only the case law principles, but also the statutory law in deciding cases. Actually, if there are both statutory law and case law governing a legal dispute, the common law courts are bound to follow the statutory law.

Statutory law refers to the laws promulgated by the

legislature with the authority to make laws, and the executive with the authority to make rules to <u>implement</u> the statutes. The laws enacted by the legislature and the executive are referred to as Acts of Parliament, legislation, statutes, regulations, <u>ordinances</u>, or enactments. Sometimes people use "statutes" referring to all the written laws described above as opposed to case law. On the other hand, case law or judge-made law refers to the body of legal rules which have been developed by courts in the course of deciding cases. The case law principles are extracted from the prior rulings in individual cases and applied in subsequent similar cases. A case decided in one of the <u>higher courts</u> which states a principle of law is called a precedent. The doctrine of *stare decisis*, which will be discussed in Part II of this book, requires that a court must follow the precedents decided by the same court and the courts above it even if it does not agree with them or the precedent was very old.

  In civil law countries, since the only <u>legal basis</u> is the written statutes, the application of law is more <u>clear-cut</u>. In common law countries, however, while statutory law and case law co-exist, which law to apply should be the first issue to address. Just as common law rules and equity rules may be contradictory, there may well be <u>conflicts</u> between case law and statutory law. The rule is that if the legislature has enacted a statute governing <u>the case at issue</u>, the rules stated in the statute must be applied to resolve the dispute. However, if the dispute is regarding a problem which the legislature has not yet attempted to resolve, case law principles will be applied to resolve the dispute. It is important to note that case law will be applied only when there is no statutory law regulating the issue before the court, or, the statutory law is in <u>violation</u> of the constitution. To some extent, the application of statutory law by common law judges is pretty much similar to the application of law by civil law judges, except that it is also a process for common law judges to make law when they <u>interpret</u> the statutory law.

  The co-existence of both statutory law and case law in common law system also leads to different approaches to the application of law. While the application of case law principles is a process of <u>reasoning</u> by <u>analogy</u> from one set of facts to another, the application of the statutory law requires a <u>deductive</u> method of reasoning, which applies a general principle to the facts of an individual case.

implement（法律的）实施

ordinance 条例

higher court 上级法院

stare decisis 遵循先例

legal basis 法律依据
clear-cut 明确的，清楚的

conflict 矛盾

the case at issue 本案的争议问题

violation 违法

interpret 解释

reasoning 推理
analogy 类推
deductive 演绎的

1.5 Summary

Being one of the two major legal systems in the world, common law originated from English law and developed in the United Kingdom, the United States, and other countries under British influence in the history. Originally, there were many small and isolated communities within England and each had its own court with local rules. With the development of the British economy, the King decided to have a more powerful centralized legal system. The whole country was divided into smaller legal circuits with each circuit court judge applying nationally unified rules made by the King. These rules gained the name of "common law" for the fact that they were applied throughout the whole nation.

When we talk about common law today, we refer to both the law and the equity which were distinctive in the history and now merged into one common law system. The few and limited law remedies in English legal history encouraged people who were not satisfied with the law court's rulings to file petitions with the King, who later established the equity court — the Court of Chancery. The basic difference between law and equity lies in their remedies. While the main remedy a law court could provide is monetary damages, an equity court had power to grant more flexible relief to the aggrieved party. Today the two systems have been merged into one court system, although different remedies remain.

Common law in the broader sense includes both case law and statutory law. Case law is judge-made law. Judges are authorized by constitutional provisions or statutes to resolve disputes and controversies between litigants. When a judge decides a case, the decision resolves the dispute before the court and it becomes law for future legal controversies that are similar. These prior decisions are called precedents and form the case law which comes down to us in the form of written court decisions. According to the doctrine of *stare decisis*, judges should follow the precedents when resolving legal controversies. In modern times, the legislature as well as the executives in common law countries have started to play a more important role in law-making process. The written laws enacted by them even preempt the case law, which means that a statute must be applied first if there is one governing the dispute. Case law will only be applied when there is not such a statute governing the dispute before the court.

Review Questions

1. What are the differences between common law system and civil law system?
2. When there is a conflict between a statute and case law, how should a common law judge apply the law?
3. How does a common law judge make the law?
4. Who has the authority to interpret the statutes enacted by the legislature?

Chapter 2
COMMON LAW COURT SYSTEM

Common law courts perform an essential function in the common law system. Before common law court judges deal with a dispute, they will first research whether there is a statute governing the issue to be litigated. If there is such a statute, they will have to apply it; at the same time it is within their province to interpret the statute. The interpretation of statutes is also a part of the law-making process. If there is no such a statute directly governing the controversy, then the judges must apply case law rules to try the case before them. The doctrine of *stare decisis* guides the judges' law-application. Where the case is a first-impression case, *i.e.*, there has never been a similar dispute decided before, the judges must make new rules, which is an important part of the common law judges' function. Overall, common law courts decide what the law means and how it should be applied to specific situations. To understand the common law court system is thus important for Chinese law students to understand the common law system. Although the United Kingdom and the United States are both common law countries, they have different court systems. A brief introduction to both is followed in this chapter.

It is to be noted that for historical reasons, as a state made up of several separate jurisdictions, the United Kingdom does not have a single unified legal system; instead, there is one system for England and Wales, another for Scotland, and a third for Northern Ireland. The court system introduced below is only of England.

2.1 The English Court System

English court system is comprised of a series of courts of hierarchical levels, with the magistrates' courts at the bottom and the Supreme Court at the top. Among them,

---

litigate 通过诉讼(解决)

province 职责

a first-impression case 无先例可循的案件

jurisdiction 法域,司法管辖区域。此处意指英国法院系统为互相独立的几个法域,每个法域内的判例仅对本法域内的法庭具有拘束力。

hierarchical 按等级划分的
the magistrates' court 治安法庭
the Supreme Court 最高法院

some courts deal only with civil cases and some deal only with criminal cases. However, most courts have jurisdiction over both civil and criminal cases.

2.1.1 Magistrates' Courts — For Both Civil and Criminal Cases

The lowest courts in the English court system are the local magistrates' courts. They are also called courts of summary jurisdiction or petty sessions. The magistrates' courts can deal with both criminal and civil disputes. The judges sitting in these courts are called "magistrates," most of whom are unpaid amateurs with only a few stipendiary magistrates. The stipendiary magistrates are professional judges appointed by certain of the larger local authorities to serve on a full or part-time basis for a suitable payment or stipend. The other magistrates are proposed for office from all walks of life on "good citizenship" grounds by local advisory committees of senior magistrates, and if acceptable, are appointed by the Lord Chancellor in the name of the Queen. All magistrates are addressed as "your Worship," or "Sir" or "Ma'am," as the case may be.

The main work of the magistrates' courts is dealing with crimes, while they also have jurisdiction over certain types of civil matters. Generally, they try over 95 percent of all the criminal cases in England and Wales. As to the civil cases, the jurisdiction of the magistrates' courts is largely confined to domestic matters, *i.e.*, civil cases dealing particularly with the family, such as the granting of separation and maintenance orders between husband and wife, adoption, and guardianship orders. The magistrates' courts also have administrative duties such as granting licenses for the sale and consumption of alcohol in public houses and places of entertainment. The losing party in a criminal case has a right of appeal to the criminal division of the Court of Appeal (*see* Chapter 2.1.5 for more details). When questions of law are involved, the magistrates may also appeal to the Divisional Court of the Queen's Bench Division (which will be further discussed in Chapter 2.1.4) by way of case stated. Any person who is a party to proceedings before a magistrates' court may question the proceedings on the basis that the magistrates erred in law.

2.1.2 County Courts — For Civil Cases Only

In order to provide efficient and cheap local justice

---

civil case 民事案件
criminal case 刑事案件

courts of summary jurisdiction (petty session) 即决法庭,小治安裁判法庭

magistrate 治安法官
amateur 外行
stipendiary magistrate 领薪治安法官

domestic matter 家庭事务

separation and maintenance order 分居令和抚养令
adoption 收养
guardianship 监护
license 执照

losing party 败诉方
right of appeal 上诉权
Court of Appeal 上诉法院;上诉法庭
question of law 法律问题
Queen's Bench Division 王座法庭

err in law 在法律问题上判断错误

for various types of civil cases, England established a system of county courts in 1846. County courts can try nearly every kind of relatively minor civil disputes and in particular claims for damages for breach of contract and tort up to £50,000, or more by agreement between the parties. The county courts are staffed by circuit judges and district judges addressed as "your Honor." Circuit judges must be barristers of at least 10 years' standing, and be appointed by the Crown. They normally sit alone but on occasions a jury of eight can be called. Circuit judges are aided by district judges, who have at least seven years' experience of advocacy qualification and are appointed by the Lord Chancellor.

Except for actions in defamation which is to be heard in the high court, other actions in contract and tort as well as personal injury actions must start in the county court unless there is a possibility that the plaintiff will recover more than £25,000. In that case the action will be heard in the high court, unless the high court transfers the case to the county court, or if the action started in the county court and the county court wishes to retain the case. The estimation shows that the largest number of cases handled by the county courts are related to debt recovery. The party not satisfied with the disposition by the county court may appeal to the Court of Appeal.

Within the county court system, there is a small claims procedure available for cases involving claims for up to £3,000 (£1,000 in personal injury claims). The proceedings are informal and apply different rules of evidence, more like that in an arbitration. Normally the loser pays both sides' costs in other civil cases, but according to the rules adopted by the small claims proceedings, each side pays its own costs of legal representation whether it wins or loses. The purpose is to discourage the parties to use lawyers in such cases.

2.1.3 Crown Court — For Criminal Cases Only

The Crown Court tries all the serious crimes by a single professional judge with a jury of twelve persons. It also hears appeals from magistrates' courts, and on these occasions lay magistrates sit with the judge. The judge may be a High Court judge, or a circuit judge who serves also as county court judge.

2.1.4 High Court — For Both Civil and Criminal Cases

The High Court is the most important lower court in England that tries all the most substantial cases. It was established by the *Judicature Act 1873*. The High Court is structured in three tiers: the Queen's Bench Division, the Chancery Division, and the Family Division. It has about 100 judges, formerly practicing senior barristers known as Queen's Counsel, appointed by the Lord Chancellor to one of the three Divisions of the Court.

Under the doctrine of *stare decisis*, a lower court should follow the higher courts' decisions. Therefore, High Court must follow the prior decisions made by the Court of Appeals and the House of Lords or the newly established Supreme Court (which will be discussed in details in Chapter 2.1.6). The decision of one Division is not binding on another, but the doctrine of precedent requires each Division to consider the decisions made by the other Divisions as persuasive authorities. All three Divisions have certain limited powers to hear appeals from subordinate courts. In hearing a case for the first time, a High Court judge sits alone. However, two or more judges sit to hear appeals from magistrates. If the Divisional Court decides that the magistrates were wrong, it can reverse or amend the decision; it can remit the case to the magistrates to continue hearing the case or discharge or convict the accused where applicable; or it can make such orders as it considers fit.

A. The Queen's Bench Division

The Queen's Bench Division (Q.B.D.) is the largest and busiest division among the High Court divisions. It was originally the court in which the Monarch sat and thus got this name. It is presided over by the Lord Chief Justice and sits in London and periodically in provincial centers. The Q.B.D. cases are heard by a single judge who is addressed as "my Lord" or "your Lordship." In addition to its other functions, as the other Divisions, the Q.B.D. also exercises the supervisory jurisdiction inherited from the old Court of King's Bench. By a procedure known as judicial review, the Queen's Bench Division in particular has powers to supervise inferior courts and tribunals by means of "prerogative orders" such as *mandamus*, prohibition, *certiorari*, and *habeas corpus*, representing the original authority of the king or queen. By judicial review, the Court may also decide cases where the validity

---

lower court 下级法院
Queen's Counsel 御用大律师；英国王室法律顾问
Court of Appeals 上诉法院
House of Lords 英国上议院, 也称贵族院。直到 2009 年 10 月, 英国上议院一直是英国最高上诉法院, 享有司法职能, 既是英格兰、威尔士、苏格兰和北爱尔兰民事案件的最终上诉法院, 也是英格兰、威尔士和北爱尔兰刑事案件的最终上诉法院。2009 年 10 月以后由英国最高法院取代。
Supreme Court 最高法院
doctrine of precedent 遵守先例原则
persuasive authority 有说服力的法律依据, 指对法庭没有约束力, 但按照法庭在具体情况下对其价值的评价, 对判决的作出具有参考、借鉴意义及某种说服力的判例或其他法律根据。例如, 下级法院或外国法院的判决、法律教科书上的论述等。区别于"有约束力的法律根据"(binding authority)。
subordinate court 下级法院
reverse the decision 撤销(原)判决
amend the decision 变更(原)判决
remit 发回重审
discharge 免除
convict 对某人作出有罪判决
the accused 刑事被告人
Monarch 君主, 帝王
judicial review 司法审查
inferior court 下级法院
tribunal 法庭, 裁判庭
prerogative order 特权令
mandamus 执行职务令, 指上级法院对私人、公司、政府或其官员、下级法院发布的命令, 要求履行属于其职责的特定行为, 或要求恢复原告被非法剥夺的权利或特权。执行职务令只在特殊情况下发布, 以纠正下级法院滥用权力或拒绝履行职责, 不同于在正常诉讼情况下对下级法院错判的改判。
prohibition 禁止令, 指上级法院禁止下级法院审理其无权管辖或超越其管辖权的事项的令状。
certiorari 调卷令, 一般是指最高法院签发给下级法院要求其将某一案件的诉讼记录移交给自己审查的一种特别令状。
habeas corpus 人身保护令, 原意为控制身体。人身保护令为一系列令状的名称, 其最初目的在于将当事人带至法庭或法官面前。16 世纪, 英国王座法庭(King's Bench)开始签发"解交审查令"(habeas corpus ad subjiciendum), 以对拘押的合宪性提出异议。该令状的基本功能在于释放受非法拘押人。

of ministerial and local government <u>edicts</u> is challenged.

B. The Chancery Division

As <u>aforementioned</u>, equity which was distinctive in common law history now has been merged with the law system and since then become a division of the English High Court, i.e., the Chancery Division. The Chancery Division is largely concerned with administering the rules and remedies of equity which had previously been handled by the Court of Chancery, in cases concerning, among other matters, the administration of land, the proving or <u>probate of wills</u>, <u>intestacies</u>, <u>trusts</u>, <u>mortgages</u>, <u>patents</u>, <u>company law</u>, <u>partnerships</u>, <u>tax</u>, and <u>bankruptcy</u>. As a <u>Court of Protection</u> it administers also the property and interests of mental patients and others under its <u>guardianship</u>. The head of the Chancery Division is the Lord Chancellor, but the Vice-Chancellor is responsible for the day-to-day running of the court.

C. The Family Division

The Family Division was created by the *Administration of Justice Act 1970* and replaced the Probate, Divorce and Admiralty Divisions. This Court has jurisdiction over <u>defended divorces</u> and other miscellaneous <u>matrimonial disputes</u>, adoption, <u>wardship</u> and guardianship of children. It is presided over by the President of the Family Division.

D. Restrictive Practices Court and Employment Appeal Tribunal

In addition to the three divisions described above, two other courts are also divisions of the High Court. Both are presided over by a High Court judge, each sitting with lay members. One of them is the <u>Restrictive Practices Court</u> which was established in 1956 to decide whether various kinds of commercial agreements restricting competition were in the public interest, and, if not, to declare them <u>void</u>. The two non-lawyers sitting with the judge are drawn from a <u>panel</u> of economists and other experts. The other is the <u>Employment Appeal Tribunal</u>(E. A. T.), which was set up in 1975 to hear appeals from industrial tribunals and to decide questions of individual rights in <u>employment</u>, notably on <u>dismissal</u>, <u>discrimination</u>, and <u>equal pay</u>. The E. A. T. lay members are nominated by management and labor organizations.

2.1.5 Court of Appeal — For Both Civil and Criminal Cases

The Court of Appeal is the most important <u>intermediate appellate court</u> in the English judicial system. It has a Civil Division and a Criminal Division. The civil division of the Court of Appeal, which sits in London, hears appeals on questions of law or fact from the county court, High Court, Restrictive Practices Court and the E. A. T. The party who is not satisfied with the decisions made by the lower courts has a right to appeal to the Court of Appeal, except that a <u>leave</u> is required in case of minor county court actions and appeals from the Divisional Court of the High Court. Appeals are usually heard by three judges, normally <u>the Master of the Rolls</u> and two Lords Justices of Appeal or High Court judges. Occasionally a full court of five or more members is <u>convened</u> to hear appeals involving novel or difficult questions of law. There are some 30 Lords Justices, under the presidency of the Master of the Rolls in civil cases and the Lord Chief Justice in criminal cases.

The Court does not <u>try the case</u> but only <u>reviews the case</u> in that when reviewing the appeal, it will not see the <u>witnesses</u> again but reach its decision on the basis of <u>transcripts</u> of their evidence. It has power to order a <u>retrial</u>, but rarely does so. Under the doctrine of *stare decisis*, the Court is bound by the prior decisions made by itself and by the Supreme Court or the former House of Lords, with very limited exceptions.

The criminal division of the Court hears appeals from the Crown Court against <u>conviction</u> or <u>sentence</u>. It normally comprises the Lord Chief Justice and two High Court judges. Its powers include that of increasing sentence or in appropriate cases ordering a retrial. It may also determine points of law referred to it by the <u>Attorney General</u> or <u>Home Secretary</u>.

2.1.6 Final Court of Appeals

Until October 2009, the House of Lords had been <u>the Highest Court of Appeal</u> in the Great Britain for controversies other than those within the jurisdiction of the <u>European Court of Justice</u>(*see* Chapter 2.1.7 for more details), and it heard appeals from both the civil and criminal divisions of the Court of Appeal, and in certain circumstances it heard appeals directly from the High Court. The House of Lords consisted of seven to eleven "Law Lords," more formally known as Lords of Appeal in

---

intermediate appellate court 中级上诉法院

leave 许可

the Master of the Rolls 掌卷法官；上诉法院民事庭庭长

convene 召集

try the case 初审法院审理案件
review the case 上诉法院审理案件
witness 证人
transcript 初审的庭审记录
retrial 重审

conviction 定罪，有罪判决
sentence 刑期

Attorney General 总检察长，其主要职责包括为王室、政府、上议院的特权委员会、御前大臣（Lord Chancellor）提供法律咨询，代表王室起诉和应诉等。凡由王室提起或对王室提起的民事诉讼均可由总检察长代替有关的政府部门提起或者对总检察长而非有关的政府部门提起。诉讼开始后，也可以由总检察长代替有关政府部门参加诉讼。此外，他还可依职权以国家的名义在高等法院王座庭提起刑事指控。

Home Secretary 内政大臣，掌管内政部（Home Office）的大臣，其职责是负责英格兰和威尔士的法律和秩序，包括执行刑法、管理警察和监狱、就赦免权（mercy）行使向英王提出建议，同时也负责管理诸如国籍、移民和引渡等其他事务。

the Highest Court of Appeal 最高上诉法院

European Court of Justice 欧盟法院，根据欧盟法律作为欧洲联盟的最高法院，掌理一般案件的法律审上诉以及特殊案件的一审。

Ordinary, *i.e.*, "by virtue of office," and under the presidency of the Lord Chancellor. The Lords were chosen from among judges of the Court of Appeal, or, exceptionally, the High Court, and given life peerages and appropriately increased salaries. Appeals were usually heard by a committee of five of their Lordships. The Lords made the decisions by majority but each Lord might give his own written opinion. Each year, the House of Lords might hear about fifteen or twenty cases. An appeal to the House of Lords was not of right and needed the permission of the court. In addition to hearing appeals from English courts, the House of Lords also heard appeals from the Superior Courts of Scotland and Northern Ireland.

Since October 2009, a newly established Supreme Court has become the final court of appeal for all United Kingdom civil cases, and criminal cases from England, Wales, and Northern Ireland. The Supreme Court was established by Part 3 of the *Constitutional Reform Act 2005* and started work on October 1, 2009. The Supreme Court, as well as being the final court of appeal, plays an important role in the development of United Kingdom law. It hears appeals on arguable points of law of general public and constitutional importance affecting the whole population, and maintains and develops the role of the highest court in the United Kingdom as a leader in the common law world. It is expected to achieve a complete separation between the United Kingdom's senior Judges and the Upper House of Parliament, emphasizing the independence of the Law Lords and increasing the transparency between Parliament and the courts. It assumes the judicial functions of the House of Lords and the jurisdiction over devolution matters that had previously been held by the Judicial Committee of the Privy Council. The impact of Supreme Court decisions extends far beyond the parties involved in any given case, shaping the society, and directly affecting people's everyday lives. For instance, in their first legal year, the Justices gave landmark rulings on access to legal advice for Scottish suspects, the rights of gay asylum seekers, and the weight to be given to prenuptial agreements.

The Supreme Court is composed of the President, Deputy President, and Puisne Justices of the Supreme Court. They are not subject to term limits, but may be removed from office on the address of Parliament. Like all British judges, Supreme Court justices are forced to retire at age 70 if first appointed to a judicial office after March 31, 1995, or at age 75 otherwise. The President and Deputy President of the Court are separately appointed to those roles. It is to be noted that the Supreme Court is open to the public and anyone can visit during opening hours. In addition, almost all the proceedings of the Supreme Court will be filmed, and sometimes broadcast. It is the only court in the United Kingdom to allow this.

2.1.7 European Court of Justice

For any litigated disputes regarding the interpretation of the European Union Law, the final court of resort in England is the European Court. Thus in England, the European Court is supreme on questions of interpretation or validity of the community law. Otherwise, the Supreme Court is the court of last resort in England.

court of last resort 终审法院

2.2 The American Court System

In the United States, each of the fifty states and the federal government has its own court system. The main courts within each system generally can deal with both civil and criminal cases, which is different from the English courts. The different court systems also intertwine at certain points, and within each court system there are usually several levels and the courts at each level perform a different and specific function.

intertwine 缠绕,交织

2.2.1 The Federal Courts

The United States Constitution and the federal statutes enacted by the U.S. Congress grant the federal courts authority to hear certain types of cases, which is called the subject-matter jurisdiction of the federal courts. Federal courts can only hear these enumerated types of cases. Generally, the jurisdiction of federal courts covers cases that involve questions of federal law, (*e.g.*, the civil actions that arise under *the Constitution*, laws, or treaties of the United States, which is called federal-question jurisdiction), cases in which the United States is a party; and cases in which the amount in controversy exceeds $75,000 if the plaintiff and defendant are citizens of different states, which is called diversity jurisdiction. U.S. Const. art. III, § 2. Federal courts

the Federal Court 联邦法院
the United States Constitution《美国宪法》
federal statute 联邦法规
U.S. Congress 美国国会
subject-matter jurisdiction 事物管辖权,也译为"对物的管辖权"
enumerate 列举

federal-question jurisdiction 联邦问题管辖权,指基于美国宪法、国会立法和条约而产生的案件,通常称为包含"联邦问题"的案件,由联邦法院管辖。
defendant 被告
diversity jurisdiction 异籍管辖权,指对不同州当事人之间诉讼的管辖权。

also have jurisdiction over cases involving admiralty or maritime law and cases involving federal crimes. When trying a case, federal courts may hear questions of state law; but while doing so, they must apply the law of the state under whose laws the claim arose. If the law of the state is unclear, the federal court must either make an educated guess about what the highest court of that state would do if confronted with the question before it or, if state law permits, certify the question to the state's highest court.

The U. S. Federal courts have three levels: a trial level, an intermediate appellate level, and a final appellate level. The U.S. Congress has also created specialized civil courts, such as federal bankruptcy courts whose jurisdiction is limited to a particular area of the law. Within each jurisdiction, the decision of the highest court is binding on the lower courts. A decision of the United States Supreme Court on a federal question would be binding on all courts that entertain the identical federal question. Judicial decisions outside the jurisdiction may be persuasive but are never binding.

A. Federal Trial Courts

Federal trial courts are called United States District Courts. Each state has within its boundaries at least one such federal district court, and some states have several. The district court's territorial jurisdiction is limited to the area of its district. The number of districts in state is determined primarily by population and the geographic size of the state. For example, Massachusetts has only one federal judicial district, which covers the whole state and is called *the United States District Court for the District of Massachusetts*. Illinois is divided into three districts and has three district courts: *the United States District Court for the Northern District of Illinois*, *the United States District Court for the Southern District of Illinois*, and *the United States District Court for the Central District of Illinois*. The federal trial courts try cases within its jurisdiction authorized by the constitution and other federal statutes.

B. Federal Intermediate Appellate Courts

Federal intermediate appellate courts are known as United States Courts of Appeals. For appellate court purposes, the United States is divided into thirteen circuits, so there are thirteen United States Courts of Appeals, eleven of which are identified by a number. Thus, the complete title of one such court is *The United States Court of Appeals for the First Circuit*. In addition, there is a circuit for the District of Columbia (*D. C. Circuit*), and a circuit known as the *Federal Circuit*. Except for the *D. C. Circuit*, each Court of Appeals circuit encompasses several states. For example, *the United States Court of Appeals for the Seventh Circuit* embraces the states of Illinois, Wisconsin, and Indiana. When a party to a lawsuit in a U.S. District Court wants to appeal that court's decision, the appeal normally goes to the U.S. Court of Appeals covering that district. For example, if you were involved in a lawsuit in a U.S. District Court in Illinois and you wanted to appeal the decision in your case, you would take your appeal to *the U.S. Court of Appeals for the Seventh Circuit*. Similarly, a party in a lawsuit in a U.S. District Court in California would take an appeal to *the U.S. Court of Appeals for the Ninth Circuit*. The Federal Circuit hears appeals from all U.S. District Courts in certain specialized kinds of cases such as international trade, patents, trademarks, and government contracts.

encompass 包含,包括

trademark 商标

C. Federal Final Appellate Court

The highest court in the U.S. federal system is *the Supreme Court of the United States*. The U.S. Supreme Court hears appeals from decisions of all the U.S. Courts of Appeals, from the highest appellate court of each state when a federal question is involved, and on extremely rare occasions directly from U.S. District Courts. In certain limited cases, the U.S. Supreme Court also has original jurisdiction and then acts as a trial court. The Supreme Court must hear certain types of cases while for other types of cases it has discretion to decide whether to hear them or not.

original jurisdiction 初审管辖权

discretion 自主裁量权

2.2.2 State Courts

In the United States, each of the 50 states has its own court system that is different from other states. Many states have three levels of courts parallel to the federal system, while some states have only two levels, one trial level and one appellate level. The courts in different states are called different names. For example, the highest court in Massachusetts is called the *Supreme Judicial Court*; in

State Court 州法院,与联邦法院(Federal Court)相对应。各州法院系统是独立的。多数州实行三级制,少数州实行二级制。

New York, it is known as the *Court of Appeals*; and in California, it is called the *Supreme Court*. The court system in a municipality or county may include criminal courts and civil courts of limited or general jurisdiction. The latter are often called circuit courts, superior courts, district courts, or county courts.

The jurisdiction of state courts is defined by the state's constitution and legislation. A trial court's jurisdiction is limited by geography and by subject matter and amount in controversy. A state court may hear questions of federal law as well as state law. When hearing a case involving federal law, the state court is bound by the decisions made by federal courts disposing similar questions.

The structure of the state court system is also a hierarchical one. Courts are organized along a vertical structure, and the position of a court within that structure has important consequences because when hearing a case of state law question, a state court must only follow the prior decisions made by itself or other state courts that are superior to it within the hierarchical state court system. However, the state courts are free to accept or reject decisions by courts of other states and decisions by federal courts interpreting their state law. Those judicial decisions outside the jurisdiction may be persuasive only.

A. Courts of Inferior Jurisdiction

Litigation generally begins with the courts of original jurisdiction. Each state may have various courts of original jurisdiction and the lowest rung of such courts of original jurisdiction in many states is called court of inferior jurisdiction. These courts have only limited jurisdiction over limited types of cases, such as misdemeanor cases or cases in which the amount of damages the plaintiff demands from the defendant does not exceed a specified sum. These courts are called *courts of common pleas* in some states or *small claims courts* in other states. There are other specialized courts of inferior jurisdiction that hear cases about one particular subject matter, such as juvenile or family law matters. The trial in the courts of inferior jurisdiction may be conducted in an informal way and the courts may not follow the strict rules of evidence. The parties often represent themselves and do not use attorneys to argue for them. The decisions of these inferior courts do not form part of the precedent and are not published.

B. Trial Courts

State trial courts are courts of general jurisdiction and may hear cases of all subject matters. Basically, a state trial court may hear civil litigation between private parties who are designated as the plaintiff and the defendant. It may also hear criminal cases which are brought by the state against a defendant or defendants.

A trial court is presided over by one judge. The trial can be conducted with or without a jury. If the trial is conducted with a jury, the jury is the trier of fact; if the trial is conducted without a jury, then the judge is to assume the function of a trier of fact. The trier of fact determines what the facts in a given dispute are and what those facts mean in terms of the law based on the evidence at trial, the examination of witnesses, and the admissions of the parties. After the facts are determined, the court then decides the case by applying the applicable law to that fact.

preside 主持，指挥

trier of fact 事实的审理官

Many cases may end up without a trial after the cases are submitted to the trial court. For example, the parties may decide to make compromise and settle their dispute outside the courtroom. Or, one of the parties may request the court to take a particular action which is called a "motion." The court will consider the motion, and if it decides to grant the motion, the trial may be ended. If a case is not ended on a motion, and the parties do not voluntarily settle their dispute, then the case will go to trial. Most state trial court decisions do not result in explanatory judicial opinions and so are not published. Although the trial court decisions are not part of the precedent, the verdicts are recorded in the court files, together with the court hearing transcript, for future use by the appellate court.

compromise 和解
settle their dispute 解决争议

motion 动议

explanatory 解释的
judicial opinion 法官意见

verdict 陪审团裁决或裁断

C. Appellate Courts

The party not satisfied with the trial court decision may ask for review by an appellate court. This review is known as an appeal. The party who appeals is usually called the appellant and the other party, the appellee or respondent. The appellate court determines whether the lower court correctly applied the relevant points of law to the facts determined at the trial level, or committed any error significant enough to require that the decision be

appeal 上诉
appellant 上诉人
appellee 被上诉人
respondent 被上诉人

reversed or modified, or a new trial be granted. Except in rare cases, appellate courts do not re-evaluate or re-determine findings of fact made at the trial level. Most states provide two levels of appellate courts: the first is an intermediate court of appeals, and the second is the highest court of appeals and is usually known as the state's supreme court — the court of last resort in the jurisdiction.

Intermediate Court of Appeals

Generally, the intermediate appellate court hears appeals from the trial courts. An appeal is normally heard by a panel of three or more judges who decide the case by majority voting and usually one of the judges from the majority writes the decision. If a judge does not agree with the majority, he or she may write a separate opinion, called a dissenting opinion or a dissent. If a judge has voted with the majority as to the outcome of the case but does not agree with other judges on certain aspects of the case, he or she may write a separate opinion to express his or her differing views, which is called a concurring opinion. The name of the judge who writes an opinion appears at the beginning of that opinion. Sometimes the opinion of the court does not bear the name of an author, but is designated a "*per curiam*" decision. This means a decision "by the court" and may be used for a shorter opinion on an issue about which there is general unanimity.

The procedure for appeal differs from the proceedings before a trial court. Since the trial court is supposed to determine the facts of the case, the appellate court will not re-evaluate the facts. The rationale is that the trial court has the best opportunity to examine the facts through hearing the testimony of the witnesses and seeing the evidence. Thus, the parties do not submit evidence or examine witnesses before the appellate court, nor does the court empanel a jury. Rather, the parties' lawyers argue to the appellate judges to persuade them that the court below did or did not commit an error or errors. Typically, this argument is made by the attorneys through the submission to the court by the attorneys of written documents called appellate briefs, and then through the oral argument made by the attorneys before the penal of the appellate court judges. In addition, the appellate court reviews the record of the proceedings below. Most of the appellate decisions are precedents and published in volumes called <u>case reporters</u> for future use.

case reporter 判例汇编

State Supreme Court — Court of Last Resort

The state supreme court is the court of last resort in the state, which hears appeals from the intermediate courts of appeals. Each state has only one court of last resort and that court is superior to all other state courts. Under certain circumstances, the state supreme court also hears appeals for certain types of issues directly from the state trial courts, even though there are intermediate courts of appeal in the state. Most litigations end with the state supreme court and there is no further appeal of the decisions of the court of last resort as to matters of state law. As discussed earlier, some states have no intermediate court of appeals. In those states, trial court decisions will be reviewed directly by the court of last resort. In either system, except for certain types of cases, appeal to the court of last resort is not of right and the highest court has discretion to choose which cases to hear.

Review Questions

1. Why is it significant that the courts in a common law country are hierarchical?
2. What are the commonalities between the British court system and the U.S. court system?
3. Is there any difference in the court proceedings between the trial court and the appellate court in the United States?
4. How is the *stare decisis* doctrine applied within a jurisdiction?

Chapter 3
SOURCES OF LAW

3.1 Sources of Law in England

The law of England today has three main sources: the European Union law, the statutory law, and case law.

3.1.1 The European Union Law

The Supreme Court is the highest court of appeal in the United Kingdom. However, the Court must give effect to directly applicable European Union law, and interpret domestic law as far as possible consistently with European Union law. It must also give effect to the rights contained in the *European Convention on Human Rights*. Under article 267 of the *Treaty on the Functioning of the European Union*, the Court must refer to the European Court of Justice in Luxembourg any question of European Union law, where the answer is not clear and is necessary for it to give judgment. In giving effect to rights contained in the *European Convention on Human Rights*, the Court must take account of any decision of the European Court of Human Rights in Strasbourg. No national court should "without strong reason dilute or weaken the effect of the Strasbourg case law." *See* Lord Bingham of Cornhill in *R. (Ullah) v. Special Adjudicator* [2004] UKHL 26. Hence, the European Union law has preemptive authority over other domestic laws in England. An individual contending that his or her *Convention rights* have not been respected by a decision of a United Kingdom court (including the Supreme Court) against which he or she has no domestic recourse may bring a claim against the United Kingdom before the European Court of Human Rights.

3.1.2 Statutory law

Statutory law is the law made by the Parliament of the United Kingdom. Parliament consists of the House of

Commons, House of Lords, and Monarch, who are all jointly responsible for any given measure. The law includes not only *Acts of Parliament* but also delegated legislations, which are the detailed rules and regulations made by government ministers under the authority given to them by the various *Acts*, to fulfill the general principles they lay down. These forms of delegated legislation still require Parliament's approval, which may be given actively or passively according to the wording of the "parent" *Act*. When considering the effect of a statute, the interpretation section and any schedules at the end which give details of its application must be considered. Since the judicial interpretation of the statutes is also part of the law, statutory law should also be considered together with those judicial interpretations.

3.1.3 Case Law

Case law is an important source of law in English legal system. As we have already noted, case law is made by judges in deciding cases before them. The rules extracted from the precedents bind the same court or the lower courts when dealing with similar disputes in the future. Although either statutory law or common law may apply to any given problem, the English judges are bound to follow statutory law if case law appears to contradict the statutory law.

3.2 Sources of Law in the United States

The Constitution of the United States is the charter of the country and the source of authority for federal laws and the federal courts. Each state has authority over persons and activities within its boundaries. State governments, in turn, delegate some authority to local governments. Each of these governmental units may, within certain constraints, make law. Generally, there are three branches of the government that make law: the legislature, the administrative agencies, and the judiciary. Each of them makes a different kind of law. Legislatures create statutory law by passing bills, which become law when signed by the executive. Agencies create administrative law, consisting of rules and decisions issued by the agencies. Finally, the judiciary makes common law, sometimes informally referred to as judge-made law, which is found in court decisions. Federal statutory,

House of Commons 英国下议院
measure 措施

delegated legislation 委任立法,指行政机关根据议(国)会的授权制定普遍性的行政管理法规的行为。

schedule 附件

bill 议案,提案,法案

administrative law 行政法

administrative, and common law apply throughout the United States; a state's statutory, administrative, and common law apply only in that state. These sources form a hierarchy with constitutions at the top and judge-made laws at the bottom.

3.2.1 Constitutions

Constitutions include *the United States Constitution* and constitutions of each state. Within a jurisdiction, its constitution is the highest authority; statutes, regulations, and common law must not conflict with the constitution. The most important source of law in the United States is *the Constitution of the United States* which separates the government into the three coordinated branches, grants certain enumerated powers to each of these branches, reserves certain powers to the states, and sets limits on the power of the federal and state governments to enact certain kinds of legislation or to engage in certain kinds of activities relating to their citizens. *The United States Constitution* sets the standards against which all federal and state law is ultimately measured, and it applies throughout the country. Each state in the United States has also adopted a constitution which sets out both the form and operation of government in that state and also places certain limits on its power. The state constitution applies only within that state's boundaries. Constitutions are normally reprinted in statutory compilations at both the federal and state levels.

3.2.2 Statutes

Statutes are another important source of law in the United States. While the constitutions address broader, more fundamental, and timeless matters of government structure and power, statutes deal with particular problems as they arise. Statutes refer to the enactments of the legislative bodies including acts of Congress, statutes of federal and state legislatures, and ordinances of local governing bodies acting within the powers conferred on them by state legislatures. Statutes create categorical rules to address particular problems. Unless and until a statute is declared to be unconstitutional, it is controlling as to the subject it encompasses.

The U.S. statutory law is found in session laws and statutory codes. The statutes are arranged in a chronological order of their enactment in the session laws,

---

compilation 汇编

ordinance 法令

categorical rule 分门别类的规则,按类别制定的规则
unconstitutional 违宪的
controlling 有约束力的,有控制力的
encompass 包含
session law 州议会法律汇编
statutory code 法典
chronological order 按照年代顺序

while arranged according to subject matter in the statutory codes, for example, all criminal laws are grouped together regardless of the dates on which the individual criminal statutes were passed. At the federal level, the session laws are found in the series called *Statutes At Large* (abbreviated as "Sta."); the codified version is found in the *United States Code* (U.S.C.) and in two commercially published editions, *United States Code Annotated* (U.S.C.A.) and *United States Code Service* (U.S.C.S). Session laws and statutory codes also exist at the state level, but states vary in their practices in organizing and publishing these. Statutes enacted by local government may be compiled in ordinance codes.

3.2.3 Administrative Regulations

The U.S. federal government and most states have many agencies with diverse responsibilities. Such agencies are authorized to promulgate rules to implement specific statutes, and the rules promulgated must be consistent with the Constitution and relevant statutes. These rules are called administrative regulations and form the source of law in the United States.

promulgate 颁布

Administrative rules are also arranged chronologically in administrative registers, and according to subject matter in administrative codes. Federal administrative rules, regardless of which agency issues them, are collected chronologically in the *Federal Register* (abbreviated as "Fed. Reg."); they are also rearranged according to specific regulatory topics in the *Code of Federal Regulations* (C.F.R.). The federal administrative agencies also make decisions interpreting and enforcing administrative rules. These decisions are available from the agencies themselves, or compiled and published by the government. Some states do not publish their administrative rules; in such a case, if you need to find them, you will have to contact the agencies themselves.

administrative register 行政法规登记册，这里指按照行政法规颁布的时间先后而编纂的行政法规汇编。

administrative code 行政法典，这里指按照行政法规所规范的内容不同而编纂的行政法规汇编。

3.2.4 Case Law

The common law or judge-made law is a very important source of law in the United States. Whenever a court is deciding a case, the law is made. When dealing with a case, a court first looks to statutes to see whether there is one specifically governing the controversy. If so, the statute should be applied. If there is no statute governing a specific area, the court then looks to prior construe 法条（法规）解释

construction 法条（法规）解释

precedents by applying the rules embodied in the case law. However, even if there is a governing statute, the court may interpret and <u>construe</u> the statute and once a constitutional provision, statute, or regulation has been construed by a court, that <u>construction</u> of the statute also becomes part of the case law.

Review Questions

1. What is the relation between the European Union Law and the Common Law in England?
2. Does a U.S. federal statute bind the state court?
3. Generally, "common law" refers to "case law." Does it mean that statutes are not part of the common law?

Chapter 4
LEGAL PROCEEDINGS

As seen from the previous chapters, some courts in the common law countries have jurisdiction over both civil and criminal cases while others deal only with one type of cases; nevertheless, disputes are almost always first heard in trial courts. Basically, a trial court has two responsibilities. First, a trial court is the trier of fact and decides what actually occurred in a case either by a jury if there is one, or by the trial court judge if no jury is involved. Sometimes the parties agree on the facts, but often they do not. The trial court achieves this responsibility through trial proceedings. A court will hear the <u>testimony</u> of witnesses and examine other <u>evidence</u> to determine which version of the facts is correct. The second responsibility of a trial court is to determine what legal rules should be applied to decide a particular case. Both parties to the dispute, represented by their attorneys, will argue their positions, but the judge makes the final decision. After the facts and the law have been determined, the trial court will then decide which party <u>prevails</u>.

The losing party may challenge the trial court decision in a higher or appellate court if that party believes the trial court judge made a mistake that affected the outcome in stating or applying the relevant legal rules. Appellate courts usually accept the <u>factual</u> determination made by the trial court and do not re-evaluate the facts of the disputes; the only remaining issues are legal ones. Therefore, there are no witnesses appearing before the appellate court and the judges decide the case mainly through reviewing the trial records and both parties' appellate briefs. Very often, the appellate court judges will hear <u>oral argument</u> made by the attorneys for both parties. After examining the legal rule or rules at issue, the appellate court will <u>uphold</u> or reverse the trial court

testimony 证词
evidence 证据

prevail 占上风,更有优势

factual 事实上的

oral argument 口头论证

uphold 支持

decision as applicable. Since the appellate court decisions form part of the precedent, the appellate court judges are concerned about different matters when making the appellate decision. Unlike trial courts whose responsibilities are limited largely to ascertaining what actually happened and doing justice in individual cases, appellate courts must think about a range of situations far beyond the facts of the case and about the broader policy implications of what the trial court has done. They are making the binding law by reviewing the decisions made by many trial courts under them, thus they help ensure that the rules are understood and applied uniformly.

The following pages will introduce the American court proceedings to illustrate the common law court practice. The persons involved in a dispute before a trial court are referred to as the "parties." The party who initiates the civil proceeding is the "plaintiff," and the party against whom the action is brought is the "defendant." In a criminal proceeding, a "prosecutor" brings an action on behalf of the State against the person accused of committing a criminal offence, who is referred to as the "accused" or the "defendant." The losing party who is not satisfied with the trial court's decision and appeals the case to a higher court is called "appellant" or "petitioner," while the party against whom an appeal is initiated is the "appellee" or "respondent."

4.1 Commencement of the Proceeding — Pretrial

4.1.1 Filing with the Court: Complaint

A legal proceeding starts when a plaintiff (or the prosecution in a criminal case) files the case with the court. There will be various written documents required to be submitted to the court or delivered alternatively by the parties to one another during the whole proceeding, until the questions of fact and questions of law to be decided in the case have been ascertained. These documents collectively are called "pleadings." The pleadings must be carefully drafted because at trial the judge may refuse to admit evidence or decide matters which were not properly pleaded. The filing of pleadings is governed strictly by rules of civil procedure or rules of the court. In order to bring a litigation, the first pleading a plaintiff is required to submit to the court is called a "complaint" (an "indictment" if it is a criminal case), which must allege facts sufficient to state a cause of action against the defendant. Here a cause of action is the legal theory upon which the plaintiff bases his or her right to bring a claim against the defendant, and it must be based upon an accepted rule of law.

indictment 公诉书

4.1.2 Service of Process

After a case is filed with court, the plaintiff must give official notice to the defendant by way of a proceeding known as "service of process." The plaintiff's lawyer should draft a <u>summons</u> or a writ of summons and take it to the <u>clerk</u> of the court, who will sign and seal it. The summons and complaint must then be "<u>served</u>," i.e., delivered to the defendant in one of the ways authorized by procedural law. In the United States, there is an informal way of service of process. The plaintiff's attorney simply mails the defendant the complaint and a special form. If the defendant signs it and mails it back, it is regarded as a "<u>waiver of service</u>," and the proceeding may proceed.

service of process 诉讼书状送达

summons 传票
clerk 书记员
serve 送达

waiver of service 放弃要求依法送达的权利

4.1.3 The Response: Motion, Answer, and Reply

Once the defendant has been properly served, he or she will have a specified period of time to provide with the court a pleading in reply to the claim(s) stated in the complaint, which may be a motion attacking the summons and complaint in some way or a <u>responsive</u> pleading, referred to as "an <u>answer</u>" in the United States and "a <u>defense</u>" in England. A motion is a request to the court that it do something while it takes no position on the truth or falsity of plaintiff's <u>allegations</u>. An answer, however, does respond to the allegations of the complaint. Through this pleading, the defendant answers the allegations in the complaint by a series of <u>admissions</u> and <u>denials</u>. If the defendant believes that he or she has a cause of action against the plaintiff, another defendant, or a new party, he or she may raise a claim against the plaintiff by means of a pleading known as a <u>counterclaim</u>, <u>cross-claim</u>, or <u>third-party claim</u>. In most cases, the pleadings stop with the answer. Nevertheless, if the defendant has filed a counterclaim, the plaintiff will respond to the allegations in the counterclaim by a pleading known as a <u>reply</u> or <u>defense to counterclaim</u>.

responsive 回应的
answer 答辩
defense 抗辩

allegation 指控,陈述

admission 承认
denial 否认

counterclaim 反诉
cross-claim 交叉诉讼请求
third-party claim 针对第三人的诉讼请求

reply 对反诉的答辩
defense to counterclaim 对反诉的抗辩

4.1.4 Discovery

After the pleadings are closed, there is an <u>interlocutory</u> stage of proceedings referred to as discovery, which provides mechanisms for a party to obtain information about the case both from other parties in the case and from third parties not in the case. There are various means of discovery, including <u>disclosure</u>, <u>inspection of documents</u>, <u>oral depositions</u>, <u>written interrogatories</u>, and physical and mental examinations. Disclosure requires the parties to reveal to each other certain basic information about the case, such as names of witnesses, existence of certain documents, the basis for damage calculations, and the like. The inspection of documents enables one party to request the other party to <u>produce</u> documents for inspection. In addition, one party can request the court to order the other party or any witnesses to answer questions <u>under oath</u> in the absence of the judge, which is called oral deposition. Written interrogatories can be used by one party to request the other party to answer questions in writing. If a motion is granted by the court, physical and mental examinations may be conducted. The purpose of discovery is to promote judicial efficiency.

4.2 Trial Date and Jury Selection

4.2.1 Trial Date Assignment

Cases are set for trial in two basic ways: individual calendars and central assignment systems. With individual calendars, each trial judge is responsible for the overall handling of every case assigned to that judge's <u>docket</u>, including setting the trial date and trying the case. In civil cases, after discovery is completed and the parties state that the case is ready to be tried, the judge will set a trial date. That date will vary, but frequently the trial date in civil cases is at least three to six months after the case is ready to be tried. Criminal cases, because of <u>speedy trial</u> requirements, usually get trial dates within three to four months of arrest or <u>arraignment</u>.

Central assignment systems are found more frequently in large urban areas. Under that system, cases are scheduled on one central calendar for trial assignment purposes. The oldest cases are at the top. It may take a long time for the newer cases to move up and ultimately get to the top of the list when it is sent to a judge for trial.

Jurisdictions having a central assignment system usually publish the trial calendar in the daily legal newspaper, and it is the lawyers' responsibility to keep track of their cases as they move up the calendar.

4.2.2 Jury Selection

If the parties do not want to settle the case outside the court, the case will go to trial on an assigned date. The trial may be a jury trial or a trial without a jury, *i.e.*, a bench trial. Jury trial is a remarkable feature of common law system whereby a jury will be the trier of facts who will determine the facts of the case. *The Seventh Amendment* to the *U.S. Constitution* provides that "[i]n suits at common law, where the value in controversy shall exceed twenty dollars, the right of trial by jury shall be preserved. ..." Thus, in the United States it is a constitutional right to be tried by a jury although the parties may agree to waive a jury trial. In some other common law countries, most civil cases, except for defamation cases, will be tried without a jury. In that case, the trier of fact will be the judge.

bench trial 法官审判

suit 这里指民事诉讼

A jury is a body of citizens with various backgrounds who are summoned by the court to decide questions of fact in a judicial proceeding. Methods of choosing the jury pool and the jurors for a particular case differ widely. In case of a jury trial, before the trial starts, the judge will first order a jury, directing the bailiff or other court personnel to go to the jury room and bring a panel of 25 to 40 or more jurors back to the courtroom. Jury selection then begins.

jury pool 候选陪审团,这里指为了确定执行陪审任务的人选,而随机抽选的人员组合,是陪审员选任程序的第一步。
juror 陪审员
bailiff 法警;法庭事务官

Usually the judge, but sometimes a court clerk or the attorneys will first tell the jurors something about the case, names of the parties and witnesses, and any other information that may help to identify persons who might not be suitable jurors. Then the jurors are questioned individually and as a group; the questioning is conducted by the judge, the lawyers, or both. The process is called jury selection, also *voir dire* examination. It is actually a process of deselection because both sides attempt to remove jurors favorable to their opponent and unfavorable to their client. In effect, attorneys are helping select their own judges of the facts in the trial.

jury selection 挑选陪审团
voir dire 陪审团资格预审程序

client 委托人

Through this process, the counsel for both parties can gather sufficient information about each juror in order to determine if that juror has prejudices or biases which may

counsel 代理人;律师

prejudice 成见,偏见
bias 偏见

interfere with a fair and impartial consideration of the evidence. They are also able to familiarize the jurors with certain facts and legal information about the case, to precondition jurors to favorably receive their legal concepts, arguments and themes, to obtain commitments, and to establish rapport and trust with the jury. Both parties may challenge jurors "for cause" and each has a number of so-called "peremptory challenges." The challenge for cause means the party who decides to dismiss or strike a juror must state a legally sufficient reason. On the other hand, a peremptory challenge allows the parties to dismiss a juror for a reason that needs not be stated. The method of using challenges and the timing of challenges differ widely among courts. Basically, jury selection is controlled by statutes, court rules, and individual judicial practices. After the jury selection process, from those called to hear the particular case, twelve, or sometimes six jurors will form a panel and be seated in the jury box.

4.2.3 Preliminary Instructions of Law

After the jurors have been selected and before the actual trial starts, the judge usually gives the jury preliminary instructions on the law. This orients the jurors and lets them know what will happen during the trial. For instance, the judge will probably summarize their duties as jurors, instruct them on how to conduct themselves during recesses, and describe how trials are conducted. The judge will instruct the jurors to follow the law, determine the facts and credibility of witnesses, and apply the facts to the law, but not to discuss the case among themselves or with others, visit the scene, or research the case in any way. The judge may also summarize the pleadings and the applicable substantive law. This usually takes only a few minutes. During this period, the attorneys for both parties may also ask the judge to order the exclusion of witnesses during the trial, which is called "separating witnesses" or "invoking the rule." This prevents witnesses from sitting in the courtroom while other witnesses are testifying.

4.3 Trial

The actual court trial starts from the opening statements made by both parties.

4.3.1 Opening Statements

Opening statements are the lawyers' opportunities to tell the jury what happened to their clients and what they expect the evidence will be during the trial. This helps the jury understand the evidence when it is actually presented. Opening statements should be factual, not argumentative, although the rules adopted in different jurisdictions and by different judges vary considerably in how much argument and discussion of law they allow in the openings. Most opening statements are based on story-telling, usually giving a chronological overview of what happened from either the plaintiff's or defendant's viewpoint. The statement should be engaging, presenting each side's case in the best possible light and drawing a picture that will make the jury want to find in that side's favor. Normally the plaintiff's attorney presents his or her opening statement first, then followed by the defendant's attorney.

argumentative 辩论性的

in the best possible light 最充分地

4.3.2 Plaintiff's Case in Chief

After both parties have had the chance to present their opening statements, the plaintiff will present his or her case in chief first since the plaintiff has the burden of proof. This is the time for the plaintiff (plaintiff's attorney) to present evidence before the jury and the judge. This means that in the plaintiff's case in chief, plaintiff (or prosecutor in a criminal case) must present sufficient proof on each element of each legal claim alleged in the complaint (or indictment in a criminal case), using every possible sources of proof. The procedure at trial will be governed by the rules of civil procedure or the rules of the court as well as the rules of the law of evidence. The plaintiff will be allowed to present evidence in support of his or her version of the facts and to call witnesses to testify on his or her behalf.

case in chief 庭审中的一方证明对方责任或抗辩己方无责的举证阶段

burden of proof 举证责任

Witnesses' testimonies are one important type of evidence. When a witness is called by the plaintiff's attorney to testify, he or she is first sworn to tell the truth by the court clerk. Once the witness is seated in the witness chair, the plaintiff's lawyer will examine him or her. This is called direct-examination or examination in chief. Direct examination is the questioning of a witness by the lawyer calling the witness. When the direct is completed, the lawyer usually says "nothing further on direct, your Honor," "pass the witness," or "your

sworn 宣誓

direct-examination 直接询问

witness," depending on local custom, then cross-examination begins. Cross-examination is the questioning of a witness by the lawyer other than the one calling the witness. In the plaintiff's case in chief, cross-examination is done by the defendant's lawyer. American rule limits the scope of the cross-examination to the subject matter of the direct; the English rule, however, allows cross-examination to go into any relevant matter. Most states in the United States adopt the American rule while some adopt English rule. When the cross-examiner announces he or she is done, the direct examiner may conduct a redirect examination but the questioning must be limited to explaining or refuting matters brought out on cross. The cross-examiner may conduct a recross-examination; similarly, the questioning must be limited to matters brought out during the redirect. The witness is then excused, and plaintiff calls another witness.

Another principal source of evidence is exhibits, including real objects such as guns, blood, drugs, or machinery; demonstrative exhibits including any diagrams, models, or maps; writings such as contracts, promissory notes, checks, or letters; and records, which may include private business and public records. In order to introduce exhibits, attorneys must first lay foundations otherwise the court will not admit the exhibits. The foundation may come from witness testimony, certification, or other methods. If an exhibit is admitted in evidence, it will be considered by jurors in determining the facts of the case.

Stipulations may also be used as evidence during trial. A stipulation is an agreement between the parties that certain facts exist and are not in dispute. This makes the presentation of undisputed evidence more efficient. Stipulations are usually made in writing and are shown or read to the jury much like any written exhibit. The judge usually instructs the jury on what a stipulation is.

Judicial notice is the fourth method of getting evidence to the jury. A judge can admit evidence through judicial notice when the fact is either well known in the jurisdiction where the trial is being held or the fact can be easily determined and verified from a reliable source. For example, a court will be judicially noticed that San Francisco is in the state of California, or, there was an earthquake impact on Japan on a certain day.

When the plaintiff has finished presenting all his or

her evidence, he or she "rests." This is done simply by standing up and announcing to the judge and jury, "Your Honor, plaintiff rests." The judge tells the jury that the plaintiff has finished presenting evidence; the judge then will probably take a recess to hear defendant's motions.

4.3.3 Defendant's Case in Chief

The same procedure will next be followed on behalf of the defendant. Defendant's case in chief has two possible components: evidence to refute plaintiff's proof, and evidence to prove any <u>affirmative defenses</u>, counterclaims, cross-claims, and third-party claims in multiple-party cases. When defendant finishes presenting all his or her evidence, he or she "rests" by standing up and announcing to the judge and jury, "Your Honor, defendant rests."

> affirmative defense 肯定性答辩，指被告并不否认原告所主张之事实的真实性，而是提出其他理由来说明为什么自己不应承担责任的答辩。

4.3.4 Closing Arguments

Plaintiff and defendant then give their closing arguments. Closing arguments are very different from opening statements. Closing arguments are the lawyers' opportunities to tell the jury what the evidence has been, how it ties into the jury instructions, and why the evidence and law compel a <u>verdict</u> in their favor. Effective closing arguments integrate the facts and law and argue that the credible evidence, when applied to the law, requires a favorable verdict. Lawyers can argue <u>inferences</u> from the facts, refer to important testimony, use admitted exhibits, tell stories, employ analogies, and use a range of other techniques to persuade the jury. In most jurisdictions the plaintiff has the right to argue first and, after defendant has argued, make a <u>rebuttal</u> argument.

> closing argument 结案陈词，指在诉讼中法官向陪审团作出指示之前，双方律师向法官或陪审团就案件证据问题所做的集中阐述，旨在解释、说明其认为己方已经证实了的、有利于自己当事人的证据，以及认为对方所没有证实的证据，与开庭陈述（opening statement）相对。
>
> verdict 裁决
>
> inference 推理
>
> rebuttal 否认；反驳；这里指控方或原告对对方当事人所举证据的反驳。

4.3.5 Jury Instructions

After both parties finish their closing arguments and other motions, the judge will need to grant jury instructions. Both parties may have requested instructions before or at the beginning of trial and then the judge must rule on which jury instructions will be submitted to the jury. Usually, however, the judge cannot reach final decisions on which instructions to submit to the jury until he or she has heard all the evidence. For that reason the instructions conference is usually held after both sides rest and before the closing arguments. During the instructions conference plaintiff and defendant argue why instructions should be given, denied, or modified. During the conference, which may be held in court (without the jury present) or in chambers, the court reporter should be present to record the objections and rulings. In most jurisdictions the lawyers must make specific objections on the record to requested instructions if they would appeal the case in the future based on an error made by the trial court judge in refusing their requested instructions.

When closing arguments are completed and the instructions are settled, the judge instructs the jury on the law that must be applied to the case. In most jurisdictions the judge will both read the instructions and give the jury a written set of the instructions to use during deliberations.

4.3.6 Verdict

After having received instructions from the judge, the jurors are sent to a conference room to confer privately together, which is referred to as deliberations. The bailiff usually carries the admitted exhibits and the written jury instructions back to the jury room for use during the deliberations. The jurors will also receive the standard instructions on how it should organize and conduct itself. Actually, the only guidelines contained therein may include that the jurors should first select a foreperson to preside over their deliberations and that the foreperson and other jurors must sign the verdict forms that reflect their decisions. How the jury organizes itself and conducts the deliberations is largely up to the jury. During the time they are conferring, no one is allowed to talk to them.

In most cases the parties do not agree with each other as regard to the facts, so the jury must first decide in such cases of conflicting factual evidence, whether one side may be lying or exaggerating, or giving evidence based upon faulty memory or poor observation of events, *etc*. After the jury has decided what it considers to be the true facts of the dispute, it then applies the applicable principles of law, as explained to them by the judge through giving the instructions, to those facts. Jurors sometimes have questions during their deliberations. They should write these questions down and the bailiff will bring them to the judge, who then confers with the lawyers on how to respond. When a response is prepared, the jury is brought back into the courtroom and given the response. Deliberations then continue.

For a decision of the jury to be valid, all of the jurors

must agree upon a decision <u>unanimously</u> or <u>by a majority</u>, depending on the jurisdiction. If they do not make their decision in one day, they are allowed to return to their homes at night after promising that they will not discuss the lawsuit with anyone. They then return the next day to confer together some more, and this procedure is followed until a decision is reached. In a complicated case, the jury may confer for several days before reaching a decision. When the jury reaches a verdict and signs the appropriate forms, it signals to the judge that it is ready to return the verdict. The lawyers, if they are not in the courthouse, are called, and everyone reappears in the courtroom. The jury is brought in, and the judge asks if the jury has reached a verdict. When the foreperson answers "yes," the foreperson is directed to give the verdict to the bailiff, who gives it to the judge, who gives it to the court clerk to be read aloud.

unanimously 一致地
by a majority 多数意见

If the jurors are not able to agree by the necessary vote on which way to decide the case, the judge usually asks the jury whether further deliberations might be useful or whether the jury is hopelessly <u>deadlocked</u>. If the latter, the judge declares a <u>mistrial</u>, excuses the jury, and the parties must then start all over again and have another trial to decide their dispute.

deadlock 陷入僵局
mistrial 无效审理

4.3.7 Motions

A motion is a request to the court that it do something. The parties may make various motions at any stage of the proceeding.

A. Pretrial Motions — <u>Summary Judgment</u>

Summary judgment is a mechanism for deciding cases for which a trial is not necessary and would serve no purpose. Theoretically, a party may make a motion for summary judgment at any stage of the proceeding; however, such motions are not ordinarily granted until after the factual development of the case is complete — that is, after discovery. At this stage, one party may move for summary judgment asserting that there is "no genuine issue as to any material fact." The rationale behind this mechanism is that a trial involves substantial financial and social costs, and little purpose is served by having one unnecessarily. If the judge grants the motion, then the case will end and no further trial will be conducted.

summary judgment 即决判决，指当当事人对案件中的主要事实不存在真正的争议或案件仅涉及法律问题时，法院不经陪审团对事实进行认定，而及早解决案件的一种方式。申请人要求即决判决，必须证明重要事实没有争点。

B. Judgment as a Matter of Law — Directed Verdict

A party at the close of the other party's case may move for judgment as a matter of law, commonly known as a directed verdict. In so moving, the party would be asking the judge to take the case away from the jury to prevent it from considering the evidence and reaching a verdict. The ground for the motion would be that the evidence presented would support only one result: there is no legally sufficient evidentiary basis for a reasonable jury to find for that party on that issue. If that is true, the judge should save everyone's time by announcing the result that a properly functioning jury would inevitably reach. To grant such a motion results in final judgment being entered against the party with the burden that he or she has failed to carry. A judge should direct a verdict only if there is no rational basis for a jury to find in favor of the party against whom the verdict is directed.

Thus, after plaintiff rests and the jury has been excused and has left the court-room, defendant usually moves for a directed verdict, asking the judge to terminate the trial in whole or part, and enter judgment for the defense, because plaintiff has failed to prove a *prima facie* case. If plaintiff has failed to present any evidence to support any element of any claim brought in the complaint or indictment, the judge should grant the motion as to that unproved claim. The standard applicable to the motion is that the judge must view the evidence "in the light least favorable to the movant." Accordingly, if there is any credible evidence, either direct or circumstantial, supporting the claim, the motion should be denied. Hence, it is up to the defendant to point out why there has been a fatal absence of proof on any required element of plaintiff's claims.

Similarly, after defendant rests and the jury has been excused and has left the courtroom, plaintiff can move for a directed verdict on any of defendant's affirmative defenses and counter-claims. The judge must again view the evidence "in the light least favorable to the movant" in ruling on the motions. If there is a failure of proof on any required element of any affirmative defense or counter-claim, the judge should grant the motion as to that defense or counterclaim.

When all the evidence is in and both sides have rested, plaintiff or defendant may again move for a directed verdict at the close of all the evidence. Again, the standard remains the same: the judge must take the evidence "in the light least favorable to the movant." In many jurisdictions a motion for a directed verdict at the close of all the evidence is required to preserve the right to move for <u>judgment notwithstanding the verdict</u> after trial.

 A judge may grant all, deny all, or grant part of the motion. For instance, a judge may grant the motion on one count of the complaint and deny the motion as to the other counts. The trial then continues.

judgment notwithstanding the verdict (J.N.O.V.) 与陪审团裁决相反的判决

C. Post-Trial Motions — J.N.O.V. and New Trial

 After a verdict is returned, a party may file written post-trial motions within certain period of time. The most common motions are a motion for judgment notwithstanding the verdict (J.N.O.V.) and a motion for a new trial.

 Either party may move for a J.N.O.V., asking the judge to <u>set aside</u> the jury's verdict and enter judgment for the other side. If a verdict is insupportable because there was simply no evidence from which a rational person could have found for the party who won the verdict, the judge may grant such a motion which is essentially a late ruling on the earlier motion for judgment as a matter of law. The grounds for a J.N.O.V. are identical to those for a pre-verdict judgment as a matter of law: "that there is no legally sufficient evidentiary basis for a reasonable jury to find for the party against whom the motion is made."

set aside 撤销,宣布无效

 A party may also at this stage ask the judge to order a new trial because of claimed errors made during the first trial. The judge may grant such a motion if he or she concludes that the process leading up to the verdict has been <u>flawed</u>, or the result of that trial, *i.e.*, the verdict, is <u>unjustifiable</u>. The most common ground for granting a new trial is that the verdict is against the weight of the evidence.

flawed 有瑕疵的
unjustifiable 不公正的

 The judge will usually schedule a hearing on the motions and allow the parties to argue orally. The judge will then rule on the motions and usually will prepare a written order.

4.3.8 Judgment

 When post-trial motions have been decided, the judge enters judgment in accordance with the jury verdict and post-trial motions. A judgment refers to a decision or ruling of the court upon the respective rights and claims of the parties in a case. Since a court must decide the case before it, judgment must be given in favor of either the plaintiff or the defendant. After the judgment is entered, the case ends in the trial court.

4.4 Appeal

The party who loses the case in the trial court can usually appeal to a higher court <u>as a matter of right</u>. A party wishing to appeal the judgment must file a timely notice of appeal with the clerk of the trial court or directly to the higher court. This act begins the appellate process. The party who appeals is referred to as the appellant or the <u>plaintiff-in-error</u>. It does not matter whether he or she was the plaintiff or the defendant in the trial court. The other party to the appeal is referred to as the appellee, respondent, or the <u>defendant-in-error</u>.

When hearing an appeal the appellate court will not re-examine the decisions of the trial court with regard to which side's contentions of facts are correct and will confines itself to reviewing the written record of the trial court. It usually does not hear witnesses or have new evidence submitted to it. The appellate court makes its decisions on the basis of written transcripts of the trial court proceedings. The trial court's determination of facts is greatly <u>deferred</u> because the trial court is regarded to be best able to decide factual matters since it actually sees the witnesses' faces, hears their voices, *etc.*, and thus can better judge whether they are lying, exaggerating, uncertain, *etc*. Arguments in the appellate courts are most often on questions of law rather than <u>questions of fact</u>. The appellate court thus usually only decides whether the trial court has applied the wrong law or has misinterpreted principles of law in making its decision.

Cases in appellate courts are usually heard by an odd-numbered panel of judges because a simple majority of the court will decide the case. Panels of three judges normally hear cases in the intermediate court of appeals. Sometimes, however, a <u>full bench</u> consisting of all the judges in the court may be <u>convened</u> to review an important case. When that happens, all the judges are sitting "*en banc*." The decision or ruling of the appellate court is also referred to as judgment, and the court will give judgment for either the appellant or the respondent. If the appellate court upholds the decision of the lower court, the judgment of the lower court is said to be affirmed. If the appellate court decides to set aside the judgment of the lower court, the judgment of the lower court is said to be reversed. If the trial court's judgment is reversed, the appellate court may either order that a new trial be conducted in the trial court or, under some circumstances order that judgment be entered for the party who lost in the trial court.

affirm 维持(原判)

reverse 推翻(原判)

If all judges on a panel agree on the decision and on the reasoning, one of them will be selected to deliver the judgment on behalf of the entire panel. This is referred to as the judgment of the court. If a judge agrees with the decision or result but does not completely agree with the reasons for the decision, he or she may choose to deliver a separate judgment of his or her own which is referred to as a concurring opinion. If a judge on a panel disagrees with the decision or result reached in the case by the majority of judges, he or she will usually deliver a dissenting opinion giving the reasons why he or she would have decided the case the opposite way. It is to be noted that in England the judgments of members of the House of Lords are often referred to as speeches.

A party dissatisfied with the appellate court's decision may in some cases appeal that decision to the court of the last resort in the jurisdiction, which has the final say in the matter. However, it is not a matter of right for the parties to make such appeals and a leave is required.

4.5 Summary

Trial procedures in the United States are complicated and vary greatly from jurisdiction to jurisdiction. However, they are identical to certain extent. During the pre-trial stage, one party must file with the court by submitting required pleadings, and then serve the other party, and the other party must submit answers within a statutorily stated period of time. A discovery procedure may be followed afterwards. After the completion of the discovery procedure, any party may move to the court for a summary judgment if the party can convince the judge that there is no genuine issue regarding the material facts. If the judge rules against such a motion, the trial will proceed.

convince 使……信服

On the assigned date of trial, the first thing is the selection of jury, and the process is also called *voir dire* examination. Through this process, the judge and attorneys may be able to get more information about the jurors' background in order to deselect those who are inappropriate for serving as jurors in the trial. The attorneys may also take this opportunity to give the potential jurors a general introduction of the case, and meanwhile get commitments from them. After the specified number of jurors has been selected, the actual trial begins.

The next event in the proceeding is for lawyers for each side to make an "opening statement" to the court. The plaintiff's lawyer is the first to make an opening statement and explain the nature of the parties' dispute and what facts and evidence the plaintiff will present to support his or her side of the case. The defendant's lawyer then has the opportunity to speak and describe the defendant's version of the dispute and the nature of the evidence which he or she will present.

Then comes the plaintiff's case-in-chief. The plaintiff's witnesses are called to give their testimony about the facts of the dispute. First they are questioned by the plaintiff's lawyer. This is called "direct examination." At this time, the plaintiff's attorney asks each witness to testify the facts which will help prove the plaintiff's version of the dispute. After the witness has answered the questions from the plaintiff's attorney, the witness is then questioned by the defendant's lawyer. This is called "cross-examination." By cross-examination, the opposing lawyer seeks to cast doubt on the witness' story. The lawyer will ask the witness questions designed to show such things as a poor memory of the events, inconsistencies or inaccuracies in the witness' testimony, doubts on the part of the witness about his or her testimony, *etc*. As a part of the proceeding, the witnesses frequently present other "evidence" in the form of written documents, such as correspondence between the parties before the dispute occurred, contract documents or invoices, public/governmental records, and also such things as photographs, maps, scale, models, or anything else that will help explain the matter being testified about. After the plaintiff rests, the defendant may move to the court for a directed verdict or a judgment as a matter of law, requesting the judge not to submit the case to the jury and instead make a judgment directly. If the court grants this motion, the trial will end at this stage. No further

---

cast doubt on 对……产生怀疑

inconsistency 前后矛盾
inaccuracy 不精确,不准确

proceeding is necessary.

However, if the court rules against this motion, the defendant will present his or her case-in-chief. The defendant presents his or her witnesses through direct-examination, and they are then subject to cross-examination by the plaintiff's attorney. Again, after the defendant rests, both parties may move for a directed verdict or judgment as a matter of law, asking the judge to make judgment without submitting the case to the jury.

After all testimony and evidence have been presented, and if the court has not granted the motion for a directed verdict, the attorneys for the parties are given an opportunity to speak and make "closing arguments." At that time, each summarizes the testimony and evidence in a manner most favorable to their side and argues why the judge or jury should decide in favor of their client.

Following the closing arguments, the judge will give the jury instructions and then send the jury into conference room for deliberations. If sufficient number of jurors have reached agreement on the disputed facts, the court will announce the verdict. After that, the parties will have another opportunity to move for a judgment notwithstanding the verdict, or a new trial. Considering all factors, the judge will make a judgment or decision, which ends the trial proceeding.

The case, however, is not over yet. The losing party may appeal the trial court's decision as a matter of right. A penal of three judges in an appellate court usually will review the appeal by examining the trial record. Since the facts have been determined by the trial court which will be given great deference, the appellate court judges will not re-evaluate the facts; instead, they will only examine the legal issues. After reading the appellate briefs submitted by both parties and hearing their oral argument, the court will affirm the lower court's decision if it decides to uphold it; or will reverse that decision if it disagrees. The reversion of the lower court's decision may result in either a new trial or a direct judgment in favor of the losing party.

Any party not satisfied with the appellate court's decision may appeal to the supreme court of the jurisdiction, *i.e.*, the court of the last resort, for relief. However, this is not a matter of right, so leave from the

Supreme Court should be obtained in order to further appeal the case

Review Questions

1. What are the differences among a complaint, an answer, a motion, and a reply?
2. Please comment on the jury system.
3. What are the differences between opening statement and closing argument?
4. What are the differences between direct-examination and cross-examination?

PART II
CASE LAW

PART I introduces the general concept of common law and its basic features, from which we know that case law is the most important source of law in common law countries. As a matter of fact, when people talk about common law, very often they mean the case law. Case law is also called judge-made law, which is different from statutory law made by legislature. Generally, statutory law refers to written statutes enacted by legislature and compiled by government in various law collection books. The application of statutory law in common law countries is similar to that in civil law countries where statutes are the primary binding legal source. Case law, instead, is in the form of court decisions and is published in various case reporters. Complied in the case reporters are hundreds of thousands court decisions made by courts in the past centuries. Part II will explain how the case law works in guiding the judicial work and where to find them.

Chapter 5
DOCTRINE OF *STARE DECISIS*

5.1 Rule of Precedent

Judges and lawyers in civil law countries seek guidance from enacted statutes in practicing law; however, a common law court looks to previous decisions on a similar issue for guidance in deciding a present case. As mentioned in earlier Chapters, the previous decisions on similar questions are known as precedents, and the rule that requires the court to follow precedents is called the rule of precedent. The rule of precedent is one of the fundamental notions of common law system, which is based on an idea that an issue, once properly decided, should not be decided again. However, the rule of precedent is not absolute. Under the doctrine of *stare decisis*, not all previous decisions are precedents.

5.2 Doctrine of *Stare Decisis*

Frequently, the rule of precedent and the doctrine of *stare decisis* are mentioned together and people tend to use them interchangeably. They are actually different. The rationale of the rule of precedent is that once a dispute is properly decided in one way, the similar disputes should not be decided in a different way in the future. The doctrine of *stare decisis* is based on the rule of precedent; however, it requires that a court follow its own decisions and the decisions of higher courts within the same jurisdiction. The term "*stare decisis*" is a shortened form of the phrase "*stare decisis et non quieta movere*," which means "to stand by precedents and not to disturb settled points." Common law judges base their reasoning and decision-making on this doctrine. They seek fairness and believe that it would only be fair that if a court has decided a particular case in one way, it should decide a subsequent case which involves similar facts and issue the same way.

The court that made the previous decision and the nature of the decision determine whether and how the previous decision is treated as a binding precedent. Even if a previous decision is a precedent, a court may or may not be bound by it because a court is only bound to follow the binding precedents instead of persuasive precedents. A precedent becomes binding on a court if it was decided by that court or a higher court in the same jurisdiction under the doctrine of *stare decisis*. When a precedent case was decided by a court other than a higher court in the same jurisdiction or the court itself, it is not binding but may be persuasive only. A court may find a persuasive precedent helpful because the reasoning of other courts may suggest solutions to a problem.

Since the doctrine of *stare decisis* requires lower courts to follow decisions of higher appellate courts, it presupposes a hierarchy of courts in the legal system so that different courts are at different positions within the hierarchy and courts at a lower position will be bound by decisions made by courts at a higher position. Judges and lawyers will need to find the case law in order to examine the binding precedents. Therefore, a reliable system of reporting and publishing court decisions is very necessary for this doctrine to apply.

The doctrine of *stare decisis* requires that a court follow only those precedents that are binding authorities and not those precedents that are only persuasive authorities. On the one hand, a court must follow a binding precedent when deciding a similar case even if the court believes the case was wrongly decided or would lead to injustice in the case before them, although the doctrine of *stare decisis* is not absolute and a court may refuse to follow a binding precedent. However, when a court decides not to follow a binding precedent, it must first explain why previous cases are inapplicable. On the other hand, the doctrine does not require a court to follow a decision from another jurisdiction or a lower court in the same jurisdiction. These decisions are not binding. Although not binding, such decisions may be persuasive. When an authority is persuasive, the court deciding a dispute is free to follow or refuse to follow it.

Theoretically, the rule of precedent and the doctrine of *stare decisis* give the continuity, cohesion, and predictability which every legal system needs because under this doctrine, it seems that judges merely need to find the law as it already exists in the law reports and apply it to the facts of the case before them. However, in reality, most cases have to be decided on their own facts and merits. The rules contained in the precedents may not be able to sufficiently cover the new problems so judges must modify or create new rules based on their own judgment to resolve them.

5.3 The Function of *Stare Decisis*

The doctrine of *stare decisis* furthers several objectives. The first objective is fairness, which requires that like cases be treated alike. Since a judge must follow precedents and must give written justification explaining why he or she decided not to follow a precedent, people believe that judges are unlikely to base their decisions on arbitrary or impermissible criteria. Therefore fairness and justice are achieved.

justification 认为正当的理由

impermissible 不应被许可的, 不应被允许的

The second objective the doctrine of *stare decisis* serves is certainty and predictability, which enables people to plan their lives and reduce the risks of becoming involved in litigation. Certainty is reflected when people in the jurisdiction know that courts will follow prior decisions made by higher courts within the same jurisdiction when trying new similar cases, and they will be able to plan their conduct accordingly to avoid being involved in litigation. Predictability is reflected when courts base their judgments on the rules and principles contained in the precedents in developing new rules governing new questions.

The doctrine of *stare decisis* also serves the purpose of efficiency. The doctrine requires courts to follow precedents so that courts do not need to reconsider the legal issues already decided, thus the efficiency of the judicial decision making is improved and the judiciary's credibility is enhanced.

The fourth objective of this doctrine is flexibility. Although the doctrine seems to be strict in requiring the courts to follow precedents, it provides some necessary flexibility to enable judges to do justice in individual cases and to develop the law to meet changing conditions and circumstances. For example, appellate courts, especially the highest appellate court within each jurisdiction, are not bound by any decisions made by courts below them in the hierarchy. Neither may the highest appellate court regard itself as strictly bound by its own decisions. This way, the highest court may be able to create new rules when necessary.

Precedents as a source of law may be construed differently by different courts. Sometimes they are construed broadly to cover a larger scope of cases, while other times they are construed narrowly so that they are applicable only to limited types of new cases. Some courts apply the doctrine rigidly while others not. In *The London Street Tramways Co. Ltd. v. London County Council*, [1898] A.C. 375 (H.L.), a case decided by the House of Lords, Lord Halsbury L.C. wrote:

> ... My lords, for my own part I am prepared to say that I adhere in terms to what has been said by Lord Campbell and assented to by Lord Wensleydale, Lord Cranworth, Lord Chelmsford and others, that a decision of this House once given upon a point of law is conclusive upon this House afterwards, and that it is impossible to raise that question again as if it was *res integra* and could be reargued, and so the House be asked to reverse its own decision. That is a principle which has been, I believe, without any real decision to the contrary, established now for some centuries, and I am therefore of opinion that in this case it is not competent for us to rehear and for counsel to reargue a question which has been recently decided ...
>
> ...
>
> My Lords, it is totally impossible, as it appears to me, to disregard the whole current of authority upon this subject, and to suppose that what some people call an "extraordinary case," an "unusual case," a case somewhat different from the common, in the opinion of each litigant in turn, is sufficient to justify the rehearing and rearguing before the final Court of Appeal of a question which has been already decided. Of course I do not deny that cases of individual hardship may arise, and there may be a current of opinion in the profession that such a judgment was erroneous; but what is that occasional interference with what is perhaps abstract justice as compared with the inconvenience — the disastrous inconvenience — of having each question subject to

being reargued and the dealings of mankind rendered doubtful by reason of different decisions, so that in truth and in fact there would be no real final Court of Appeal? My Lords, "*interest rei publicae*" that there should be "*finis litium*" at some time, and there could be no "*finis litium*" if it were possible to suggest in each case that it might be reargued, because it is "not an ordinary case," whatever that may mean. Under these circumstances I am of opinion that we ought not to allow this question to be reargued.

  My Lords, I only wish to say one word in answer to a very ingenious argument which the learned counsel set before your Lordships. It is said that this House might have omitted to notice an Act of Parliament, or might have acted upon an Act of Parliament which was afterwards found to have been repealed. It seems to me that the answer to that ingenious suggestion is a very manifest one — namely, that that would be a case of a mistake of fact. If the House were under the impression that there was an Act when there was not such an Act as was suggested, of course they would not be bound, when the fact was ascertained that there was not such an Act or that the Act had been repealed, to proceed upon the hypothesis that the Act existed. They would then have ascertained whether it existed or not as a matter of fact, and in a subsequent case they would act upon the law as they then found it to be, although before they had been under the impression, on the hypothesis I have put, either on the one hand that an Act of Parliament did not exist, or on the other hand that an Act had not been repealed (either case might be taken as an example) and acted accordingly. But what relation has that proposition to the question whether the same question of law can be reargued on the ground that it was not argued or not sufficiently argued, or that the decision of law upon the argument was wrong? It has no application at all.

  Under these circumstances it appears to me that your Lordships would do well to act upon that which has been universally assumed in the profession, so far as I know, to be the principle, namely, that *a decision of this House upon a question of law is conclusive, and that nothing but an Act of Parliament can set right that which is alleged to be wrong in a*

interest rei publicae 公共利益
finis litium 终局诉讼

ingenious 精妙的

repeal 撤销,废除
manifest 显然的,明白的

hypothesis 假设

proposition 主张,观点

judgment of this House. For these reasons, my Lords, I move your Lordships that this appeal be dismissed with costs.

(*Emphasis added*).

This had been a leading authority on the doctrine of *stare decisis* in the House of Lords of England until it issued the *1966 Practice Statement* (*Judicial Precedent*). The Lords focused on the possibility for the House to reconsider and reargue an issue previously decided in an 1894 case. The conclusion of the House was that once an issue had been previously decided by itself, the House should not reconsider it. The rigidity of the application of the doctrine of *stare decisis* can be seen from this case. Apparently, this rigidity had defeated the flexibility objective of the doctrine and brought some problems which came into the House's attention. It took several decades for the House of Lords to reconsider it and ultimately decide to change it. Sixty-eight years after the above case was decided, the House changed the situation and announced a *Practice Statement* in 1966:

Their Lordships regard the use of precedent as an indispensable foundation upon which to decide what is the law and its application to individual cases. It provides at least some degree of certainty upon which individuals can rely in the conduct of their affairs, as well as a basis for orderly development of legal rules.

Their Lordships nevertheless recognize that too rigid adherence to precedent may lead to injustice in a particular case and also unduly restrict the proper development of the law. They propose, therefore, to modify their present practice and, while treating former decisions of this House as normally binding, to depart from a previous decision when it appears right to do so.

In this connection they will bear in mind the danger of disturbing retrospectively the basis on which contracts, settlements of property and fiscal arrangements have been entered into and also the especial need for certainty as to the criminal law.

This announcement is not intended to affect the use of precedent elsewhere than in this House.

Lord Gardiner L. C. , *The Practice Statement* (*judicial Precedent*), [1966] 1 W. L. R. 1234 (H. L.)

It is fair to say that since 1966, the House of Lords could depart from the prior precedents decided by itself when "it appear[ed] right to do so." The last sentence contained in the *Statement* above explicitly emphasized that the *Statement* only applied to the House instead of other courts below the House.

Traditionally, English courts apply the doctrine of *stare decisis* more rigidly than American courts. In the United States, although all lower courts must follow the precedents decided by a higher court within the same jurisdiction and the higher court should follow its own precedents, the higher court may avoid applying a precedent by determining that the facts in the present case are sufficiently dissimilar from the precedent case. In doing so, the court distinguishes the precedent. In addition, if a higher court determines that a precedent was wrongly decided or outdated, the higher court may overrule the precedent and create a new rule in its opinion. However, a justification must be stated to explain why the precedent is overruled and why a new rule is necessary.

distinguish 分辨,区分

5. 4 Courts Affected by *Stare Decisis*

Stare decisis affects three types of courts: the lower courts in a jurisdiction, the higher courts in a jurisdiction, and the courts in other jurisdictions. The following sections explain the impact of the doctrine on those courts.

5. 4. 1 The Courts in England
A. Lower Courts

Since within each jurisdiction the court system is a hierarchical one with the lowest courts at the bottom and the court of the last resort at the top, *stare decisis* provides that a lower court is bound to follow decisions of courts which are superior to it within the jurisdiction. Since lower courts are located at the bottom of the hierarchy, they are bound by decisions of all the courts superior to them within the same jurisdiction. Accordingly, they do not need to follow a decision made by a court below it within the jurisdiction; neither do they need to follow a decision made by a court of another jurisdiction. Specifically, the High Court and other lower courts in England are bound to follow decisions of the Court of Appeal and the Supreme Court (formerly the House of Lords). The Court of Appeal is bound to follow decisions of the Supreme Court.

B. Higher Courts

While a lower court is bound to follow decisions made by a higher court, a higher court is not bound to follow decisions made by a lower court within the hierarchy of the jurisdiction. However, a higher court is generally bound to follow its own decisions. But this rule is not strictly applied and different courts have different practices in this regard. As we have seen from the case *The London Street Tramways Co., Ltd. v. The London County Council*, [1898] A. C. 375, the House of Lords had considered itself strictly bound by its own decisions. However, from 1966, the House of Lords decided to adopt a more flexible approach. Since then, the highest court in England would be able to depart from its previous decisions when it determines that it is right to do so. As a matter of fact, the Judicial Committee of the Privy Council has never considered itself strictly bound by its own decisions. Neither is there any rule regarding whether an intermediate appellate court in England should be bound by its own prior decisions. These ambiguities leave much room for appellate courts to determine whether they are bound by their own prior decisions in deciding new cases.

5.4.2 The Courts in the United States
A. Federal Courts

The decisions of the Supreme Court of the United States are binding on all courts in all jurisdictions for matters of constitutional and other federal law, although the Supreme Court is not strictly bound to its own decisions. A federal court of appeals is bound only by its own decisions and those of the Supreme Court. The decisions of federal courts of appeals do not bind each other. A federal district court is bound by its own decisions, decisions of court of appeals of the circuit in which the district court is located, and decisions of the Supreme Court. It is not bound by decisions of any other district court or decisions of other federal courts of appeals.

As discussed in earlier sections, the U. S. federal courts also have jurisdiction over the state law cases where the parties have diversity citizenship. When dealing with diversity suits, the federal court must apply state law and thus follow state courts' decisions on state <u>substantive law</u> questions.

substantive law 实体法

B. State Courts

Since state courts also have jurisdiction over federal issues, they are bound by federal courts' interpretations of federal law when federal law issues are litigated before them. When dealing with state law issues, a state court must follow precedents decided by the higher courts in the state. Accordingly, a state trial court must follow precedents decided by court of appeals and the highest court of that state. An appellate court of the state must follow decisions of the state's supreme court and itself, but it is not bound by decisions of the other appellate courts if there are multiple courts of appeals in that state, because those courts are not superior to it, although the decisions made by them usually are very persuasive.

5.5 Components of a Judicial Decision

Under the doctrine of *stare decisis*, a court is bound to follow the prior decisions made by higher courts within the same jurisdiction or by the court itself when the causes of action of the precedents are the same as the cause of action of the new case, and when the material facts of the precedents are similar to the facts before the court. However, even if a court is bound to follow a precedent, not everything said by a court in its opinion has authority as precedent. A judicial opinion may be very long, but is composed of two main parts: <u>*ratio decidendi*</u> and <u>*obiter dictum*</u>.

Ratio decidendi, also called "<u>holding</u>" of a decision, is the proposition of law which was necessary for its decision on the facts of that particular case; therefore, it is the part of a decision which establishes legal principles and rules which carry binding authority under the doctrine of *stare decisis*. It explains the reason or ground for the decision.

The remaining language in the opinion is referred to as *obiter dictum* or *dicta*, which carries less weight in

ratio decidendi 主旨意见；法庭判决中确立的法律原则，也叫"holding"，与附带意见(*dicta*)相对

obiter dictum 同"*dicta*"，附带意见，指法官在作出判决的过程中就某一与案件并不直接相关的法律问题所作的评论，它并非为本案判决所必要，因此不具有判例的拘束力，与"holding"或"*ratio decidendi*"相对。

holding 判例的主旨意见，判决中确立的法律原则

legal argument. "*Obiter dictum*" or "*dicta*" means "a saying by the way," referring to all languages contained in the decision that are not part of the holding. This part of the opinion includes statements or observations made by a court in its judgment which were not necessary for its decision, and thus does not have binding authority on later courts. Statements that are *dicta* are not always unimportant, however. Sometimes the *dicta* in a case become more important in later years than the holding of the case because *dicta* reflect other judges' concerns and often indicate how a court would rule in the future, given a particular set of facts.

5.6 Types of Judicial Decisions

A judicial decision or opinion is a statement by judges explaining why they decided the case the way they did. Since there is not a unified format of how to draft an opinion, different judges write opinions differently based on their personal writing styles. No matter how different the opinions may be, each opinion is expected to contain a summary of the procedural history of the case, a statement of facts, an explanation of the reasons that lead to the conclusion, and the conclusion of the decision. The different parts of an opinion will be discussed later in Part III. This section will focus on the different types of opinion that could be written by judges in deciding a case.

The judicial opinions given by civil law judges generally contain no indication as to which judge drafted the opinion or how many judges on the panel agreed on the decision. Common law court opinions, however, generally make it clear in the beginning of the opinion which judge wrote the opinion and who agreed on and joined the opinion. This opinion is the one agreed by majority judges on the panel, and is called majority opinion. If there are judges who do not agree on the majority decision, they may write separate opinion(s) expressing their views. Common law judges believe that doing so encourages judicial responsibility. Therefore, it is not uncommon that a common law case opinion is followed by several different opinions.

5.6.1 Majority Opinion

Within the common law court system, a case appealed to an appellate court is usually reviewed by a panel of three or more judges. The final result of the case will be determined by voting of all the judges. If the judges agree unanimously on the proposition of law and the disposition of the dispute, one of them will draft the opinion, explaining the reasoning of the court. This opinion is the opinion of the court. However, if the judges do not agree on how a dispute should be resolved or why a particular decision should be reached, then one of the judges in the majority will write the opinion for the court. This opinion is sometimes referred to as the majority opinion or simply the opinion of the court. The majority opinion of a case is the precedent that lawyers and judges will look to when dealing with new cases before them.

5.6.2 Dissenting Opinion

A dissenting opinion, or simply a dissent, is written by a judge or judges who do not agree on the proposition of law by the majority of judges. It is reasonable and understandable that not all judges agree on one proposition of law. Some legal reasoning contained in the majority's opinion seems unreasonable because there are honest intellectual differences about what the law means or what direction it should take. The analytical process leading to the proposition may also be unreasonable or with limitations. A dissenting opinion often points out these shortcomings contained in the majority opinion and it will lead to a disposition of the case different from that reached by the majority. Therefore, the existence of dissents promotes judicial justice and alerts the courts and lawyers when dealing with similar cases in the future.

5.6.3 Concurring Opinion

A concurring opinion is written by a judge who agrees on the disposition of the case by the majority but does not agree on the proposition of law contained in the majority opinion. Its analytical approach is similar to that of a dissent; however, a dissenting opinion may lead to different disposition of the case while a concurring opinion will lead to the same result but for a different reason. The concurring judges just feel that they need to write a separate opinion to express their own reasoning. Sometimes, a concurring opinion may try to limit the scope of the majority opinion and to explore problems that it presents. It may also encourage the losing party to pursue further proceedings because it points out the weak spots in the majority's opinion. The losing party may find useful support from a concurring opinion (as well as a dissenting opinion) for appeal. See the following comments on dissenting and concurring opinions:

> Unlike *dicta*, which may indicate how a court would rule in the future, a concurring or dissenting opinion indicates only that a judge disagreed strongly enough to write a separate opinion. Nevertheless, these opinions can be a valuable resource. Often, a dissenting or concurring opinion sharpens the focus of the debate. It may offer a different interpretation of precedent, emphasize social policies disregarded by the majority, or frame the legal question in a different way. A court that is considering a change in the law of its jurisdiction or facing an issue of first impression will read concurring and dissenting opinions on the issue in question with great interest. And dissenting opinions in an earlier case are sometimes adopted by a majority of the court in later cases.

John C. Dernbach *et al*, A PRACTICAL GUIDE TO LEGAL WRITING & LEGAL METHOD 36 (2d Ed., Rothman & Co. 1994) (hereinafter, "Dernbach, A PRACTICAL GUIDE").

5.7 Different Ways to Use Precedents

Since the doctrine of *stare decisis* is a fundamental concept of common law system, courts are strictly bound to follow precedents, and if there is a binding authority, a court must follow that authority in deciding similar cases before it. The application of this doctrine seems to be absolute; yet in practice, it is a flexible concept because a judicial opinion may be interpreted in different ways. Actually, a court has freedom to overrule its previous decisions and thus decide a case by a rule different from the one it had previously adopted, although the court may be reluctant to admit this. As a matter of fact, judges may follow, distinguish, or overrule even a binding precedent.

5.7.1 Following Prior Precedents

Under the doctrine of *stare decisis*, a court must follow the *ratio decidendi* of a precedent. It implies that following precedent is mandatory. If a court determines that the material fact of the case before it is very similar to that of a binding precedent, the court must follow the prior precedent required by *stare decisis*.

5.7.2 Distinguishing Prior Precedents

While requiring courts to follow prior precedents, the doctrine of *stare decisis* does not require courts to follow a precedent if the factual situations or the issues of the present case are different from those of the precedent. If that happens, the prior precedent is distinguishable and need not be followed. Accordingly, if a court is unwilling to follow a precedent, the court can try to distinguish the precedent. The most common method of distinguishing a precedent is to claim that the facts of the precedent case are different from the facts of the present case; therefore, the proposition of law of the precedent should not be applied to the present case. A precedent can also be distinguished if the cause of action or issue presented in the precedent case is different from that presented in the present case.

cause of action 案由, 诉因

5.7.3 Overruling Prior Precedents

When a court distinguishes a precedent, the court only says that the precedent is not applicable to the new problem for various reasons, but the precedent is still valid and will be applied to similar cases in the future. However, if a court overrules a precedent, the court actually announces that the precedent is no longer valid and the rule should be changed. Normally the court would be very reluctant to change the law because they believe the legislature is supposed to change the law that is inapplicable owing to the change of circumstances. Therefore, if there is an adverse precedent and the court would not like to apply it to the case before it, the court will always try to distinguish it. However, if the court cannot distinguish such an adverse precedent, the court may overrule the precedent. Nevertheless, even if the court decides to overrule it, they would not like to use the term "overrule" when describing what they are doing; instead, they would carefully choose the words in describing the process as "to depart from" (as the House of Lords did in their 1966 *Statement*) or "not to follow" the prior decision.

change of circumstances 情势变更

A precedent may be overruled because the rule contained in the earlier decision has become outdated owing to changed conditions and thus the reasons and rationale for it may no longer exist. Or, if the rule of the precedent is applied, injustice may occur to the parties in the case at hand. Other reasons include that the precedent rule may be impeding the proper development of the law, has produced undesirable results, or that the precedent was based on what is now recognized as poor reasoning. Sometimes the judges' interpretation of law has changed so that they have a different view toward the precedent rule.

Review Questions

1. What is the difference between the rule of precedent and the doctrine of *stare decisis*?
2. Under what circumstances may a court distinguish a precedent?
3. Are the consequences the same when a court distinguishes a precedent or overrules a precedent?
4. Explain the differences among the majority opinion, concurring opinion, and dissenting opinion.

Chapter 6
COMMON LAW REASONING

Case law is not created by legislature but is a body of rules and principles found exclusively in judicial decisions. Although many scholars have collected the common law rules and translated them into restatements or black letter law, the reasoning of each opinion on which these rules are based forms the core of common law rules and principles. When researching on whether or how a precedent might apply to a case in hand, common law lawyers must first study the reasons contained in the judicial opinion.

In performing law-making function, a common law court is required to consider a case based on various principles. First, the court must dispose the present case before it in favor of one of the parties, and announce which party wins the case and which party loses the case upon completion of the trial. When disposing the case, the court must consider fairness and justice and its impact on society instead of fairness between the two parties. Second, the doctrine of *stare decisis* requires a court to follow the precedents with similar factual situations and the rule of precedent requires a court to consider prior cases that are not binding but with similar facts. If there is such a precedent case and if that case cannot be adequately distinguished, the court must apply the *ratio decidendi* of that precedent to the facts of the case at hand, even if it believes the result will be unfair or unjust. Third, while conducting common law reasoning, the court must consider the impact of its decision on future development of the law, especially if the court is the highest court in a jurisdiction.

With these principles in mind, lawyers analyze their cases by using various types of reasoning.

---

restatement 重述

black letter law 黑体字法，非正式用语，用来表示被法院普遍接受的或体现在某一特定司法管辖区的制定法中基本的法律原则。

completion 完成，结束

6.1 Typical Types of Common Law Reasoning

6.1.1 Deductive and Inductive Reasoning

Deductive reasoning refers to the reasoning from an established general rule of law to the particular facts of a case in common law analysis. For example, if there is a well-established and clear rule of law contained in a precedent case which is applicable under the doctrine of *stare decisis* to the issue before a court, the court will examine the facts of the two cases. If the court finds no material differences in the facts, it will apply the rule of law in the precedent case to the case at hand. This reasoning process is sometimes used by the subsequent courts to expand or limit the proposition of law in the precedent case to cover different fact situations.

On the contrary, inductive reasoning is a method of reasoning from particular to general. In common law analysis, when there is no clear-established rule governing the issue before a court, the court may look to the rules or decisions in the precedent cases within narrow categories to form a general rule which covers a new broader category of fact situations. The precedent cases may establish rules of law which govern only narrow categories of fact situations, but the present case may not fit into those narrow categories. The precedents may have been decided on very narrow grounds which are not applicable in the present case. In such circumstances lawyers will examine the precedents to determine whether they have common characteristics and to determine whether there is implicit in them a general rule of law which governs a broader category of fact situations. If so, they may argue that when the cases are considered together, a general rule of law can be derived from them which is wide enough to include the facts of existing precedents and of the present case.

6.1.2 Analogy and Distinction

Under the doctrine of *stare decisis*, judges decide cases according to principles laid down in earlier similar cases. In order to resolve a new legal problem, judges and lawyers must find those prior cases and analyze the impact that those cases will have on the decision in their own case. Thus, lawyers are always comparing cases by drawing analogies and making distinctions between them. When comparing the cases, a lawyer should compare both the facts and the underlying policies in different cases.

Analogy is a process to extend a rule of law to a fact situation not covered by the express words of the rule when such fact situation is within the policy underlying the rule. When the precedent cases are in the same category of fact situations as the present case, but there is no rule of law found to exist on the legal question before the court, analogy will then be used to determine what rules of law exist to govern the same question in other categories of fact situations. If any such rules of law are found, lawyers may argue that the rule of law in the other categories of fact situations should be applied to this category because the policy considerations underlying the rule are the same. Facts and the underlying policies are important elements used to determine whether a case is analogous to your case, but they are not the only elements. You must also determine that the issues the court dealt with must be the same or similar in significant ways to the issues in your case.

Distinction is a process to avoid the impact and restrict the application of a rule of law contained in the precedents to the fact situation of the present case. This type of reasoning is employed when you decide that the cases are different and that the decision in the precedent case should not control the proposition of your problem. There are various ways that you can distinguish a case. For example, you can distinguish a precedent by establishing that the facts of a precedent case and the present case are materially different so that a different rule should apply to the present case. You may also argue that although the rules contained in the precedent case is applicable, the particular factual situations of the present case require a different outcome. Since it is impossible for two cases to be exactly the same, each case has some differences from other cases. Therefore, you must be very careful when distinguishing cases. Even if you do, the differences between the factual situations of the cases must be significant.

Analogy and distinction are not simply matters of locating obvious similarities and differences. You should also "spot threads running through entire lines of cases that the courts themselves may not have made explicit, and use these threads to weave sophisticated arguments for or against the application of these cases." Dernbach, A PRACTICAL GUIDE 69. By comparing and contrasting your case with the precedents, you can determine whether the rules of the precedent cases fit your case, so that you will be able to predict the probable outcome of your own case. This is a creative process, which is a very important skill for lawyers. After all, "the more analogous these cases are, the more precedent and *stare decisis* dictate the application of their conclusions to the present case. The more distinguishable they are, the more inapplicable they should be." *Id*.

6.1.3 Arguments in Common Law Reasoning

Lawyers may use various arguments, as part of the common law reasoning, to argue their cases. For example, you may argue that a general principle of law will be served if a case is decided in a particular way, or, a general principle of law is different from a rule of law or proposition of law. A rule of law or proposition of law often refers to the rule of law applied to the particular factual situation in the case; however, a general principle of law is the fundamental principle in the legal system and covers broader subjects than a rule of law or proposition of law. If you can convince the judge, he or she may use a general principle of law as a basis for creating new legal rules or in selecting which legal rule should be applied in a particular case.

You may also make a policy argument, arguing that the disposition of your case in a particular way would hurt or enhance the interests or values underlying a legal rule or legal principle. Since the concept is often vague and ambiguous, English judges are generally reluctant to admit in the judicial opinion that they made the decision based on policy reasons. However, it is not difficult for a U.S. judge to admit it.

Another type of argument lawyers may use is the common sense, fairness, and justice argument. If you think a rule of law should be applied, you may argue that it is either based upon common sense, or it is fair or just to apply it. However, if you want to argue that a rule of law should not be adopted, you may claim that the application of the rule will lead to unfairness and injustice to the parties to the present case.

Sometimes, practical consequences arguments may also be used in the common law reasoning. When your argument is based on the practical consequences, you are actually arguing that the application of a certain rule of law will lead to a highly impractical or undesirable result. A common example of a practical consequences argument is the so-called "floodgates argument," referring to the situation where once the rule is adopted, it would lead to a proliferation of claims, or a flood of litigation. Examples include tort cases where a court must decide whether to expand an existing category recognizing a duty of care or to create a new category recognizing a duty of care.

You may also base your argument on the balance of the interests of the two sides to the dispute. In doing so, you should claim various factors that the court should consider and give different weight in deciding the case. In addition, you may argue that the logical consequence of the application of a certain rule of law may lead to absurdity. Such an argument is called arguments *ad absurdum*.

6.2 Techniques and Arguments Used with Case Authorities

Reasoning in common law cases often revolves around case authorities, *i.e.*, precedents. If the precedent is favorable to your case, then it is a favorable authority and you would like to apply the authority in your case. However, if the precedent is favorable to your opponent's case, it is an adverse authority to your case and you would not like to apply it at all; instead, you would rather distinguish or discredit it.

6.2.1 Favorable Authorities

When a precedent is favorable to your client's case, this precedent is a favorable authority. You may want to use the favorable authorities to support your case by arguing that since there are no material differences between the facts of the precedent and the present case, the doctrine of *stare decisis* requires that the *ratio decidendi* of the precedent be applied in your case. Sometimes the facts of the precedent case are not exactly the same as the facts of the present case, you may still want to argue that the rule of the precedent should be applied to your case because the *ratio decidendi* of the precedent should be expanded to cover the facts of your case, or the principles and policies underlying the decision in the precedent case are equally applicable in the present case at hand. In order to strengthen your argument, you

floodgates argument 水闸理论，指若某些法律规则一旦适用，就会导致大量案件适用该规则
proliferation 扩散，泛滥

duty of care 注意义务

balance of the interests 利益平衡

absurdity 荒谬的结果
ad absurdum 荒谬

case authority 作为先例的案例

favorable authority 对（自己的）案子的解决有利的先例

adverse authority 对（自己的）案子的解决不利的先例
discredit 不适用，怀疑

may also want to credit the favorable authorities by arguing that the precedent case was decided by an eminent court or that the judgment cited was written by an eminent judge and the case was exceptionally well reasoned. Also it may add weight to the favorable authority if it has been followed in subsequent cases and has received favorable comments from academic writers.

6.2.2 Adverse Authorities

When a precedent is adverse to your client's case, you do not want to apply the rule of the case, but want to distinguish it. In order to distinguish such a case, you must convince the court that the *ratio decidendi* of the precedent should not be applied in the present case because there is a material fact in the present case which was not present in the precedent case; or there was a material fact in the precedent case which is not present in the present case. In addition to distinguishing the facts of the cases, you may also want to distinguish the issue if the issue in the present case is not the same as that in the precedent case. If so, the *ratio decidendi* of the precedent case is not applicable to the issue in the case at hand either. Lawyers and judges also use a variety of arguments to discredit or cast doubt on the authority of precedents which are against them, especially if the precedents are older cases from lower courts.

6.3 Illustration of the Common Law Reasoning

Below are a series of English and American cases discussing the creation and development of the strict liability rule. When reading the cases, pay attention to how the *stare decisis* doctrine works in the development of the rule, and locate the various arguments which contributed to the process. You may also find the different styles and other differences between the judicial opinions written by English judges and American judges. Otherwise you are only required to get the general idea about the common law reasoning at this moment. The following Part will discuss the different components of a judicial opinion, how to read and summarize a case, and how to analyze a case. After you have studied Part III, especially Chapter 8, and obtained more knowledge about the common law analysis approach, you may want to come back to revisit these cases, brief them, and use the legal analysis approaches adopted by the judges.

6.3.1 Fletcher v. Rylands — The Establishment of the Rule

If your neighbor constructed a reservoir without any fault but later the reservoir flooded and damaged your property, is your neighbor liable for your damage? The case below was aimed at resolving such a legal issue.

Fletcher v. Rylands
L. R. 1 Exch. 265 (1866)

Blackburn J.

This was a special case stated by an arbitrator, under an order of *nisi prius* court, in which the question for the Court is stated to be, whether the plaintiff is entitled to recover any, and, if any, what damages from the defendants, by reason of the matters thereinbefore stated.

In the Court of Exchequer, the Chief Baron and Martin B. were of opinion that the plaintiff was not entitled to recover at all, Bramwell B. being of a different opinion. The judgment in the Exchequer was consequently given for the defendants, in conformity with the opinion of the majority of the court. The only question argued before us was, whether this judgment was right, nothing being said about the measure of damages in case the plaintiff should be held entitled to recover. We have come to the conclusion that the opinion of Bramwell B. was right, and that the answer to the question should be that the plaintiff was entitled to recover damages from the defendants, by reason of the matters stated in the case, and consequently, that the judgment below should be reversed, but we cannot at present say to what damages the plaintiff is entitled.

It appears from the statement in the case, that the plaintiff was damaged by his property being flooded by water, which, without any fault on his part, broke out of a reservoir constructed on the defendants' land by the defendants' orders, and maintained by the defendants.

It appears from the statement in the case, that the coal under the defendants' land had, at some remote period, been worked out; but this was unknown at the time when the defendants gave directions to erect the reservoir, and the water in the reservoir would not have escaped from the defendants' land, and no mischief would

---

reservoir 水库,蓄水池

arbitrator 仲裁员
nisi prius court 由一名法官和陪审团审理案件事实问题的初级法院
entitle 赋予权利
recover 获得赔偿
thereinbefore 在上文
the Court of Exchequer 财税法庭

for the defendant 支持被告

the measure of damages 关于损害赔偿的标准

mischief 伤害

have been done to the plaintiff, but for this latent defect in the defendants' subsoil. And it further appears that the defendants selected competent engineers and contractors to make their reservoir, and themselves personally continued in total ignorance of what we have called the latent defect in the subsoil; but that these persons employed by them in the course of the work became aware of the existence of the ancient shafts filled up with soil, though they did not know or suspect that they were shafts communicating with old workings.

It is found that the defendants, personally, were free from all blame, but that in fact proper care and skill was not used by the persons employed by them, to provide for the sufficiency of the reservoir with reference to these shafts. The consequence was that the reservoir when filled with water burst into the shafts, the water flowed down through them into the old workings, and thence into the plaintiff's mine, and there did the mischief.

The plaintiff, though free from all blame on his part, must bear the loss, unless he can establish that it was the consequence of some default for which the defendants are responsible. The question of law therefore arises, what is the obligation which the law casts on a person who, like the defendants, lawfully brings on his land something which, though harmless whilst it remains there, will naturally do mischief if it escapes out of his land. It is agreed on all hands that he must take care to keep in that which he has brought on the land and keeps there, in order that it may not escape and damage his neighbors, but the question arises whether the duty which the law casts upon him, under such circumstances, is an absolute duty to keep it in at his peril, or is, as the majority of the Court of Exchequer have thought, merely a duty to take all reasonable and prudent precautions, in order to keep it in, but no more. If the first be the law, the person who has brought on his land and kept there something dangerous, and failed to keep it in, is responsible for all the natural consequences of its escape. If the second be the limit of his duty, he would not be answerable except on proof of negligence, and consequently would not be answerable for escape arising from any latent defect which ordinary prudence and skill could not detect.

Supposing the second to be the correct view of the law, a further question arises subsidiary to the first, viz., whether the defendants are not so far identified with the contractors whom they employed, as to be responsible for the consequences of their want of care and skill in making the reservoir in fact insufficient with reference to the old shafts, of the existence of which they were aware, though they had not ascertained where the shafts went to.

We think that the true rule of law is, that the person who for his own purposes brings on his lands and collects and keeps there anything likely to do mischief if it escapes, must keep it in at his peril, and, if he does not do so, is *prima facie* answerable for all the damage which is the natural consequence of its escape. He can excuse himself by showing that the escape was owing to the plaintiff's default; or perhaps that the escape was the consequence of *vis major*, or the act of God; but as nothing of this sort exists here, it is unnecessary to inquire what excuse would be sufficient. The general rule, as above stated, seems on principle just. The person whose grass or corn is eaten down by the escaping cattle of his neighbor, or whose mine is flooded by the water from his neighbor's reservoir, or whose cellar is invaded by the filth of his neighbor's privy, or whose habitation is made unhealthy by the fumes and noisome vapors of his neighbor's alkali works, is damnified without any fault of his own; and it seems but reasonable and just that the neighbor, who has brought something on his own property which was not naturally there, harmless to others so long as it is confined to his own property, but which he knows to be mischievous if it gets on his neighbor's, should be obliged to make good the damage which ensues if he does not succeed in confining it to his own property. But for his act in bringing it there no mischief could have accrued, and it seems but just that he should at his peril keep it there so that no mischief may accrue, or answer for the natural and anticipated consequences. And upon authority, this we think is established to be the law whether the things so brought be beasts, or watery or filth, or stenches.

The case that has most commonly occurred, and which is most frequently to be found in the books, is as to the obligation of the owner of cattle which he has brought on his land, to prevent their escaping and doing mischief. The law as to them seems to be perfectly settled from early times; the owner must keep them in at his peril, or he will be answerable for the natural consequences of their escape; that is with regard to tame beasts, for the grass

want of care 注意义务

prima facie 初步证明,表面证据。指表面上充分有效的证据,在法律上足以证明当事人的请求或答辩所依据的事实。但对方当事人可以提出反证加以反驳,在此情况下,审判人员应对各种证据进行综合比较与权衡。
vis major 不可抗力
the act of God 天灾,属于不可抗力

on principle 原则上
just 正义的,公平的
cattle 牛

cellar 酒窖
invade 入侵
filth 脏物
privy 厕所
habitation 住所
fumes 烟气
noisome vapor 臭烟
alkali works 碱性物质
damnify 损害

mischievous 有害的
make good the damage 赔偿损失
ensue 接着发生

accrue 产生,形成

anticipated consequence 预期的状况

beast 畜生
watery 都是水的
stench 恶臭

settled 稳定的,稳固的

tame beast 被驯服的畜或兽

they eat and trample upon, though not for any injury to the person of others, for our ancestors have settled that it is not the general nature of horses to kick, or bulls to gore; but if the owner knows that the beast has a vicious propensity to attack man, he will be answerable for that too.

As early as the *Year Book*, 20 Ed. 4. 11. *Placitum* 10, Brian C. J., lays down the doctrine in terms very much resembling those used by Lord Holt in *Tenant v. Goldwin* (1704) 2 Ld. Raym. 1089, 1 Salk. 360 which will be referred to afterwards. It was trespass with cattle. Plea that the defendant's land adjoined a place where defendant had common, that the cattle strayed from the common, and defendant drove them back as soon as he could. It was held a bad plea. Brian C.J. says:

"It behoves him to use his common so that he shall do no hurt to another man, and if the land in which he has common be not enclosed, it behoves him to keep the beasts in the common and out of the land of any other."

He adds, when it was proposed to amend by pleading that they were driven out of the common by dogs, that although that might give a right of action against the master of the dogs, it was no defense to the action of trespass by the person on whose land the cattle went. In the recent case of *Cox v. Burbidge* (1863) 13 C. B. (N. S.) 430 at p.438; 32 L.J. (C.P.) 89, Williams J., says,

"I apprehend the general rule of law to be perfectly plain. If I am the owner of an animal in which by law the right of property can exist, I am bound to take care that it does not stray into the land of my neighbor, and I am liable for any trespass it may commit, and for the ordinary consequences of that trespass. Whether or not the escape of the animal is due to my negligence is altogether immaterial."

So in *May v. Burdett* (1846) 9 Q.B. 101, 112, the Court, after an elaborate examination of the old precedents and authorities, came to the conclusion that,

"a person keeping a mischievous animal, with knowledge of its propensities, is bound to keep it secure *at his peril.*"

And in 1 *Hole's Pleas of the Crown* 430, Lord Hale states that where one keeps a beast, knowing its nature or habits are such that the natural consequence of his being loose is that he will harm men, the owner

"must at his peril keep him up safe from doing hurt, for though he use his diligence to keep him up, if he escape and do harm, the owner is liable to answer damages";

though, as he proceeds to show, he will not be liable criminally without proof of want of care.

In these latter authorities the point under consideration was damage to the person, and what was decided was, that where it was known that hurt to the person was the natural consequence of the animal being loose, the owner should be responsible in damages for such hurt, though where it was not known to be so, the owner was not responsible for such damages; but where the damage is, like eating grass or other ordinary ingredients in damage feasant, the natural consequence of the escape, the rule as to keeping in the animal is the same ...

As has been already said, there does not appear to be any difference in principle, between the extent of the duty cast on him who brings cattle on his land to keep them in, and the extent of the duty imposed on him who brings on his land, water, filth, or stenches, or any other thing, which will, if it escape, naturally do damage, to prevent their escaping and injuring his neighbor, and the case of *Tenant v. Goldwin*, is an express authority that the duty is the same, and is, to keep them in at his peril.

As Martin B. in his judgment below appears not to have understood that case in the same manner as we do, it is proper to examine it in some detail ... Salkeld, who had been counsel in the case, reports the judgment much more concisely, but to the same effect; he says (1 Salk. 361):

"The reason he gave for his judgment was because it was the defendant's wall, and the defendant's filth, and he was bound of common right to keep his wall so as his filth might not damnify his neighbor, and that it was a trespass on his neighbor, as if his beasts should escape, or one should make a great heap on the border of his ground, and it should tumble and roll down upon his neighbor's, ... he must repair the wall of his house of office, for he whose dirt it is must keep it that it may not trespass."

... Martin B, in the Court below says that he thinks this was a case without difficulty, because the defendant had, by letting judgment go by default, admitted his liability to repair the wall, and that he cannot see how it is an authority for any case in which no such liability is admitted. But a perusal of the report will show that it was because Lord Holt and his colleagues thought (no matter for this purpose whether rightly or wrongly) that the liability was *not* admitted, that they took so much trouble to consider what liability the law would raise from the admitted facts, and it does therefore seem to us to be a very weighty authority in support of the position that he who brings and keeps anything, no matter whether beasts, or filth, or clean water, or a heap of earth or dung, on his premises, must at his peril prevent it from getting on his neighbor's, or make good all the damage which is the natural consequence of its doing so.

No case has been found in which the question as to the liability for noxious vapors escaping from a man's works by inevitable accident has been discussed, but the following case will illustrate it. Some years ago several actions were brought against the occupiers of some alkali works at Liverpool for the damage alleged to be caused by the chlorine fumes of their works. The defendants proved that they at great expense erected contrivances by which the fumes of chlorine were condensed, and sold as muriatic acid, and they called a great body of scientific evidence to prove that this apparatus was so perfect that no fumes possibly could escape from the defendants' chimneys. On this evidence it was pressed upon the jury that the plaintiff's damage must have been due to some of the numerous other chimneys in the neighborhood; the jury, however, being satisfied that the mischief was occasioned by chlorine, drew the conclusion that it had escaped from the defendants' works somehow, and in each case found for the plaintiff. No attempt was made to disturb these verdicts on the ground that the defendants had taken every precaution which prudence or skill could suggest to keep those fumes in, and that they could not be responsible unless negligence were showing; yet, if the law be as laid down by the majority of the Court of Exchequer, it would have been a very obvious defense. If it had been raised, the answer would probably have been that the uniform course of pleading in actions on such nuisances is to say that the defendant caused the noisome vapors to arise on his premises, and suffered them to come on the plaintiffs, without stating there was any want of care of skill in the defendant, and that the case of *Tenant v. Goldwin* showed that this was founded on the general rule of law, that he whose stuff it is must keep it that it may not trespass. There is no difference in this respect between chlorine and water; both will, if they escape, do damage, the one by scorching, and the other by drowning, and he who brings them there must at his peril see that they do not escape and do that mischief ...

  But it was further said by Martin B. that when damage is done to personal property, or even to the person, by collision, either upon land or at sea, there must be negligence in the party doing the damage to render him legally responsible; and this is no doubt true, and as was pointed out by Mr. Hellish during his argument before us, this is not confined to cases of collision, for there are many cases in which proof of negligence is essential, as for instance, where an unruly horse gets on the footpath of a public street and kills a passenger: *Hammack v. White* (1862) 11 C. B. (N.S.) 588, 31 L.J. (C.P.) 129; or where a person in a dock is struck by the falling of a bale of cotton which the defendant's servants are lowering, *Scott v. London Dock Company* (1865) 3 H. & C. 596, 34 L.J. (Ex.) 17, 220; and many other similar cases may be found. But we think these cases distinguishable from the present. Traffic on the highways, whether by land or sea, cannot be conducted without exposing those whose persons or property are near it to some inevitable risk; and that being so, those who go on the highway, or have their property adjacent to it, may well be held to do so subject to their taking upon themselves the risk of injury from that inevitable danger; and persons who by the license of the owner pass near to warehouses where goods are being raised or lowered, certainly do so subject to the inevitable risk of accident. In neither case, therefore, can they recover without proof of want of care or skill occasioning the accident; and it is

nuisance 妨害

scorch 烧焦
drown 溺亡
see 确保

collision 碰撞

unruly 难以驾驭的
footpath 人行道

bale 一大捆

warehouse 仓库

believed that all the cases in which inevitable accident has been held an excuse for what *prima facie* was a trespass, can be explained on the same principle, *viz.*, that the circumstances were such as to show that the plaintiff had taken that risk upon himself. But there is no ground for saying that the plaintiff here took upon himself any risk arising from the uses to which the defendants should choose to apply their land. He neither knew what these might be, nor could he in any way control the defendants, or hinder their building what reservoirs they liked, and storing up in them what water they pleased, so long as the defendants succeeded in preventing the water which they were brought from interfering with the plaintiff's property.

The view which we take of the first point renders it unnecessary to consider whether the defendants would or would not be responsible for the want of care and skill in the persons employed by them, under the circumstances stated in the case.

We are of opinion that the plaintiff is entitled to recover, but as we have not heard any argument as to the amount, we are not able to give judgment for what damages. The parties probably will empower their counsel to agree on the amount of damages; should they differ on the principle, the case may be mentioned again.

Judgment for the plaintiff.

In this case, the plaintiff's property was flooded, without any fault on his part, by water which broke out of a reservoir constructed on the defendants' land by the defendants' orders and maintained by the defendants. The trial court decided that the plaintiff lost the case and was not entitled to any compensation. However, the appellate court did not agree. It reversed the case and granted a judgment for the plaintiff. In reviewing the case, the court formulated the rule of law as "that the person who for his own purposes brings on his lands and collects and keeps there anything likely to do mischief if it escapes, must keep it in at his peril, and, if he does not do so, is *prima facie* answerable for all the damage which is the natural consequence of its escape." After this case was decided, it became a binding precedent as to all the lower courts and the court itself. However, it is not binding to a higher court within the jurisdiction. Therefore, the rule established by Judge Blackburn in this case was further reviewed by the House of Lords, who then modified it.

6.3.2 Rylands *v.* Fletcher — Modification of the Rule

Two years later, this case was reviewed by the House of Lords, who modified the rule formulated by the lower court and affirmed it.

Rylands *v.* Fletcher
L. R. 3 H. L. 330 (1868)

The Lord Chancellor (Lord Cairns)

My Lords, in this case the Plaintiff is the occupier of a mine and works under <u>a close of land</u>. The Defendants are the owners of a <u>mill</u> in his neighborhood, and they proposed to make a reservoir for the purpose of keeping and storing water to be used about their mill upon another close of land, which, for the purposes of this case, may be taken as being adjoining to the close of the Plaintiff, although, in point of fact, some intervening land lay between the two. Underneath the close of land of the Defendants on which they proposed to construct their reservoir there were certain old and <u>disused</u> mining passages and works. There were five vertical shafts, and some horizontal shafts communicating with them. The vertical shafts had been filled up with soil and rubbish, and it does not appear that any person was aware of the existence either of the vertical shafts or of the horizontal works communicating with them. In the course of the working by the Plaintiff of his mine, he had gradually worked through the <u>seams of coal</u> underneath the close, and had come into contact with the old and disused works underneath the close of the Defendants.

In that state of things the reservoir of the Defendants was constructed. It was constructed by them through the agency and inspection of an engineer and contractor. Personally, the Defendants appear to have taken no part in the works, or to have been aware of any want of security connected with them. As regards the engineer and the contractor, we must take it from the case that they did not exercise, as far as they were concerned, that reasonable care and caution which they might have exercised, taking notice, as they appear to have taken notice, of the vertical shafts filled up in the manner which I have mentioned. However, my Lords, when the reservoir was constructed, and filled, or partly filled,

a close of land 一片土地
mill 磨坊

disused 废弃不用的

seams of coal 丰富的煤矿

with water, the weight of the water bearing upon the disused and imperfectly filled-up vertical shafts, broke through those shafts. The water passed down them and into the horizontal workings, and from the horizontal workings under the close of the Defendants it passed on into the workings under the close of the Plaintiff, and flooded his mine, causing considerable damage, for which this action was brought.

The Court of Exchequer, when the special case stating the facts to which I have referred, was argued, was of opinion that, the Plaintiff had established no cause of action. The Court of Exchequer Chamber before which an appeal from this judgment was argued, was of a contrary opinion, and the Judges there unanimously arrived at the conclusion that there was a cause of action, and that the Plaintiff was entitled to damages.

My Lords, the principles on which this case must be determined appear to me to be extremely simple. The Defendants, treating them as the owners or occupiers of the close on which the reservoir was constructed, might lawfully have used that close for any purpose for which it might in the ordinary course of the enjoyment of land be used; and if, in what I may term the natural user of that land, there had been any accumulation of water either on the surface or underground, and if, by the operation of the laws of nature, that accumulation of water had passed off into the close occupied by the Plaintiff, the Plaintiff could not have complained that that result had taken place. If he had desired to guard himself against it, it would have lain upon him to have done so, by leaving, or by interposing some barrier between his close and the close of the Defendants in order to have prevented that operation of the laws of nature.

As an illustration of that principle, I may refer to a case which was cited in the argument before your Lordships, the case of *Smith v. Kenrick* (1849) 7 C. B. 515 in the Court of Common Pleas.

On the other hand if the Defendants, not stopping at the natural use of their close, had desired to use it for any purpose which I may term a non-natural use, for the purpose of introducing into the close that which in its natural condition was not in or upon it, for the purpose of introducing water either above or below ground in quantities and in a manner not the result of any work or operation on or under the land, and if in consequence of their doing so, or in consequence of any imperfection in the mode of their doing so, the water came to escape and to pass off into the close of the Plaintiff, then it appears to me that that which the Defendants were doing they were doing at their own peril; and, if in the course of their doing it, the evil arose to which I have referred, the evil, namely, of the escape of the water and its passing away to the close of the Plaintiff and injuring the Plaintiff, then for the consequence of that, in my opinion, the Defendants would be liable. As the case of *Smith v. Kenrick* is an illustration of the first principle to which I have referred, so also the second principle to which I have referred is well illustrated by another case in the same Court, the case of *Baird v. Williamson* (1863) 15 C. B. (N. S.) 317, which was also cited in the argument at the Bar.

My Lords, these simple principles, if they are <u>well founded</u>, as it appears to me they are, really dispose of this case.

well founded 有良好基础的

The same result is arrived at on the principles referred to by Mr. Justice Blackburn in his judgment, in the Court of Exchequer Chamber, where he states the opinion of that Court as to the law in these words:

> "We think that the true rule of law is, that the person who, for his own purposes, brings on his land and collects and keeps there anything likely to do mischief if it escapes, must keep it in at his peril; and if he does not do so, is *prima facie* answerable for all the damage which is the natural consequence of its escape. He can excuse himself by showing that the escape was owing to the Plaintiffs default; or, perhaps, that the escape was the consequence of *vis major*, or the act of God; but as nothing, of this sort exists here, it is unnecessary to inquire what excuse would be sufficient. The general rule, as above stated, seems on principle just. The person whose grass or corn is eaten down by the escaping cattle of his neighbor, or whose mine is flooded by the water from his neighbor's reservoir, or whose cellar is invaded by the filth of his neighbor's privy, or whose habitation is made unhealthy by the fumes and noisome vapors of his neighbor's alkali works, is damnified without any fault of his own; and it seems but reasonable and just that the neighbor who has

brought something on his own property (which was not naturally there), harmless to others so long as it is confined to his own property, but which he knows will be mischievous if it gets on his neighbor's, should be obliged to make good the damage which ensues if he does not succeed in confining it to his own property. But for his act in bringing it there no mischief could have accrued, and it seems but just that he should at his peril keep it there, so that no mischief may accrue, or answer for the natural and anticipated consequence. And upon authority this we think is established to be the law, whether the things so brought be beasts, or water, or filth, or stenches."

My Lords, in that opinion, I must say I entirely concur. Therefore, I have to move your Lordships that the judgment of the Court of Exchequer Chamber be affirmed, and that the present appeal be dismissed with costs.

Lord Cranworth

My Lords, I concur with my noble and learned friend in thinking that the rule of law was correctly stated by Mr. Justice Blackburn in ... delivering the opinion of the Exchequer Chamber. If a person brings or accumulates, on his land anything which, if it should escape, may cause damage to his neighbor, he does so at his peril. If it does escape, and cause damage, he is responsible, however careful he may have been, and whatever precautions he may have taken to prevent the damage.

In considering whether a Defendant is liable to a Plaintiff for damage which the Plaintiff may have sustained, the question in general is not whether the Defendant has acted with due care and caution, but whether his acts have occasioned the damage. This is all well explained in the old case of *Lambert v. Bessey* (1680) T. Raym. 421, reported by Sir Thomas Raymond. And the doctrine is founded on good sense. For when one person, in managing his own affairs, causes, however innocently, damage to another, it is obviously only just that he should be the party to suffer. He is bound *sic uti suo ut non laedat alienum*. This is the principle of law applicable to cases like the present, and I do not discover in the authorities which were cited anything conflicting with it.

The doctrine appears to me to be well illustrated by the two modern cases in the Court of Common Pleas referred to by my noble and learned friend. I <u>allude</u> to the two cases of *Smith v. Kenrick*, and *Baird v. Williamson*. In the former the owner of a coal mine on the higher level worked out the whole of his coal, leaving no barrier between his mine and the mine on the lower level, so that the water <u>percolating through</u> the upper mine flowed into the lower mine, and obstructed the owner of it in getting his coal. It was held that the owner of the lower mine had no ground of complaint. The Defendant, the owner of the upper mine, had a right to remove all his coal. The damage sustained by the Plaintiff was occasioned by the natural flow or <u>percolation</u> of water from the upper <u>strata</u>. There was no obligation on the Defendant to protect the Plaintiff against this. It was his business to erect or leave a sufficient barrier to keep out the water, or to adopt proper means for so conducting the water as that it should not <u>impede</u> him in his workings. The water, in that case, was only left by the Defendant to flow in its natural course.

But in the later case of *Baird v. Williamson* the Defendant, the owner of the upper mine, did not merely suffer the water to flow through his mine without leaving a barrier between it and the mine below, but in order to work his own mine beneficially he pumped up quantities of water which passed into the Plaintiffs mine in addition to that which would have naturally reached it, and so occasioned him damage. Though this was done without negligence, and in the due working of his own mine, yet he was held to be responsible for the damage so occasioned. It was in consequence of his act, whether skillfully or unskillfully performed, that the Plaintiff had been damaged, and he was therefore held liable for the consequences. The damage in the former case may be treated as having arisen from the act of God; in the latter, from the act of the Defendant.

Applying the principle of these decisions to the case now before the House, I come without hesitation to the conclusion that the judgment of the Exchequer Chamber was right. The Plaintiff had a right to work his coal through the lands of Mr. Whitehead, and up to the old workings. If water naturally rising in the Defendants' land (we may treat the land as the land of the Defendants for the purpose of this case) had by percolation found its way

allude 暗指；顺便提及

percolate through 渗透过

percolation 渗透
strata 地层

impede 阻碍，妨碍

down to the Plaintiffs mine through the old workings, and so had impeded his operations, that would not have afforded him any ground of complaint. Even if all the old workings had been made by the Plaintiff, he would have done no more than he was entitled to do; for, according to the principle acted on in *Smith v. Kenrick*, the person working the mine, under the close in which the reservoir was made, had a right to win and carry away all the coal without leaving any wall or barrier against Whitehead's land. But that is not the real state of the case. The Defendants, in order to effect an object of their own, brought on to their land or on to land which for this purpose may be treated as being theirs, a large accumulated mass of water, and stored it up in a reservoir. The consequence of this was damage to the Plaintiff, and for that damage, however skillfully and carefully the accumulation was made, the Defendants, according to the principles and authorities to which I have adverted, were certainly responsible.

  I concur, therefore, with my noble and learned friend in thinking that the judgment below must be affirmed, and that there must be judgment for the Defendant in Error.

  Judgment of the Court of Exchequer Chamber affirmed.

Lord Cairns wrote the majority opinion in which the rule formulated by the lower court was modified as to exclude the "natural user" of the land. "The Defendants, treating them as the owners or occupiers of the close on which the reservoir was constructed, might lawfully have used that close for any purpose for which it might in the ordinary course of the enjoyment of land be used; and if, in what I may term the natural user of that land, there had been any accumulation of water either on the surface or underground, and if, by the operation of the laws of nature, that accumulation of water had passed off into the close occupied by the Plaintiff, the Plaintiff could not have complained that that result had taken place."

  Lord Cranworth wrote a concurring opinion, expressed his slightly different view by formulating a general principle of law relating to the use of land: "In considering whether a Defendant is liable to a Plaintiff for damage which the Plaintiff may have sustained, the question in general is not whether the Defendant has acted with due care and caution, but whether his acts have occasioned the damage." He based his analysis on the Latin phrase *sic uti suo ut non laedat alienum*. Both Lord Cairns and Lord Cranworth cited *Smith v. Kenrick* and *Baird v. Williamson*, you will find more detailed description of the two cases in Lord Cranworth's opinion.

After the case was reviewed by the House of Lords, the strict liability rule, as modified by the House of Lords in this case, has been established and is binding to all courts (including the House itself) in England. Theoretically, all lower courts and the House itself must follow this rule in deciding similar cases in the future. However, the courts treated the rule differently as illustrated below.

6.3.3 Rickards *v.* Lothian — Exceptions to the Rule

Now the story is changed. If your property was damaged by water overflown from your neighbor's lavatory basin owing to a third person's malicious mischief, is your neighbor liable for your damage? The case below occurred in Australia and was reviewed by the Privy Council, who held that the rule in *Rylands v. Fletcher* did not apply.

lavatory basin 洗脸盆
malicious mischief 故意毁坏财物行为

Rickards *v.* Lothian

[1913] **A. C.** 263 (Privy Council)

Lord Moulton

The appellants in this case are the personal representatives of Harry Rickards, who was the defendant in an action for damages brought by the respondent against him in the Melbourne County Court for damages occasioned to the stock in trade of the plaintiff, who was the tenant of the second floor of certain premises belonging to the defendant, by an overflow from a lavatory basin situated on an upper floor of the same premises. Though the sum involved is not large, the legal questions raised by the case are of considerable importance, and the litigation has been characterized by remarkable differences of judicial opinion upon them. Upon the findings of the jury the judge at the trial directed judgment to be entered for the plaintiff for 156 *l.*, the amount of the damages found by the jury. On appeal to the Supreme Court of Victoria that judgment was set aside and judgment entered for the defendant in accordance with the views of a majority of that Court. This decision was reversed on appeal by the

personal representative 身后代理人

tenant 承租人
premise 房屋及附属部件

damages 赔偿金

set aside 撤销

High Court of Australia in accordance with the views of a majority of that Court, and the present appeal is brought by leave from that decision of the High Court of Australia. The circumstances out of which the action arose were as follows:

Their Lordships are of opinion that there was abundant evidence to support the finding of the jury that the plugging of the pipes was the malicious act of some person, and indeed it is difficult to see how upon the evidence any other conclusion could reasonably have been arrived at. ...

It is clear that on these findings the plaintiff did not make good his claim as a claim in an ordinary action of negligence. ...

The principal contention, however, on behalf of the plaintiff was based on the doctrine customarily associated with the case of *Fletcher v. Rylands* (1866) L. R. 1 Ex. 265; (1868) L. R. 3 H. L. 330. It was contended that it was the defendant's duty to prevent an overflow from the lavatory basin, however caused, and that he was liable in damages for not having so done, whether the overflow was due to any negligent act on his part or to the malicious act of a third person.

The legal principle that underlies the decision in *Fletcher v. Rylands* was well known in English law from a very early period, but it was explained and formulated in a strikingly clear and authoritative manner in that case and therefore is usually referred to by that name. It is nothing other than an application of the old maxim "*Sic utere tuo ut alienum non laedas.*" The defendants in that action had constructed a reservoir on their land to collect and hold water for the purpose of working their mill. Under that land were situated underground workings of an abandoned coal mine the existence of which was unknown to everybody. After the reservoir had been filled the water found its way down to those underground workings through some old shafts and escaping through them flooded the plaintiff's colliery. The defendants had been guilty of no negligence either in the construction or use of the reservoir, and they contended that in the absence of negligence they were not liable. The plaintiff contended on the other hand that the defendants having brought and stored the water upon their land for their own purposes were bound to keep it safely there, and that if it escaped to adjoining lands and did damage the defendants were liable for the breach of this duty whether or not it was due to negligence.

The argument took place on a special case stated by an arbitrator setting forth the facts and the contentions of the parties. It was heard in the first instance before the Court of Exchequer, which by a majority decided in favor of the defendants, Bramwell B. dissenting. Error was brought from this judgment, and the Court of Exchequer Chamber reversed the decision of the Court of Exchequer by a unanimous judgment which was read by Blackburn J. On appeal to the House of Lords the judgment of the Exchequer Chamber was affirmed; both Cairns L. C, and Lord Cranworth expressly approving of Blackburn J. 's statement of the law on the subject in the judgment appealed from. The formulation of the principle which is to be found in that judgment is therefore of the highest authority as well from the fact that it received the express approval of the ultimate tribunal as from the eminence of the judges who took part in the decision.

tribunal 法庭,裁判庭,审判庭

So far as is necessary for the present case the law on the point is thus laid down by Blackburn J.:

> "We think that the true rule of the law is that the person who, for his own purposes, brings on his land and collects and keeps there anything likely to do mischief if it escapes, must keep it in at his peril; and if he does not do so, is *prima facie* answerable for all the damage which is the natural consequence of its escape. He can excuse himself by showing that the escape was owing to the plaintiff's default; or, perhaps, that the escape was the consequence of *vis major*, or the act of God; but as nothing of this sort exists here, it is unnecessary to inquire what excuse would be sufficient."

It will be seen that Blackburn J., with characteristic carefulness, indicates that exceptions to the general rule may arise where the escape is in consequence of *vis major*, or the act of God, but declines to deal further with that question because it was unnecessary for the decision of the case then before him. A few years later the question of law thus left undecided in *Fletcher v. Rylands* came up for decision in a case arising out of somewhat similar circumstances. The defendant in *Nichols v. Marsland* (1876) 2 Ex. D. 1 had formed on her land certain ornamental pools which contained large quantities of water. A sudden and unprecedented rainfall occurred, giving rise to a flood of such magnitude that the jury found that it could not reasonably have been anticipated. This flood caused the lakes to burst their dams, and the plaintiff's adjoining lands were flooded. The jury found that there was no negligence in the construction or maintenance of the lakes. But they also found that if such a flood could have been anticipated the dams might have been so constructed that the flooding would have been prevented. Upon these findings the judge at the trial directed a verdict for the plaintiff, but gave leave to move to enter a verdict for the defendant. On the argument of the rule the Court of Exchequer directed the verdict to be entered for the defendant, and on appeal to the Exchequer Chamber that judgment was unanimously affirmed.

The judgment of the Court of Exchequer Chamber was read by Mellish L. J. After pointing out that the facts of the case rendered it necessary to decide the point left undecided in *Fletcher v. Rylands*, he proceeds to lay down the law thereupon in the following language:

"... The ordinary rule of law is that when the law creates a duty, and the party is disabled from performing it without any default of his own, by the act of God, or the King's enemies, the law will excuse him; but when a party by his own contract creates a duty, he is bound to make it good notwithstanding any accident by inevitable necessity. We can see no reason why that rule should not be applied to the case before us. The duty of keeping the water in and preventing its escape is a duty imposed by the law, and not one created by contract. If, indeed, the making a reservoir was a wrongful act in itself, it might be right to hold that a person could not escape from the consequences of his own wrongful act. But it seems to us absurd to hold that the making or the keeping a reservoir is a wrongful act in itself. The wrongful act is not the making or keeping the reservoir, but the allowing or causing the water to escape. If, indeed, the damages were occasioned by the act of the party without more as where a man accumulates water on his own land, but, owing to the peculiar nature or condition of the soil, the water escapes and does damage to his neighbor — the case of *Rylands v. Fletcher* establishes that he must be held liable. The accumulation of water in a reservoir is not in itself wrongful; but the making it and suffering the water to escape, if damage ensue, constitutes a wrong. But the present case is distinguished from that of *Rylands v. Fletcher* in this, that it is not the act of the defendant in keeping this reservoir, an act in itself lawful, which alone leads to the escape of the water, and so renders wrongful that which but for such escape would have been lawful. It is the supervening *vis major* of the water caused by the flood, which, superadded to the water in the reservoir (which of itself would have been innocuous), causes the disaster. A defendant cannot, in our opinion, be properly said to have caused or allowed the water to escape, if the act of God or the Queen's enemies was the real cause of its escaping without any fault on the part of the defendant. If a reservoir was destroyed by an earthquake, or the Queen's enemies destroyed it in conducting some warlike operation, it would be contrary to all reason and justice to hold the owner of the reservoir liable for any damage that might be done by the escape of the water. We are of opinion therefore that the defendant was entitled to excuse herself by proving that the water escaped through the act of God."

supervening 随后发生的
superadd 添加,再加上

innocuous 无害的

the Queen's enemy 外敌

Their Lordships are of opinion that all that is there laid down as to a case where the escape is due to "*vis major* or the King's enemies" applies equally to a case where it is due to the malicious act of a third person, if indeed that case is not actually included in the above phrase. To follow the language of the judgment just recited — a defendant cannot in their Lordships' opinion be properly said to have caused or allowed the water to escape if the malicious act of a third person was the real cause of its escaping without any fault on the part of the defendant.

It is remarkable that the very point involved in the present case was expressly dealt with by Bramwell B. in delivering the judgment of the Court of Exchequer in the same case. He says:

"What has the defendant done wrong? What right of the plaintiff has she infringed? She has done nothing wrong. She has infringed no right. It is not the defendant who let loose the water and sent it to destroy the brides. She did indeed store it, and store it in such quantities that if it was let loose it would do as it did, mischief. But suppose a stranger let it loose, would the defendant be liable? If so, then if a mischievous boy bored a hole in a cistern in any London house, and the water did mischief to a neighbor, the occupier of the house would be liable. That cannot be. Then why is the defendant liable if some agent over which she has no control lets the water out? ... I admit that it is not a question of negligence. A man may use all care to keep the water in ... but would be liable if through any defect, though latent, the water escaped. ... But here the act is that of an agent he cannot control."

Following the language of this judgment their Lordships are of opinion that no better example could be given of an agent that the defendant cannot control than that of a third party surreptitiously and by a malicious act causing the overflow.

The same principle is affirmed in the case of *Box v. Jubb* (1879) 4 Ex. D. 76. In that case the defendants had a reservoir on their land which was connected both for supply and discharge with a watercourse or main drain. Through the sudden emptying of another reservoir into the drain at a higher level than their reservoir and by the blocking of the main drain below, the defendants' reservoir was made to overflow, and damage was done to the lands of the plaintiff. The defendants were guilty of no negligence either in the construction or maintenance of the reservoir, and the acts which led to its overflow were done by persons over whom they had no control. In giving judgment Kelly C. B. says:

"The question is, what was the cause of this overflow? Was it anything for which the defendants are responsible? Did it proceed from their act or default, or from that of a stranger over which they had no control? The case is abundantly clear on this, proving beyond a doubt that the defendants had no control over the causes of the overflow and no knowledge of the existence of the obstruction. The matters complained of took place through no default or breach of duty of the defendants, but were caused by a stranger over whom and at a spot where they had no control. It seems to me to be immaterial whether this is called *vis major* or the unlawful act of a stranger; it is sufficient to say that the defendants had no means of preventing the occurrence. I think the defendants could not possibly have been expected to anticipate that which happened here and the law does not require them to construct their reservoir and the sluices and gates leading to it to meet any amount of pressure which the wrongful act of a third person may impose."

sluice 水闸

Their Lordships agree with the law as laid down in the judgments above cited, and are of opinion that a defendant is not liable on the principle of *Fletcher v. Rylands* for damage caused by the wrongful acts of third persons.

But there is another ground upon which their Lordships are of opinion that the present case does not come within the principle laid down in *Fletcher v. Rylands*. It is not every use to which land is put that brings into play that principle. It must be some special use bringing with it increased danger to others, and must not merely be the ordinary use of the land or such a use as is proper for the general benefit of the community. To use the language of Lord Robertson in *Eastern and South African Telegraph Co. v. Cape Town Tramways Companies* [1902] A.C. 393, the principle of *Fletcher v. Rylands* "subjects to a high liability the owner who uses his property for purposes other than those which are natural." This is more fully expressed by Wright J. in his judgment in *Blake v. Woolf* [1898] 2 Q.B. 426. In that case the plaintiff was the occupier of the lower floors of the defendant's house, the upper floors being occupied by the defendant himself. A leak occurred in the cistern at the top of the house which without any negligence on the part of the defendant caused the plaintiffs premises to be flooded. In giving judgment for the defendant Wright J. says:

leak 漏水

"The general rule as laid down in *Rylands v. Fletcher* is that *prima facie* a person occupying land has an absolute right not to have his premises invaded by injurious matter, such as large quantities of water which his neighbor keeps upon his land. That general rule is, however, qualified by some exceptions, one of which is that, where a person is using his land in the ordinary way and damage happens to the adjoining property without any default or negligence on his part, no liability attaches to him. The bringing of water on to such premises as these and the maintaining a cistern in the usual way seems to me to be an ordinary and reasonable user of such premises as these were; and, therefore, if the water escapes without any negligence or default on the part of the person bringing the water in and owning the cistern, I do not think that he is liable for any damage that may ensue."

This is entirely in agreement with the judgment of Blackburn J. in *Ross v. Fedden* (1872) L. R. 7 Q. B. 661. In that case the defendants were the occupiers of the upper floor of a house of which the plaintiff occupied the lower floor. The supply and overflow pipes of a water-closet which was situated in the defendants' premises and was for their use and convenience got out of order and caused the plaintiffs' premises to be flooded. Negligence was negatived. In giving judgment in favor of the defendants Blackburn J. says:

"I think it is impossible to say that defendants as occupiers of the upper storey of a house were liable to the plaintiff under the circumstances found in the case. The water-closet and the supply pipe are for their convenience and use, but I cannot think there is any obligation on them at all hazards to keep the pipe from bursting or otherwise getting out of order. The cause of the overflow was the valve of the supply pipe getting out of order and the escape pipe being choked with paper, and the judge has expressly found that there was no negligence; and the only ground taken by the plaintiff is that the plaintiff and defendants being occupiers under the same landlord, the defendants being the occupiers of the upper storey, contracted an obligation binding them in favor of the plaintiff, the occupier of the lower storey, to keep the water in at their peril. I do not agree to that; I do not think the maxim, '*Sic utere tuo ut alienum non laedas*' applies. Negligence is negatived; and probably, if the defendants had got notice of the state of the pipe and valve and had done nothing, there might have been ground for the argument that they were liable for the consequences; but I do not think the law casts on the defendants any such obligation as the plaintiff contends for."

Their Lordships are in entire sympathy with these views. The provision of a proper supply of water to the various parts of a house is not only reasonable, but has become, in accordance with modern sanitary views, an almost necessary feature of town life. It is recognized as being so desirable in the interests of the community that in some form or other it is usually made obligatory in civilized countries. Such a supply cannot be installed without causing some concurrent danger of leakage or overflow. It would be unreasonable for the law to regard those who install or maintain such a system of supply as doing so at their own peril, with an absolute liability for any damage resulting from its presence even when there has been no negligence. It would be still more unreasonable if, as the respondent contends, such liability were to be held to extend to the consequences of malicious acts on the part of third persons. In such matters as the domestic supply of water or gas it is essential that the mode of supply should be such as to permit ready access for the purpose of use, and hence it is impossible to guard against willful mischief. Taps may be turned on, ball-cocks fastened open, supply pipes cut, and waste-pipes blocked. Against such acts no precaution can prevail. It would be wholly unreasonable to hold an occupier responsible for the consequences of such acts which he is powerless to prevent, when the provision of the supply is not only a reasonable act on his part but probably a duty. Such a doctrine would, for example, make a householder liable for the consequences of an explosion caused by a burglar breaking into his house during the night and leaving a gas tap open. There is, in their Lordships' opinion, no support either in reason or authority for any such view of the liability of a landlord or occupier. In having on his premises such means of supply he is only using those premises in an ordinary and proper manner, and, although he is bound to exercise all reasonable care,

sanitary 有关卫生和健康的

absolute liability 无过错责任

tap 龙头
ball-cock 浮球阀

he is not responsible for damage not due to his own default, whether that damage be caused by inevitable accident or the wrongful acts of third persons.

On the above grounds their Lordships are of opinion that the direction of the learned judge at the trial to the effect that "if the plugging up were a deliberately mischievous act by some outsider unless it were instigated by the defendant himself, the defendant would not be responsible," was correct in law, and that upon the finding of the jury that the plugging up was the malicious act of some person the judge ought to have directed the judgment to be entered for the defendant.

The appeal must therefore be allowed and judgment entered for the defendant in the action with costs in all the Courts, and the plaintiff must pay the costs of this appeal, and their Lordships will humbly advise His Majesty accordingly.

It is discussed in Part I that the Privy Council historically provided legal opinions to the Commonwealth countries. This case was appealed from the High Court of Australia to the Privy Council. The plaintiff was the tenant of the second floor of certain premises belonging to the defendant. An overflow from a lavatory basin situated on an upper floor of the same premises was caused by a third person which destroyed the plaintiff's stock in trade. The plaintiff sued the defendant for damages based on the rule of *Fletcher v. Rylands*. The Privy Council, however, reasoned that the rule established by the House of Lords left some undecided points so that it could not cover this case. The Lords discussed the exceptions to the rule of *Fletcher v. Rylands*, including the exception pointed out by Blackburn J. as well as the exception untouched by him. Among other things, the Lords agreed that if the damage was caused by act of God or by any third person that was beyond the control of the defendant, the latter is not liable for the damage suffered by the plaintiff. Study the reasoning part of the opinion to see how the Lords treated the authorities that were favorable or adverse to their opinion, and whether the Privy Council justified itself for not following the rule.

6.3.4 Read *v.* Lyons — Interpretation and Application of the Rule

This time you are inside your neighbor's backyard and

are personally injured by your neighbor's activity occurred inside his premise. Is your neighbor liable for your personal injury arising out of the activity? Does the strict liability rule formulated by the House of Lords in *Rylands v. Fletcher* cover this situation?

Over eighty years after *Rylands v. Fletcher* was decided, the House of Lords was facing such a case. The Lords delivered multiple opinions on it. In the majority opinion, Lord Simon pointed out that there were two elements of the rule in *Rylands v. Fletcher*: one is the "escape" of the thing that did harm, while the other is the "non-natural use" of the defendant's premise. Believing that the first element was not satisfied, he thought it unnecessary to consider whether the second element was met, although he expressed his view as *dicta* that he did not think it a non-natural use for the property owner to operate a munitions factory on his premise. Lord MacMillan wrote a separate opinion attacking the strict liability rule. He also mentioned the different treatment of property damage and personal injury as *dicta*. When reading the opinions, analyze the majority opinion's reasoning approach to see how the Lords treated different authorities. Also study other opinions, trying to distinguish whether they are concurring or dissenting opinions.

munitions factory 兵工厂

Read *v*. Lyons
[1947] A. C. 156 (H. L.)

Viscount Simon

... My Lords, no negligence was averred, or proved against the respondents ... and thus the simple question for decision is whether in these circumstances the respondents are liable, without any proof or inference that they were negligent, to the appellant in damages ....

Cassels J. who tried the case, considered that it was governed by *Rylands v. Fletcher* (1866) L. R. 1 Ex. 265, (1868) L. R. 3 H. L. 330, and held that the respondents were liable, on the ground that they were carrying on an ultra-hazardous activity and so were under what is called a "strict liability" to take successful care to avoid causing harm to persons whether on or off the premises. The Court of Appeal reversed this decision, Scott L. J. in an elaborately reasoned judgment holding that a person on the premises had, in the absence of any proof of

aver 断言

inference 推理

ultra-hazardous activity 极度危险活动

on or off the premises 在或不在建筑物内

elaborately 精巧的

negligence, no cause of action, and that there must be an escape of the damage-causing thing from the premises and damage caused outside before the doctrine customarily associated with the case of *Rylands v. Fletcher* can apply.

I agree that the action fails. The appellant was a person present in the factory in pursuance of a public duty (like an ordinary factory inspector) and was consequently in the same position as an invitee. The respondents were managers of the factory as agents for the Ministry of Supply and had the same responsibility to an invitee as an ordinary occupier in control of the premises. The duties of an occupier of premises to an invitee have been analyzed in many reported cases, but in none of them, I think, is there any hint of the proposition necessary to support the claim of the appellant in this case. The fact that the work that was being carried on was of a kind which requires special care is a reason why the standard of care should be high, but it is no reason for saying that the occupier is liable for resulting damage to an invitee without any proof of negligence at all.

Blackburn J., in delivering the judgment of the Court of Exchequer Chamber in *Fletcher v. Rylands* (1866) L. R. 1 Ex. 265, 279, laid down the proposition that

> "the person who for his own purposes brings on his lands and collects and keeps there anything likely to do mischief if it escapes, must keep it in at his peril, and, if he does not do so, is *prima facie* answerable for all the damage which is the natural consequence of its escape."

It has not always been sufficiently observed that in the House of Lords, when the appeal from *Fletcher v. Rylands* was dismissed and Blackburn J.'s pronouncement was expressly approved, Lord Cairns L. C. emphasized another condition which must be satisfied before liability attaches without proof of negligence. This is that the use to which the defendant is putting his land is "a non-natural use" (L. R. 3 H. L., 330, 338-9). Blackburn J. had made a parenthetic reference to this sort of test when he said (L. R. 1 Exch. 265, 280):

> "it seems but reasonable and just that the neighbor, who has brought something on his own property, which was not naturally there, harmless to others so

long as it is confined to his own property, but which he knows to be mischievous if it gets on his neighbor's, should be obliged to make good the damage which ensues if he does not succeed in confining it to his own property."

I confess to finding this test of "non-natural" user (or of bringing on the land what was not "naturally there," which is not the same test) difficult to apply. Blackburn J., in the sentence immediately following that which I have last quoted, treats cattle-trespass as an example of his generalization. The <u>pasturing</u> of cattle must be one of the most ordinary uses of land, and strict liability for damage done by cattle enclosed on one man's land if they escape thence into the land of another, is one of the most ancient propositions of our law. It is in fact a case of pure trespass to property, and thus constitutes a wrong without any question of negligence. See *per* Lord Coleridge C.J. in *Ellis v. Loftus Iron Co.* (1874) L.R. 10 C.P. 10, 12. The circumstances in *Fletcher v. Rylands* did not constitute a case of trespass because the damage was <u>consequential</u>, not direct. It is to be noted that all the counts in the declaration in that case set out allegations of negligence (*see* L.R. 1 Ex. 265) but in the House of Lords Lord Cairns begins his opinion by explaining that ultimately the case was treated as determining the rights of the parties independently of any question of negligence.

The classic judgment of Blackburn J., besides deciding the issue before the court and laying down the principle of duty between neighboring occupiers of land on which the decision was based, sought to group under a single and wider proposition other instances in which liability is independent of negligence, such for example as liability for the bite of a defendant's monkey, *May v. Burdett* (1846) 9 Q.B. 101; *see* also the case of a bear on a chain on the defendant's premises, *Besozzi v. Harris* (1858) 1 F. & F. 92. There are instances, no doubt, in our law in which liability for damage may be established apart from proof of negligence, but it appears to me logically unnecessary and historically incorrect to refer to all these instances as <u>deduced</u> from one common principle. The conditions under which such a liability arises are not necessarily the same in each class of case. Lindley L.J. issued a valuable warning in *Green v. Chelsea Waterworks Co.* (1894) 70 L.T. 547, 549, when he said of *Rylands*

pasturing 放牧

consequential 间接的

deduce 推断

v. Fletcher that that decision

"is not to be extended beyond the legitimate principle on which the House of Lords decided it. If it were extended as far as strict logic might require, it would be a very oppressive decision."

It seems better, therefore, when a plaintiff relies on *Rylands v. Fletcher*, to take the conditions declared by this House to be essential for liability in that case and to ascertain whether these conditions exist in the actual case.

Now, the strict liability recognized by this House to exist in *Rylands v. Fletcher* is conditioned by two elements which I may call the condition of "escape" from the land of something likely to do mischief if it escapes, and the condition of "non-natural use" of the land. This second condition has in some later cases, which did not reach this House, been otherwise expressed, e. g., as "exceptional" user, when such user is not regarded as "natural" and at the same time is likely to produce mischief if there is an "escape." Dr. Stallybrass, in a learned article on *Dangerous Things and Non-Natural User of Land* in 3 CAMBRIDGE LAW JOURNAL, p. 376, has collected the large variety of epithets that have been judicially employed in this connexion. The American *Restatement of the Law of Torts*, vol. 3, section. 519, speaks of "ultra-hazardous activity," but attaches qualifications which would appear in the present instance to exonerate the respondents. It is not necessary to analyze this second condition on the present occasion, for in the case before us the first essential condition of "escape" does not seem to me to be present at all. "Escape," for the purpose of applying the proposition in *Rylands v. Fletcher*, means escape from a place where the defendant has occupation of or control over land to a place which is outside his occupation or control. Blackburn J. several times refers to the defendant's duty as being the duty of "keeping a thing in" at the defendant's peril and by "keeping in" he does not mean preventing an explosive substance from exploding but preventing a thing, which may inflict mischief from escaping from the area which the defendant occupies or controls. In two well-known cases the same principle of strict liability for escape was applied to defendants who held a franchise to lay pipes under a highway and to conduct water (or gas) under pressure through them (*Charing Cross Electricity Supply Co. v. Hydraulic Power Co.* [1914] 3 K. B. 772; *Northwestern Utilities Ltd. v. London Guarantee & Accident Co. Ltd.* [1936] A. C. 108).

In *Howard v. Furness Moulder Argentine Lines Ltd.* (1936) 41 Com. Cas. 290, 296, Lewis J. had before him a case of injury caused by an escape of steam on board a ship where the plaintiff was working. The learned judge was, I think, right in refusing to apply the doctrine of *Rylands v. Fletcher*, on the ground that the injuries were caused on the premises of the defendants. Apart altogether from the judge's doubt (which I share) whether the owners of the steamship by generating steam therein are making a non-natural use of their steamship, the other condition upon which the proposition in *Rylands v. Fletcher* depends was not present, any more than it is in the case with which we have now to deal. Here there is no escape of the relevant kind at all and the appellant's action fails on that ground.

In these circumstances it becomes unnecessary to consider other objections that have been raised, such as the question whether the doctrine of *Rylands v. Fletcher* applies where the claim is for damages for personal injury as distinguished from damages to property. It may be noted, in passing, that Blackburn J. himself when referring to the doctrine of *Rylands v. Fletcher* in the later case of *Cattle v. Stockton Waterworks Co.* (1875) L. R. 10 Q. B. 453, 457, leaves this undealt with: he treats damages under the *Rylands v. Fletcher* principle as covering damages to property, such as workmen's clothes or tools, but says nothing about liability for personal injuries.

On the much litigated question of what amounts to "non-natural" use of land, the discussion of which is also unnecessary in the present appeal, I content myself with two further observations. The first is that when it becomes essential for the House to examine this question it will, I think, be found that Lord Moulton's analysis in delivering the judgment of the Privy Council in *Richards v. Lothian* [1913] A. C. 263 is of the first importance. The other observation is as to the decision of this House in *Rainham Chemical Works Ltd. v. Belvedere Fish Guano Co. Ltd.* [1921] 2 A. C. 465, to which the appellant's counsel in the present case made considerable reference in support of the proposition that manufacturing explosives was a "non-natural" use of land. This was a case of damage to adjoining property: it is reported in the Court of Appeal and in the court of first instance, where it was tried by Scrutton L. J., sitting as an additional judge of the King's Bench Division I find in Scrutton L. J. 's judgment (*id.* 212) that he understood it to be admitted before him that the person in possession of and responsible for the D. N. P. was liable under the doctrine of *Rylands v. Fletcher* for the consequences of its explosions. The point therefore was not really open for argument to the contrary before the House of Lords, where Lord Carson begins his opinion ([1921] 2 A. C. 465, 491, 492) by stating that "it was not seriously argued," and that the real point to be determined was as to the liability of two directors of the appellant company. The opinion of Lord Buckmaster, which covers many pages, is almost exclusively concerned with establishing the directors' liability, and on the other point his observation (*id.* 471) merely is that the making of munitions "was certainly not the common and ordinary use of the land." I think it not improper to put on record with all due regard to the admission and *dicta* in that case, that if the question had hereafter to be decided whether the making of munitions in a factory at the Government's request in time of war for the purpose of helping to defeat the enemy is a "non-natural" use of land, adopted by the occupier "for his own purposes," it would not seem to me that the House would be bound by this authority to say that it was. In this appeal the question is immaterial, as I hold that the appellant fails for the reason that there was no "escape" from the respondents' factory. I move that the appeal be dismissed with costs.

Lord MacMillan

My Lords, nothing could be simpler than the facts in this appeal; nothing more far-reaching than the discussion of fundamental legal principles to which it has given rise. ...

In my opinion the appellant's statement of claim discloses no ground of action against the respondents. The action is one of damages for personal injuries. Whatever may have been the law of England in early times I am of opinion that as the law now stands an allegation of negligence is in general essential to the relevancy of an action of reparation for personal injuries. The gradual development of the law in the matter of civil liability is discussed and traced by the late Sir William Holdsworth with ample learning and lucidity in his *History of English Law*, vol. 8, pp. 446 *et seq*; and need not here be rehearsed. Suffice it to say that the process of evolution has been from the principle that every man acts at his peril and is liable for all the consequences of his acts to the principle that a man's freedom of action is subject only to the obligation not to infringe any duty of care which he owes to others. The emphasis formerly was on the injury sustained and the question was whether the case fell within one of the accepted classes of common law actions; the emphasis now is on the conduct of the person whose act has occasioned the injury and the question is whether it can be characterized as negligent. I do not overlook the fact that there is at least one instance in the present law in which the primitive rule survives, namely, in the case of animals *ferae naturae* or animals *mansuetae naturae* which have shown dangerous proclivities. The owner or keeper of such an animal has an absolute duty to confine or control it so that it shall not do injury to others and no proof of care on his part will absolve him from responsibility. But this is probably not so much a vestigial relic of otherwise discarded doctrine as a special rule of practical good sense. At any rate, it is too well established to be challenged. But such an exceptional case as this affords no justification for its extension by analogy.

The appellant in her printed case in this House thus poses the question to be determined: "Whether the manufacturer of high-explosive shells is under strict liability to prevent such shells from exploding and causing harm to persons on the premises where such manufacture is carried on as well as to persons outside such premises." Two points arise on this statement of the question. In the first place the expression "strict liability," though borrowed from authority, is ambiguous. If it means the absolute liability of an insurer irrespective of negligence then the answer in my opinion must be in the negative. If it means that an exacting standard of care is incumbent on manufacturers of explosive shells to prevent the occurrence of accidents causing personal injuries I should answer the question in the affirmative, but this will not avail the appellant. In the next place, the question as stated would seem to assume that liability would exist in the present case to persons injured outside the defendants'

lucidity 明晰

animals *ferae naturae* 野生动物
animals *mansuetae naturae* 驯养动物
proclivity 倾向

absolve 免除责任
a vestigial relic 退化的遗留物

discard 抛弃

absolute liability 绝对责任

incumbent 职责

avail 有益于

premises without any proof of negligence on the part of the defendants. Indeed, Cassels J. in his judgment records that [(1944) 170 L. T. 418, 420]:

> "It was not denied that if a person outside the premises had been injured in the explosion the defendants would have been liable without proof of negligence."

I do not agree with this view. In my opinion persons injured by the explosion inside or outside the defendants' premises would alike require to aver and prove negligence in order to render the defendants liable.

In an address characterized by much painstaking research Mr. Paull for the appellant sought to convince your lordships that there is a category of things and operations dangerous in themselves and that those who harbor such things or carry on such operations in their premises are liable apart from negligence for any personal injuries occasioned by these dangerous things or operations. I think that he succeeded in showing that in the case of dangerous things and operations the law has recognized that a special responsibility exists to take care. But I do not think that it has ever been laid down that there is absolute liability apart from negligence where persons are injured in consequence of the use of such things or the conduct of such operations. In truth it is a matter of degree. Every activity in which man engages is fraught with some possible element of danger to others. Experience shows that even from acts apparently innocuous injury to others may result. The more dangerous the act the greater is the care that must be taken in performing it. This relates itself to the principle in the modern law of torts that liability exists only for consequences which a reasonable man would have foreseen. One who engages in obviously dangerous operations must be taken to know that if he does not take special precautions injury to others may very well result. In my opinion it would be impracticable to frame a legal classification of things as things dangerous and things not dangerous, attaching absolute liability in the case of the former but not in the case of the latter. In a progressive world things which at one time were reckoned highly dangerous come to be regarded as reasonably safe. The first experimental flights of aviators were certainly dangerous but we are now assured that travel by air is little if at all more dangerous than a railway journey.

Accordingly, I am unable to accept the proposition that in law, the manufacture of high-explosive shells is a dangerous operation which imposes on the manufacturer an absolute liability for any personal injuries which may be sustained in consequence of his operations. Strict liability, if you will, is imposed upon him in the sense that he must exercise a high degree of care, but that is all. The sound view, in my opinion, is that the law in all cases exacts a degree of care commensurate with the risk created. It was suggested that some operations are so intrinsically dangerous that no degree of care however scrupulous can prevent the occurrence of accidents and that those who choose for their own ends to carry on such operations ought to be held to do so at their peril. If this were so, many industries would have a serious liability imposed on them. Should it be thought that this is a reasonable liability to impose in the public interest it is for Parliament so to enact. In my opinion it is not the present law of England.

The mainstay of Mr. Paull's argument was his invocation of the doctrine of *Rylands v. Fletcher*, and especially the passage in the judgment of Blackburn J., so often quoted, approved and followed. Adopting the language of Blackburn J. he said that the respondents here brought on their lands and collected and kept there things likely to do mischief. But the immediately following words used by that eminent judge did not suit so well, for, according to him, the things must be things likely to do mischief if they escape and the duty is to keep them in at peril. In the present case it could not be said that anything had escaped from the respondents' premises or that they had failed in keeping in anything. Mr. Paull was accordingly constrained to paraphrase the words of Blackburn J. and read them as if he had said "likely to do mischief if not so controlled as to prevent the possibility of mischief." He invoked, as did Blackburn J. (L.R. 1 Ex. 265, 280) the case of straying cattle as an illustration of such liability. That again, in my opinion, is a special survival with an[sic] historical background and affords no analogy to the present case.

The doctrine of *Rylands v. Fletcher*, as I understand it, derives from a conception of mutual duties of adjoining or neighboring landowners and its congeners are trespass

sound view 正确的观点
exact 要求
commensurate with 与……相当

scrupulous 严谨的

mainstay 支柱
invocation 调用;适用;启动

congener 同类的人

and nuisance. If its foundation is to be found in the injunction *sic utere tuo ut alienum non laedas*, then it is manifest that it has nothing to do with personal injuries. The duty is to refrain from injuring not *alium* but *alienum*. The two prerequisites of the doctrine are that there must be the escape of something from one man's close to another man's close and that that which escapes must have been brought upon the land from which it escapes in consequence of some non-natural use of that land, whatever precisely that may mean. Neither of these features exists in the present case. I have already pointed out that nothing escaped from the defendants' premises and were it necessary to decide the point I should hesitate to hold that in these days and in an industrial community it was a non-natural use of land to build a factory on it and conduct there the manufacture of explosives. I could conceive it being said that to carry on the manufacture of explosives in a crowded urban area was evidence of negligence, but there is no such case here and I offer no opinion on the point.

It is noteworthy that in *Rylands v. Fletcher* all the counts in the declaration alleged negligence and that on the same page of the report on which his famous *dictum* is recorded Blackburn J. states that

> "... the plaintiff ... must bear the loss, unless he can establish that it was the consequence of some default for which the defendants are responsible."

His decision for the plaintiff would thus logically seem to imply that he found some default on the part of the defendants in bringing on their land and failing to confine there an exceptional quantity of water. Notwithstanding the width of some of the pronouncements, particularly on the part of Lord Cranworth I think that the doctrine of *Rylands v. Fletcher* when studied in its setting is truly a case on the mutual obligations of the owners or occupiers of neighboring closes and is entirely inapplicable to the present case, which is quite outside its ambit.

It remains to say a word about the case of *Rainham Chemical Works Ltd. v. Belvedere Fish Guano Co. Ltd.*. There are several features to be noted. Perhaps most important is the fact that the application of the doctrine of *Rylands v. Fletcher* was not contested except on the ground that it was not non-natural to use land in war-time for the manufacture of explosives. Lord Carson said (*Id*. 491) that the liability of the defendant company "was not seriously argued." In the next place it was a case of damage to adjoining property. The explosion caused loss of life but we find nothing in the case about any claim for personal injuries. It is true that Lord Buckmaster stated (*Id*. 471) (that was not contested, except to the limited extent I have indicated) that the use of the land for the purpose of making munitions was "certainly not the common and ordinary use of the land" and thus brought the case within the doctrine of *Rylands v. Fletcher*, but that was a finding of fact rather than of law. In his enunciation of the doctrine he clearly confined it to the case of neighboring lands. And the case is open to this farther observation that the real contest was not whether there was liability but who was liable, in particular whether two directors of the company which was carrying on the manufacture of munitions were in the circumstances liable as well as the company itself. The case clearly affords no precedent for the present appellant's claim.

enunciation 表达

Your Lordships' task in this House is to decide particular cases between litigants and your Lordships are not called upon to rationalize the law of England. That attractive if perilous field may well be left to other hands to cultivate. It has been necessary in the present instance to examine certain general principles advanced on behalf of the appellant because it was said that consistency required that these principles should be applied to the case in hand. Arguments based on legal consistency are apt to mislead for the common law is a practical code adapted to deal with the manifold diversities of human life and as a great American judge has reminded us "the life of the law has not been logic; it has been experience." For myself, I am content to say that in my opinion no authority has been quoted from case or text-book which would justify your Lordships, logically or otherwise, in giving effect to the appellant's plea. I would accordingly dismiss the appeal.

perilous 危险的

advance 提出

manifold diversity 千差万别

Lord Porter

My Lords, the point for decision by your Lordships in this case may be stated in a sentence. It is, are the occupiers of a munitions factory liable to one of those working in that factory who is injured in the factory itself by an explosion occurring there without any negligence on the part of the occupiers or their servants?

Normally at the present time in an action of tort for personal injuries if there is no negligence there is no liability. To this rule however the appellant contends that there are certain exceptions, one of the best known of which is to be found under the principle laid down in *Rylands v. Fletcher*. The appellant relied upon that case and naturally put it in the forefront of his argument. To make the rule applicable, it is at least necessary for the person whom it is sought to hold liable to have brought on to his premises or at any rate to someplace over which he has a measure of control, something which is dangerous in the sense that, "if it escapes, it will do damage." Possibly a further requisite is that to bring the thing to the position in which it is found is to make a non-natural use of that place. Such at any rate appears to have been the opinion of Lord Cairns L. C. and this limitation has more than once been repeated and approved. *See Richards v. Lothian* [1913] A. C. 263, 280, *per* Lord Moulton. Manifestly these requirements must give rise to difficulty in applying the rule in individual cases and necessitate at least a decision as to what can be dangerous and what is a non-natural use. Indeed, there is a considerable body of case law dealing with these questions and a series of findings or assumptions as to what is sufficient to establish their existence. Amongst dangerous objects have been held to be included, gas, explosive substances, electricity, oil, fumes, rusty wire, poisonous vegetation, vibrations, a flagpole and even dwellers in caravans. Furthermore, in *Musgrove v. Pandelis* [1919] 2 K. B. 43 it was held that a motor car brought into a garage with full tanks was a dangerous object, a conclusion, which as Romer L. J. pointed out in *Collingwood v. Home & Colonial Stores Ltd*. (1936) 155 L. T. 550, 553 involves the propositions "(1) that a motor car is ... a dangerous thing to bring into a garage, and (2) that the use of one's land for the purpose of erecting a garage and keeping a motor car there is not an ordinary or proper user of the land."

My Lords, if these questions ever come directly before this House it may become necessary to lay down principles for their determination. For the present I need only say that each seems to be a question of fact subject to a ruling of the judge as to whether the particular object can be dangerous or the particular use can be non-natural and in deciding this question I think that all the

rusty wire 生锈的铁丝
vibration 摆动
flagpole 旗杆
caravans 大蓬车

circumstances of the time and place and practice of mankind must be taken into consideration so that what might be regarded as dangerous or non-natural may vary according to those circumstances.

I do not, however, think that it is necessary for your Lordships to decide these matters now, in as much as the defense admits that high-explosive shells are dangerous things and, whatever view may be formed as to whether the filling of them is or is not a non-natural use of land, the present case can, in my opinion, be determined upon a narrower ground. In all cases which have been decided, it has been held necessary, in order to establish liability, that there should have been some form of escape from the place in which the dangerous object has been retained by the defendant to some other place not subject to his control. In *Rylands v. Fletcher* it was water, in *Rainham Chemical Works Ltd. v. Belvedere Fish Guano Co. Ltd.*, it was explosive matter, in *National Telephone Co. v. Baker* [1933] 2 Ch. 186, it was electricity, in *Northwestern Utilities Ltd. v. London Guarantee & Accident Co. Ltd.*, it was gas which escaped from the defendants' mains into property belonging to the plaintiff, and so on, in the other instances. In every case, even in *Charing Cross Electricity Supply Co. v. Hydraulic Power Co.*, there was escape from the container in which the defendants had a right to carry the dangerous substance, and which they had at least a license to use, and also an escape into property over which they had no control. Such escape is, I think, necessary if the principle of *Rylands v. Fletcher* is to apply. The often quoted words of Blackburn J. in that case in the Court of Exchequer Chamber (L.R. 1 Ex. 265, 280) are

> "it seems but reasonable and just that the neighbor, who has brought something on his own property which was not naturally there, harmless to others so long as it is confined to his own property, but which he knows to be mischievous if it gets to his neighbor's, should be obliged to make good the damage which ensues if he does not succeed in confining it to his own property,"

and in *Howard v. Furness Houlder Argentine Lines Ltd.*, Lewis J. so decided in a judgment with the result of which I agree. The limitations within which the judgment of

Blackburn J. confines the doctrine have all been the subject of discussion, more particularly as to who is a neighbor, whether knowledge of the danger is a condition of liability and how far personal injuries are covered, but I know of no case where liability was imposed for injury occurring on the property in which the dangerous thing was confined.

It was urged upon your Lordships that it would be a strange result to hold the respondents liable if the injured person was just outside their premises but not liable if she was just within them. There is force in the objection, but the liability is itself an extension of the general rule and, in my view, it is undesirable to extend it further. As Lindley L. J. said in *Green v. Chelsea Waterworks Co.* (1894) 70 L. T. 547, 549

> "That case (*Rylands v. Fletcher*) is not to be extended beyond the legitimate principle on which the House of Lords decided it. If it were extended as far as strict logic might require, it would be a very oppressive decision."

Much of the width of principle which has been ascribed to it is derived not from the decision itself but from the illustrations by which Blackburn J. supported it. Too much stress must not in my opinion be laid upon these illustrations. They are but instances of the application of the rule of strict liability, having for the most part separate historical origins and though they support the view that liability may exist in cases where neither negligence, nuisance nor trespass are to be found, yet it need not as I think necessarily be said that they form a separate coherent class, in which liability is created by the same elements throughout.

I would add that in considering the matter now in issue before your Lordships it is not in my view necessary to determine whether injury to the person is one of those matters in respect of which damages can be recovered under the rule. Atkinson J. thought it was — *see Shiffman v. Order of St. John of Jerusalem* [1936] 1 All E. R. 557, and the language of Fletcher Moulton L. J. in *Wing v. London General Omnibus Co.* [1909] 2 K. B. 652, 665, where he says

> "This cause of action is of the type usually described

ascribe 把……归于

by reference to the well-known case of *Rylands v. Fletcher*. For the purposes of today it is sufficient to describe this class of actions as arising out of cases where by excessive use of some private right a person has exposed his neighbor's property or person to danger."

is to the same effect, and, although the jury found negligence on the part of the defendants in *Miles v. Forest Rock Granite Co. (Leicestershire) Ltd.* (1918) 34 T. L. R. 500, the Court of Appeal applied the rule in *Rylands v. Fletcher* in support of a judgment in favor of the plaintiff for 850 pounds in respect of personal injuries. Undoubtedly the opinions expressed in these cases extend the application of the rule and may some day require examination.

For the moment, it is sufficient to say that there must be escape from a place over which a defendant has some measure of control to a place where he has not. In the present case there was no such escape and I would dismiss the appeal.

Appeal dismissed.

6.3.5 Turner v. Big Lake Oil Co. — The Impact of the Rule on the U. S. Courts

The English case *Rylands v. Fletcher* originated the doctrine of strict liability for abnormally dangerous activities. As illustrated above, the *Rylands* rule is that a person who brings on his or her land anything that was not naturally there, and which is likely to do mischief if it escapes, must keep it in at his or her peril, and if he or she does not do so, is *prima facie* liable for all the damage that is the natural consequence of its escape. The general principle the courts have derived from *Rylands* is that where a person chooses to use an abnormally dangerous instrumentality, that person is strictly liable without showing negligence for any injury proximately caused by that instrumentality.

A precedent decided by a court outside the jurisdiction is not binding in the United States, thus a U. S. court is not bound to follow a precedent decided by a "foreign" court. However, the rule of precedent requires a court to consider the precedents that are not binding, yet may have persuasive authority in deciding similar cases. Will a U. S. court adopt the strict liability rule formulated in *Rylands v. Fletcher*?

instrumentality 手段

When your neighbor operated oil wells and discharged salt water which polluted your land and water and subsequently killed your live stock and plants, is your neighbor liable for your damage? The question seems similar to the questions presented by the line of cases we have discussed so far, yet the case occurred in the United States. Read the opinion below for how the rule in *Rylands v. Fletcher* had been discussed in the courts of the United States. You will also find the different styles and features of the judicial opinions written by British judges and American judges.

Supreme Court of Texas
Turner *et al. v.* Big Lake Oil Co. *et al.*
128 Tex. 155, 96 S.W.2d 221
July 15, 1936

Cureton, Chief Justice

The primary question for determination here is whether or not the defendants in error, without negligence on their part, may be held liable in damages for the destruction or injury to property occasioned by the escape of salt water from ponds constructed and used by them in the operation of their oil wells. The facts are stated in the opinion of the Court of Civil Appeals (62 S.W.2d 491), and will be but briefly noted in this opinion.

The defendants in error in the operation of certain oil wells in Reagan County constructed large artificial earthen ponds or pools into which they ran the polluted waters from the wells. On the occasion complained of, water escaped from one or more of these ponds, and, passing over the grass lands of the plaintiffs in error, injured the turf, and after entering Garrison Draw flowed down the same into Centralia Draw. In Garrison Draw there were natural water holes, which supplied water for the livestock of plaintiffs in error. The pond, or ponds, of water from which the salt water escaped were, we judge from the map, some six miles from the stock water holes to which we refer. The plaintiffs in error brought suit, basing their action on alleged neglect on the part of the defendants in error in permitting the levees and dams, etc., of their artificial ponds to break and overflow the land of plaintiffs in error, and thereby pollute the waters to which we have above referred and injure the turf in the pasture of plaintiffs in error. The question was submitted

turf 草皮

levee 堤

to a jury on special issues, and the jury answered that the defendants in error did permit salt water to overflow from their salt ponds and lakes down Garrison Draw and on to the land of the plaintiffs in error. However, the jury acquitted the defendants in error of negligence in the premises. The questions and answers are shown in the opinion of the Court of Civil Appeals, and will not be here repeated.

acquit 宣告无罪

Various questions are raised in this court, but we are well satisfied with the opinion of the Court of Civil Appeals, and will take occasion to discuss only two issues.

The plaintiffs in error in their application say that the Court of Civil Appeals in its opinion has held that in order for plaintiffs in error to recover because the defendants in error permitted salt water to overflow their land, kill the vegetation, and pollute the water of their live stock, "they must allege and prove some specific act of neglect or must allege and prove that the water polluted was a water course." In this conclusion we think the Court of Civil Appeals stated the correct rule. *Gulf, C. & S. F. R. Co. v. Oakes*, 94 Tex. 155, 58 S. W. 999; *Galveston, H. & S. A. R. Co. v. Currie*, 100 Tex. 136, 96 S. W. 1073; *Farnham on Waters*, vol. 3, p. 2546, s 875; *Thompson on Negligence*, vol. 1, ss 696, 706, 707.

The Court of Civil Appeals quite correctly determined that the rules of law applicable to the pollution of streams and water courses or public waters were not applicable here, for reasons which that court stated. So the immediate question presented is whether or not defendants in error are to be held liable as insurers, or whether the cause of action against them must be predicated upon negligence. We believe the question is one of first impression in this court, and so we shall endeavor to discuss it in a manner in keeping with its importance.

predicate 预示

Upon both reason and authority we believe that the conclusion of the Court of Civil Appeals that negligence is a prerequisite to recovery in a case of this character is a correct one. There is some difference of opinion on the subject in American jurisprudence brought about by differing views as to the correctness or applicability of the decision of the English courts in *Rylands v. Fletcher*, L. R. 3 H. L. 330. The doctrine of this case is correctly stated ... as follows: "In *Rylands v. Fletcher*, L. R. 3 H. L. 330, affirming L. R. 1 Exch. 265, which is the leading case, the plaintiff was the lessee of mining privileges

lessee 承租人

which had passages communicating with abandoned mines under the land of a mill owner who built a reservoir over some shafts which had been filled in, and the pressure of the water forced the same through these shafts and injured plaintiff's mines. The defendant did not know that the mines were being worked underneath the land. It was said that the failure on the part of the engineer or contractor to block up these abandoned shafts was an act of negligence for which the defendant would be liable. But it was held that the defendant was liable on the ground that he had brought on his premises, and stored, a dangerous substance without restraining it. Cranworth, J., said: 'The defendants, in order to effect an object of their own, brought onto their land, or onto land which for this purpose may be treated as being theirs, a large accumulated mass of water, and stored it up in a reservoir. The consequence of this was damage to the plaintiff, and for that damage, *however skillfully and carefully the accumulation was made*, the defendants, according to the principles and authorities to which I have adverted, were certainly responsible.'" (*Italics ours*.)

The italicized portion of the above quotation shows that in fact the case was one of negligence, and that the damages could have been placed upon that ground. The distinguished judge who wrote the opinion in truth went beyond and outside the facts of his case in holding that there could be liability without negligence. This *dictum*, however, with some modification, became the rule of decision in England and in some of the American courts. *See Thompson on Negligence*, vol. 1, ss 697 to 703, inclusive. In a qualified sense, therefore, *Rylands v. Fletcher* may be regarded as a statement of the common-law rule; not, however, of such universal acceptance as to be controlling on the American courts.

While the rule has been followed to some extent in this country, in general the American courts base liability, where dams have broken, on negligence, either in the original construction of the reservoir or in failing properly to provide against all such contingent damages as might reasonably be anticipated. 67 *Corpus Juris*, p. 916, s 356; *Thompson on Negligence*, Vol. 1, ss 696, 706, 707; *Sedgwick on Damages* (8th Ed.) vol. 1, p. 34, s 33.

This court long since repudiated the general rule announced in *Rylands v. Fletcher*. Associate Justice Williams, in the case of *Gulf, C. & S. F. R. Co. v.*

Oakes, cited above, a case involving the planting and subsequent spreading of Bermuda grass, after stating the rule in *Rylands v. Fletcher*, <u>decline</u>d to follow the same, and in part said:

decline 谢绝

There have been subsequent decisions in England which some authorities regard as relaxing the rule in *Flectcher v. Rylands*, but it is unnecessary to refer especially to them. Cooley, *Torts*, pp. 677-680. The rule laid down was largely deduced from prior rulings, establishing absolute liability for damages caused by fires kindled on one's premises, and spreading to those of another; by injuries <u>inflict</u>ed by one, in his lawful <u>self-defense</u> against another, upon an innocent bystander; and by animals straying from the lands of their owners upon those of others. The law has become settled, in this country at least, that there is no liability in the two first instances without negligence on the part of the person permitting the fire to spread or inflicting the injury, and, in the case of animals, the law is entirely different in this and other states. *Clarendon, etc., Co. v. McClelland Bros.*, 86 Tex. 179, 23 S.W. 576, 1100.

inflict 处罚
self-defense 自卫

By making the liability absolute, the rule in *Fletcher v. Rylands*, taken literally, imposes an unqualified restriction upon the right of an owner of land to put it to a use lawful in itself, and this is the aspect in which it has the most direct bearing upon the question before us. It so applies the maxim, "*sic utere tuo*," etc., as to make the owner of land liable, in all cases, for loss or damage suffered by another in consequence of the escape of anything brought by the owner upon his land, which, in escaping, is likely to do mischief. Of course, the broad proposition was laid down with reference to such things as the court had in mind, and should not, even if accepted as generally correct, be applied indiscriminately to other facts which, in their nature, are essentially different. Even if the rule stated were a just one, as defining the duty of one storing so dangerous and destructive an element as water is when moving in large volume, it should be applied with careful discrimination to things which, like grass, spread slowly and are subject to more or less control. The fact that the proposition, as abstractly stated, cannot be justly applied to all subjects which its terms embrace, is enough to show that it is incorrect as a statement of a general principle of law. Accordingly, it has not met with general acceptance in this country; most of the authorities holding that liability for such injuries must be based upon negligence or other culpability on the part of the person sought to be held responsible. The authorities are so numerous as to make a review, or even the citation of them all, impracticable. Cooley, *Torts*, pp. 776, 777; 1 *Thomp. Neg.* 96; *Pennsylvania Coal Co. v. Sanderson*, 113 Pa. 126, 6 A. 453; *Losee v. Buchanan*, 51 N. Y. 476; *Brown v. Collins*, 53 N. H. 442; *Marshall v. Welwood*, 38 N. J. Law, 339.

As noted by Associate Justice Funderburk in *Cosden Oil Co. v. Sides* (Tex. Civ. App.) 35 S. W. (2d) 815, 816, 818, this court in *Galveston, H. & S. A. R. Co. v. Currie*, supra, in an opinion also by Associate Justice Williams, interpreted and applied its holding in the *Oakes Case*, saying in part:"In the absence of some positive law forbidding or regulating the keeping or use of the thing, the fundamental question is one of negligence vel non, depending, as in other cases of negligence, upon the inquiry whether or not there has been a neglect or violation of the duty which the law imposes upon all persons to use due care in the use of their property or the conduct of their business to avoid injury to others. Some of the older cases in England seem to assert the absolute liability of an insurer, but it is settled in this state that the question is one of negligence (*Gulf, C. & S. F. Ry. Co. v. Oakes*, 94 Tex. 155, 58 S. W. 999)."

In the *Cosden Oil Co. Case*, cited above, the Court of Civil Appeals had before it a case involving damage to land brought about by the flow of "oils, waste oil and products." The court in an able opinion by Associate Justice Funderburk held, correctly we think, that no right of recovery was shown independently of the existence of negligence.

In the case of *Rigodn v. Temple Water Works Co.*, 11 Tex. Civ. App. 542, 32 S. W. 828, 829, involving damages due to the falling of a water tower and tank, the Court of Civil Appeals applied the rule of negligence as a predicate for damages, although the exact question here involved may have not been presented in that case.

As pointed out in the quotation above from Judge Williams' opinion in the *Oakes Case*, our courts hold that one who uses fire, an <u>agency</u> as dangerous as water, is not an insurer of his neighbors' safety, but is only liable for damages due to negligence. 19 Tex. Jur., p. 660, s 2, and cases cited in the notes; *Missouri Pac. Ry. Co. v. Platzer*, 73 Tex. 117, 11 S. W. 160; *Missouri, K. & T. Ry. Co. v. Carter*, 95 Tex. 461, 483, 68 S. W. 159; *Pfeiffer v. Aue*, 53 Tex. Civ. App. 98, 115 S. W. 300 (*writ refused*).

As to liability for trespass by animals, we have likewise departed from the common law rule, because unsuited to our conditions. 2 Tex. Jup. p. 751, s 15, p. 755, s 19; *Clarendon Land, etc., Co. v. McClelland Bros.*, 89 Tex. 483, 34 S. W. 98, 35 S. W. 474; *Pace v. Potter*, 85 Tex. 473, 22 S. W. 300.

We have also discarded the common law of liability for injuries to an innocent bystander by one in his lawful self-defense against another, and hold that civil liability in such instances can be predicated only upon negligence. *Gulf, C. & S. F. Ry. Co. v. Oakes*, 94 Tex. 155, 158, 58 S. W. 999; *Koons. v. Rook* (Tex. Com. App.) 295 S. W. 592.

The storage and use of explosives is clearly within the rule of absolute liability laid down in *Rylands v. Fletcher*; but, as to these, we have also changed from the common-law rule, and predicate liability upon negligence, in the absence of controlling statutes or facts so obvious as to constitute a nuisance as a matter of law. 19 Tex. Jur. p. 458, s 4; p. 459, s 5; p. 461, s 7; p. 462, s 8; p. 464, s 9.

Associate Justice Williams in the opinion in the *Oakes Case, supra*, states that the rule of absolute liability announced in *Rylands v. Fletcher* was largely deduced from prior rulings establishing absolute liability for damages caused: (1) by fires kindled on one's premises and spreading to those of another; (2) by injuries inflicted by one in his lawful defense against another upon an innocent bystander; and (3) by animals straying from the lands of their owners upon those of others.

As shown above, in these three instances, as well as others where in England the same rule was applied, we have departed from the common law, and only <u>award damages</u> when predicated upon Negligence.

Since we have <u>repudiated</u> the bases of the rule

agency 媒介物

award damages 授予损害赔偿

repudiate 拒绝接受

announced in *Rylands v. Fletcher*, it follows as a necessary corollary that we should not apply the rule in cases such as the one before us. It is true that the *Oakes Case*, in which Justice Williams announced in general terms our repudiation of the absolute liability doctrine, was not a water case; but the reasons for its repudiation there are equally cogent here. No good reason can be assigned for declining to follow the common-law rule as applied to damages due to fires, to the destruction of property by animals, and to injuries to an innocent bystander by one engaged in his own defense, the basis of the rule applied to the water case of *Rylands v. Fletcher*, and then apply the repudiated rule in the type of case before us. In general, we believe, it may be said that the doctrine of absolute liability announced in *Rylands v. Fletcher* has been likewise generally repudiated in the United States, although some states in at least a modified form adhere to it. Authorities *supra*.

Thompson, in his masterly work on *Negligence*, vol. 1, s 694 *et seq.*, reviews at length the English common-law rule of absolute liability in the use and control of agencies, which from their nature have a tendency to escape control and get upon land of adjoining owners, and there produce injury, which he says make those who employ such agencies "liable as an insurer." He then states that the American rule is to the contrary; that here liability can only arise from negligence. He says:

Sec. 706. But the American Doctrine Decisively Against that Case (*Rylands v. Fletcher*) in Respect of Liability for Escape of Water. Where water is collected in reservoirs, behind dams, in canals or in ditches, in the ordinary manner for the purpose of being used as a motive power, in navigation, in irrigation, in mining, or for any other convenient and lawful end, the rule, in reason and according to the decisive weight of American judicial opinion, is different. There is nothing unlawful in collecting water for such purposes; and hence, in case it escapes and does mischief, the person so collecting it can only be held liable on the ground of something unlawful in the manner in which he has built or maintained his structure, that is, on the principle of negligence ... It follows, therefore, that if a dam breaks away, to the injury of property below, the owner will not be liable unless the person injured can show negligence; and if it appears in proof that the dam was well and properly built, upon a proper model, he will not be liable merely from the fact that it gave way; but otherwise, if it broke away in consequence of having been improperly constructed, or maintained in unsafe condition.

Sec. 707. Rule of Diligence in Restraining Water is Ordinary Care. The rule of diligence which the law puts upon an owner or occupier of land in restraining water artificially collected thereon is the rule described as ordinary or reasonable care; and here, as in other cases, this rule of care varies in proportion to the danger likely to accrue to others from the escape of water. It may be discharged by slight attention in some cases, and it may require the most exacting and unremitting attention, care and skill in others. The rule of diligence here exacted is, as in other cases, ordinary care which men employ where the risk is their own; ...

Judge Thompson then says, and with this we concur: "For this rule of ordinary care exacts here, as in other cases, a degree of vigilance, attention, and skill in proportion to the probabilities of danger. In an action for damages caused by the breaking away of a dam, it will not do for the owner to say that he built it strong enough to resist ordinary freshets; he must build it strong enough to resist those extraordinary freshets which sometimes occur, and which are therefore reasonably to be anticipated."

A review of the decisions made the basis of Judge Thompson's text, as well as those subsequent, leads to the conclusion stated by him, that the American rule in cases of the character before us requires negligence as the basis of the recovery of damages; that the doctrine of *Rylands v. Fletcher* is not the common-law rule as applied generally in this country to cases of the character before us. This conclusion is not only supported by Thompson and the various cases cited in *Sedgwick* and the notes to 15 L.R.A.(N.S.) 541, *supra*, but the editor of the notes in the latter declares: "The weight of authority in this country is that the defendant maintaining a water ditch or tank, or operating and using water pipes, will not be liable for damages caused to others from the escape of the

digence 勤勉
ordinary care 一般注意

reasonable care 合理注意

exacting 严格的
unremitting 不懈的

vigliance 警觉

freshet 洪汛

water from his premises in the absence of negligence."

Likewise *Corpus Juris* (vol. 67, p. 915, s 356) states: "The English rule has been followed to some extent in this county; but in general the American courts base the liability on negligence, either in the original construction of the reservoir or other receptacle, in subsequently allowing it to become defective, or in failing properly to provide against all such contingent damages as might reasonably be anticipated."

The American conception of the common law is the rule of decision with us, rather than the rule as understood and applied in England. 9 Tex. Jur. p. 307, s 9; *Dickson v. Strickland*, 114 Tex. 176, 265 S. W. 1012. Applying the common-law rule as deducible generally from the decisions of the American courts, we are compelled to say that negligence is a necessary basis for actions of the character before us.

Another rule with reference to the adoption of the English common law is that in adopting it as the rule of decision we have done so only in so far as consistent with the conditions which obtain in this state. 9 Tex. Jur. p. 310, s 12; *Motl v. Boyd*, 116 Tex. 82, 115, 286 S. W. 458.

In *Rylands v. Fletcher* the court predicated the absolute liability of the defendants on the proposition that the use of land for the artificial storage of water was not a natural use, and that, therefore, the landowner was bound at his peril to keep the waters on his own land. *Rylands v. Fletcher*, L. R. 3, H. L. 330. This basis of the English rule is to be found in the meteorological conditions which obtain there. England is a pluvial country, where constant streams and abundant rains make the storage of water unnecessary for ordinary or general purposes. When the court said in *Rylands v. Fletcher* that the use of land for storage of water was an unnatural use, it meant such use was not a general or an ordinary one; not one within the contemplation of the parties to the original grant of the land involved, nor of the grantors or grantees of adjacent lands, but was a special or extraordinary use, and for that reason applied the rule of absolute liability. This conclusion is supported by the fact that those jurisdictions which adhere to the rule in *Rylands v. Fletcher* do not apply that rule to dams or reservoirs constructed in rivers and streams, which they say is a natural use, but apply the principle of negligence. 27 R. C. L. p. 1207, s 125. In other words, the impounding of water in stream-ways, being an obvious and natural use, was necessarily within the contemplation of the parties to the original and adjacent grants, and damages must be predicated upon negligent use of a granted right and power; while things not within the contemplation of the parties to the original grants, such as unnatural uses of the land, the landowner may do only at his peril. As to what use of land is or may be a natural use, one within the contemplation of the parties to the original grant of land, necessarily depends upon the attendant circumstances and conditions which obtain land, necessarily depends upon the attendant or the initial terms of those grants.

In Texas we have conditions very different from those which obtain in England. A large portion of Texas is an arid or semiarid region. West of the 98th meridian of longitude, where the rainfall is approximately 30 inches, the rainfall decreases until finally, in the extreme western part of the state, it is only about 10 inches. This land of decreasing rainfall is the great ranch or livestock region of the state, water for which is stored in thousands of ponds, tanks, and lakes on the surface of the ground. The country is almost without streams; and without the storage of water from rainfall in basins constructed for the purpose, or to hold waters pumped from the earth, the great livestock industry of West Texas must perish. No such condition obtains in England. With us the storage of water is a natural or necessary and common use of the land, necessarily within the contemplation of the state and its grantees when grants were made, and obviously the rule announced in *Rylands v. Fletcher*, predicated upon different conditions, can have no application here.

Again, in England there are no oil wells, no necessity for using surface storage facilities for impounding and evaporating salt waters therefrom. In Texas the situation is different. Texas has many great oil fields, tens of thousands of wells in almost every part of the state. Producing oil is one of our major industries. One of the by-products of oil production is salt water, which must be disposed of without injury to property or the pollution of streams. The construction of basins or ponds to hold this salt water is a necessary part of the oil business. In Texas much of our land was granted without mineral reservation to the state, and where minerals were reserved, provision has usually been made for leasing and operating. It

impounding 滤网

attendant 伴随的

arid 干旱的
semiarid 半干旱的
meridian 子午线
longtitude 经线

perish 消亡

evaporate 蒸发

follows, therefore, that as to these grants and leases the right to mine in the usual and appropriate way, as, for example, by the construction and maintenance of salt water pools such as here involved, incident to the production of oil, was contemplated by the state and all its grantees and mineral lessees, that being a use of the surface incident and necessary to the right to produce oil. 40 *Corpus Juris*, p. 752, s 74.

From the foregoing it is apparent that we decline to follow and apply in this case the rule of absolute liability laid down in *Rylands v. Fletcher*, because: (a) the rule has been generally repudiated by this court in *Gulf, C. & S. F. R. Co. v. Oakes*, 94 Tex. 155, 58 S. W. 999, and *Galveston, H. & S. A. R. Co. v. Currie*, 100 Tex. 136, 96 S. W. 1073; (b) the basis of the rule drawn from its application in England in cases of fire, damage by livestock, and injuries to an innocent bystander have been repudiated by us; (c) the conditions which obtain here are so different from those of England that the rule should not be applied here; (d) and because the rule of negligence, instead of absolute liability, while not obtaining universally in the United States, is of such general application as to constitute, as Thompson says, the "American Rule," in effect the common-law rule as applied in America, which is the common law which we follow rather than that declared by the English courts.

Against the adoption of the negligence rule in cases of this character, we are cited to a number of cases which it is claimed conflict therewith. We do not find it necessary to discuss all of them by name.

The pipe line cases can have no application here, for the reason that these cases generally have some form of contract as a basis, or else the facts show injury due to an obvious nuisance. Nor are we prepared to say that the conveyance of oil by pipe lines is an unnatural use of land, and that the rule of absolute liability should be applied to them. Pipe lines are but a means of transportation, and certainly it was within the contemplation of the state and the original grantees of all lands that the latter could be used to carry transportation agencies. Besides, it appears that the opinion of Associate Justice Sharp in *Lone Star Gas Co. v. Hutton* (Tex. Com. App.) 58 S. W. 2d 19, 20, strongly indicates that in that type of case the rule of negligence should be applied. Nor is it necessary for us to discuss cases of the pollution of public waters or <u>riparian</u>

riparian 河边的

streams, as these are predicated upon statutes or <u>riparian rights</u> protected by law from invasion.

Other cases to which our attention has been directed are nuisance cases, where the undisputed facts showed an <u>actionable</u> nuisance. Nor need we discuss cases where injury was the necessary result of the operation of some business, regardless of care or a failure to use care. We do think, however, that the cases of *Texas & P. R. Co. v. O'Mahoney* (Tex. Civ. App.) 50 S. W. 1049, *Id.*, 24 Tex. Civ. App. 631, 60 S. W. 902, and *Texas & P. R. Co. v. Frazer* (Tex. Civ. App.) 182 S. W. 1161, deserve discussion because <u>writs of error</u> were refused by this court.

In the last appeal of the *O'Mahoney Case*, 24 Tex. Civ. App. 631, 60 S. W. 902, the Court of Civil Appeals held that where the railroad company constructed an artificial lake or pond on its own land, by means of a dam, and <u>diverted</u> a natural stream thereto through a ditch, and maintained the water therein so high that by reason of its pressure the water percolated through the dam and destroyed plaintiff's land, and caused sickness, *etc.*, the railroad company was liable for damages, regardless of the question of negligence in the construction of the dam. In making this holding the court used some language and cited some authorities [sic] rule of absolute liability, announced in *Rylands v. Fletcher*, although the *Rylands Case* was not cited. We shall not quote the court's statement of the facts, since the opinion is available.

It is obvious from the statement made by the court that the railroad company had not only created a nuisance as a matter of undisputed fact, but had, in violation of the *Constitution*, substantially taken a portion of O'Mahoney's property; and, of course, in such a case proof of negligence was not necessary. 31 Texas Jur. p. 421, s 11.

In its essential aspects the case of *Texas & P. Ry. Co. v. Frazer*, *supra*, was one of the diversion of surface waters from their place of natural flow in such manner as to injure the owner of the lower estate. In addition to the water diverted by the <u>barrow pits</u> of the railroad company, it had constructed a levee and ditch 1,400 yards long, apparently around at least a part of the town of Toyah, which carried the water from its natural drainage way on the north side of the railway track to the company's reservoir on the south side of the track. The

riparian right 河岸权,指水流沿岸土地所有权人享有的权利

actionable 可诉的

writ of error 复审令

divert 转移

barrow pit 手工运输的露天矿

case was not one where the company had merely erected a dam in a natural basin to impound waters which would naturally flow into it. This tortous act of the railway company in diverting surface water from its natural course, and concentrating it above the plaintiff's land in this case, was the real basis of the action, and as to which there was no dispute. Had no reservoir been constructed and the diverted waters been thrown upon the plaintiff's land to his damage, he would have had a cause of action without the necessity of alleging negligence. The diversion of the water and throwing it on the plaintiff's land to his damage would have been an invasion of his rights, just as though his property had been bodily taken. *Bunch v. Thomas*, 121 Tex. 225, 229, 49 S. W. 2d 421.

Nor do we believe that the facts that the diverted water was collected in a reservoir before being cast on the plaintiff's land changes the rule. It was merely one of the instrumentalities of the wrongful diversion by which the diverted agency was concentrated and rendered more destructive. 67 *Corpus Juris*, p. 877, s 300.

That the Court of Civil Appeals considered the case as essentially one of the diversion of surface waters is shown by the fact that it sustained the action of the trial court in refusing a charge upon the defense of unprecedented rainfall, upon the ground that such a plea was no defense when surface waters had been diverted to the plaintiff's injury, citing the case of *Galveston, H. & S. A. R. Co. v. Riggs* (Tex. Civ. App.) 107 S. W. 589.

If the case had been one simply of impounding water, and the court thought that the principles of *Rylands v. Fletcher* should rule it, then an act of God, such as an unprecedented rainfall, would have been a defense. *Thompson on Negligence*, vol. 1, s 700. But where the act of God combined with the negligence or actionable conduct of the defendant as a proximate cause to bring about the injury and damage, *vis major* is not a defense, and of course the holding of the Court of Civil Appeals was correct. 1 Tex. Jur. p. 700, s 5; 67 *Corpus Juris*, p. 931, s 385; *Patterson v. Speer* (Mo. App.) 229 S. W. 275, 276.

We have heretofore stated that this court refused to grant writs of error in both the *O'Mahoney* and *Frazer Cases*. At the time the Supreme Court refused these writs of error, it was compelled by its jurisdictional statutes to either grant or refuse the applications. Since the

heretofore 迄今为止

judgments were correct, it is obvious that it was the court's duty to refuse the writs. Such refusals are not to be construed as an approval of all the reasons assigned by the Courts of Civil Appeals for their legal conclusions. The refusals, however, were obviously correct on the grounds we have stated above.

The plaintiffs in error insist that the waters of Garrison Draw, if not the waters of a stream, the pollution of which is prohibited by law, are nevertheless public waters under *R. S.* art. 7467, to which the anti-pollution statutes apply. The statute in so far as here involved reads:

> "Art. 7467. Property of the State. The waters of the ordinary flow and underflow and <u>tides</u> of every flowing river or natural stream, of all lakes, bays or arms of the Gulf of Mexico, and the storm, flood or rain waters of every river or natural stream, <u>canyon</u>, <u>ravine</u>, <u>depression</u> or <u>watershed</u>, within the State of Texas, as, are hereby declared to be the property of the State, and the right to the use thereof may be acquired by <u>appropriation</u> in the manner and for the uses and purposes hereinafter provided, and may be taken or diverted from its natural channel for any of the purposes expressed in this chapter."

tide 潮汐

canyon 峡谷
ravine 沟壑
depression 地坑
watershed 分水岭

appropriation 土地征用

The contention here is that this article makes the water from rainfall while on the watershed, or in ravines and draws, and while it is still regarded in law and fact as surface water, and before it has reached a riparian or public stream, public waters, the pollution of which is prohibited by positive enactment.

The statute is capable of this construction if it alone were to be looked for its meaning. It must be interpreted, however, in the light of the Constitution and of the common law and Mexican civil law under which lands have been granted in this State. *Miller v. Letzerich*, 121 Tex. 248, 49 S. W. 2d 404.

Under both the common law and the Mexican civil law, the owners of the soil on which rains may fall and surface waters gather are the <u>proprietor</u>s of the water so long as it remains on their land, and prior to its passage into a natural water course to which riparian rights may attach. *Farnham on Water Rights*, vol. 3, s 883, and cases cited in the note; *Miller v. Letzerich*, 121 Tex.

proprietor 所有权人

248, 254, 256, 49 S. W. 2d 404; *Hall's Mexican Law* (1885) p. 402, s 1372.

No citation of authority is necessary to demonstrate that the right of a landowner to the rainwater which falls on his land is a property right which vested in him when the grant was made. Being a property right, the Legislature is without power to take it from him or to declare it public property and subject by appropriation or otherwise to the use of another. This is so regardless of the question as to whether the grant was made by Texas or Mexico. *Miller v. Letzerich*, 121 Tex. 248, 49 S. W. 2d 404.

If article 7467, quoted above, is to be construed so as to make surface waters public waters and subject to appropriation, then it would be clearly void, because in violation of the State Constitution. Article 7469 declares that the provisions of article 7467 and related provisions shall not prejudice vested rights. Interpreting article 7467 we would, in order to sustain its validity, be compelled to say that it has no application to lands granted prior to the enactment of the statute, in so far as it attempts to take from the grantees their rights to surface waters and to make them public waters subject to appropriation. Whether or not the article in this respect could be applied under our Constitution to grants made subsequent to the passage of the law is not before us in this case, and no opinion is expressed relative thereto. There is no contention here that the surface waters alleged to have been polluted were on lands granted by the state subsequent to the enactment of article 7467.

Article 7467 has no application to the facts of this case, and the surface waters involved were not public waters, the pollution of which was prohibited by express statutory enactment.

Revised Statutes, art. 7589a [enacted by *Acts 1927*, c. 56, s 1, amended by *Acts 1935*, c. 334, s 1 (*Vernons' Ann. Civ. St.* art. 7589a)], relating to the diversion or impounding of surface waters, has no application to this case. We do not understand from the pleadings that the suit was brought for the wrongful diversion or impounding of surface waters to another's injury.

The judgments of the Court of Civil Appeals and of the district court are *affirmed*.

Above is a case decided by a U. S. court discussing the

vested right 既得权利
sustain its validity 维持其有效性

rule in *Rylands*. Although a U.S. court is not bound to follow a foreign authority, the Chief Justice used many paragraphs to explain why the *Rylands* rule was rejected and why the English rule should not be applied to this case. Please note that the Justice described the *Rylands* rule as "absolute liability" instead of "strict liability." (What is the difference between the two?) In order to support his reasoning, the Chief Justice cited numerous authorities throughout the opinion. Compare the factual situations of this case to the *Rylands* case and read the court's discussion of the rule carefully.

6.3.6 Foster *v*. Preston Mill Co. — A Later Case Decided By a U.S. Court

Suppose your neighbor conducted blasting operations and the explosions scared the mink you raised in your farm. As a result, the mink killed their kittens. Is your neighbor liable for your loss? Is the strict liability rule formulated in *Rylands* applicable here? The American judges had been reluctant to adopt the strict liability rule in deciding cases. Again, they refused to adopt it in the following case.

mink 水貂

Supreme Court of Washington, Department 1
Foster v. Preston Mill Co.
44 Wash.2d 440, 268 P.2d 645
March 19, 1954

Hamley, Justice

Blasting operations conducted by Preston Mill Company frightened mother mink owned by B. W. Foster, and caused the mink to kill their kittens. Foster brought this action against the company to recover damages. His second amended complaint, upon which the case was tried, sets forth a cause of action on the theory of absolute liability, and, in the alternative, a cause of action on the theory of nuisance.

blast operation 爆破作业

After a trial to the court without a jury, judgment was rendered for plaintiff in the sum of $1,953.68. The theory adopted by the court was that, after defendant received notice of the effect which its blasting operations were having upon the mink, it was absolutely liable for all damages of that nature thereafter sustained. The trial court concluded that defendant's blasting did not constitute a public nuisance, but did not expressly rule on

public nuisance 妨害公共利益

the question of private nuisance. Plaintiff concedes, however, that, in effect, the trial court decided in defendant's favor on the question of nuisance. Defendant appeals.

Respondent's mink ranch is located in a rural area one and one-half miles east of North Bend, in King County, Washington. The ranch occupies seven and one half acres on which are located seven sheds for growing mink. The cages are of welded wire, but have wood roofs covered with composition roofing. The ranch is located about two blocks from U.S. highway No. 10, which is a main east-west thoroughfare across the state. Northern Pacific Railway Company tracks are located between the ranch and the highway, and Chicago, Milwaukee, St. Paul & Pacific Railroad Company tracks are located on the other side of the highway about fifteen hundred feet from the ranch.

The period of each year during which mink kittens are born, known as the whelping season, begins on about May 1st. The kittens are born during a period of about two and one-half weeks, and are left with their mothers until they are six weeks old. During this period, the mothers are very excitable. If disturbed by noises, smoke, or dogs and cats, they run back and forth in their cages and frequently destroy their young. However, mink become accustomed to disturbances of this kind, if continued over a period of time. This explains why the mink in question were apparently not bothered, even during the whelping season, by the heavy traffic on U.S. highway No. 10, and by the noise and vibration caused by passing trains. There was testimony to the effect that mink would even become accustomed to the vibration and noise of blasting, if it were carried on in a regular and continuous manner.

Appellant and several other companies have been engaged in logging in the adjacent area for more than fifty years. Early in May, 1951, appellant began the construction of a road to gain access to certain timber which it desired to cut. The road was located about two and one-quarter miles southwest of the mink ranch, and about twenty-five hundred feet above the ranch, along the side of what is known as Rattle-snake Ledge.

It was necessary to use explosives to build the road. The customary types of explosives were used, and the customary methods of blasting were followed. The most powder used in one shooting was one hundred pounds, and usually the charge was limited to fifty pounds. The procedure used was to set off blasts twice a day — at noon and at the end of the work day.

Roy A. Peterson, the manager of the ranch in 1951, testified that the blasting resulted in a tremendous vibration. The mother mink would then run back and forth in their cages and many of them would kill their kettens. Peterson also testified that on two occasions the blasts had broken windows.

Appellant's expert, Professor Drury Augustus Pfeiffer, of the University of Washington, testified as to tests made with a pin seismometer, using blasts as large as those used by appellant. He reported that no effect on the delicate apparatus was shown at distances comparable to those involved in this case. He said that it would be impossible to break a window at two and one-fourth miles with a hundred-pound shot, but that it could cause vibration of a lightly-supported cage. It would also be audible. Charles E. Erickson, who had charge of the road construction for appellant in 1951, testified that there was no glass breakage in the portable storage and filing shed which the company kept within a thousand feet of where the blasting was done. There were windows on the roof as well as on the sides of this shed.

Before the 1951 whelping season had far progressed, the mink mothers, according to Peterson's estimate, had killed thirty-five or forty of their kittens. He then told the manager of appellant company what had happened. He did not request that the blasting be stopped. After some discussion, however, appellant's manager indicated that the shots would be made as light as possible. The amount of explosives used in a normal shot was then reduced from nineteen or twenty sticks to fourteen sticks.

Officials of appellant company testified that it would have been impractical to entirely cease road-building during the several weeks required for the mink to whelp and wean their young. Such a delay would have made it necessary to run the logging operation another season, with attendant expense. It would also have disrupted the company's log production schedule and consequently the operation of its lumber mill.

In this action, respondent sought and recovered judgment only for such damages as were claimed to have been sustained as a result of blasting operations conducted

pin seismometer 针式地动仪
blast 爆破

audible 听得见的

wean 使断奶

attendant 随之产生的

after appellant received notice that its activity was causing loss of mink kittens.

The primary question presented by appellant's assignments of error is whether, on these facts, the judgment against appellant is sustainable on the theory of absolute liability.

The modern doctrine of strict liability for dangerous substances and activities stems from Justice Blackburn's decision in *Rylands v. Fletcher*, 1 Exch. 265, decided in 1866 and affirmed two years later in *Fletcher v. Rylands*, L. R. 3 H. L. 330. *Prosser on Torts*, 449, § 59. As applied to blasting operations, the doctrine has quite uniformly been held to establish liability, irrespective of negligence, for property damage sustained as a result of casting rocks or other debris on adjoining or neighboring premises. *Patrick v. Smith*, 75 Wash. 407, 134 P. 1076; *Schade Brewing Co. v. Chicago, M. & P. S. R. Co.*, 79 Wash. 651, 140 P. 897; *Bedell v. Goulter*, Or., 261 P. 2d 842; *Exner v. Sherman Power Const. Co.*, 2 Cir., 54 F. 2d 510. But *see Klepsch v. Donald*, 4 Wash. 436, 30 P. 991.

There is a division of judicial opinion as to whether the doctrine of absolute liability should apply where the damage from blasting is caused, not by the casting of rocks and debris, but by concussion, vibration, or jarring. 92 *A. L. R.* 741, annotation. This court has adopted the view that the doctrine applies in such cases. *Patrick v. Smith, supra*. In the *Patrick* case, it was held that contractors who set off an exceedingly large blast of powder, causing the earth for a considerable distance to shake violently, were liable to an adjoining owner whose well was damaged and water supply lost, without regard to their negligence in setting off the blast, although there was no physical invasion of the property. For excellent expositions of this view, *see Exner v. Sherman Power Const. Co., supra*; and *Bedell v. Goulter, supra*.

However the authorities may be divided on the point just discussed, they appear to be agreed that strict liability should be confined to consequences which lie within the extraordinary risk whose existence calls for such responsibility. *Prosser on Torts*, 458, § 60; Harper, *Liability Without Fault and Proximate Cause*, 30 Mich. L. Rev. 1001, 1006; 3 *Restatement of Torts*, 41, § 519. This limitation on the doctrine is set forth in *Restatement of Torts, supra*:

Except as stated in §§ 521-4, one who carries on an ultrahazardous activity is liable to another whose person, land or chattels the actor should recognize as likely to be harmed by the unpreventable miscarriage of the activity for harm resulting thereto from that which makes the activity ultrahazardous, although the utmost care is exercised to prevent the harm.

This restriction which has been placed upon the application of the doctrine of absolute liability is based upon considerations of policy. As Professor Prosser has said:

> ... It is one thing to say that a dangerous enterprise must pay its way within reasonable limits, and quite another to say that it must bear responsibility for every extreme of harm that it may cause. The same practical necessity for the restriction of liability within some reasonable bounds, which arises in connection with problems of "proximate cause" in negligence cases, demands here that some limit be set.... This limitation has been expressed by saying that the defendant's duty to insure safety extends only to certain consequences. More commonly, it is said that the defendant's conduct is not the "proximate cause" of the damage. But ordinarily in such cases no question of causation is involved, and the limitation is one of the policy underlying liability.

Prosser on Torts, 457, § 60.

Applying this principle to the case before us, the question comes down to this: Is the risk that any unusual vibration or noise may cause wild animals, which are being raised for commercial purposes, to kill their young, one of the things which make the activity of blasting ultrahazardous?

We have found nothing in the decisional law which would support an affirmative answer to this question. The decided cases, as well as common experience, indicate that the thing which makes blasting ultrahazardous is the risk that property or persons may be damaged or injured by coming into direct contact with flying debris, or by being directly affected by vibrations of the earth or concussions of the air.

chattel 动产
unpreventable miscarriage 无法避免的不履行

exercise the utmost care 履行最高注意义务

bound 限制
proximate cause 近因，指实质性原因，即伤害或损害是作为或不作为的直接结果或合理结果，亦即如果没有该原因，则结果不会产生。

decisional law 判例法

Where, as a result of blasting operations, a horse has become frightened and has trampled or otherwise injured a person, recovery of damages has been upheld on the theory of negligence. *Klein v. Phelps Lumber Co.*, 75 Wash. 500, 135 P. 226; *Peterson v. General Geophysical Co.*, Cal. App., 185 P. 2d 56; *Bassett v. Moberly Paving Brick Co.*, 219 Mo. App. 81, 268 S. W. 645; *Missouri Iron & Metal Co. v. Cartwright*, Tex. Civ. App., 207 S. W. 397. Contra: *Uvalde Construction Co. v. Hill*, 142 Tex. 19, 175 S. W. 2d 247, where a milkmaid was injured by a frightened cow. But we have found no case where recovery of damages caused by a frightened farm animal has been sustained on the ground of absolute liability.

If, however, the possibility that a violent vibration, concussion, or noise might frighten domestic animals and lead to property damages or personal injuries be considered one of the harms which makes the activity of blasting ultrahazardous, this would still not include the case we have here.

The relatively moderate vibration and noise which appellant's blasting produced at a distance of two and a quarter miles was no more than a usual incident of the ordinary life of the community. *See 3 Restatement of Torts*, 48, § 522, comment a. The trial court specifically found that the blasting did not unreasonably interfere with the enjoyment of their property by nearby landowners, except in the case of respondent's mink ranch.

It is the exceedingly nervous disposition of mink, rather than the normal risks inherent in blasting operations, which therefore must, as a matter of sound policy, bear the responsibility for the loss here sustained. We subscribe to the view expressed by Professor Harper (30 Mich. L. Rev. 1001, 1006, *supra*) that the policy of the law does not impose the rule of strict liability to protect against harms incident to the plaintiff's extraordinary and unusual use of land. This is perhaps but an application of the principle that the extent to which one man in the lawful conduct of his business is liable for injuries to another involves an adjustment of conflicting interests. *Exner v. Sherman Power Const. Co.*, *supra*.

It may very well be that, under the facts of a particular case, recovery for damages of this kind may be sustained upon some theory other than that of absolute liability. In *Hamilton v. King County*, 195 Wash. 84, 79 P. 2d 697, for example, recovery of such damages was sanctioned on the ground that defendant had trespassed upon plaintiff's land in doing the blasting which caused the disturbance.

Likewise, if the facts warrant, it is possible that such damages may be predicated upon a violation of *RCW* 70.74.250, *cf.* Rem. 1941 Sup., § 5440-25, requiring notice to be given at certain times of the year when blasting is to be undertaken within fifteen hundred feet of any fur farm or commercial hatchery, except in certain cases. In *Maitland v. Twin City Aviation Corp.*, 254 Wis. 541, 37 N. W. 2d 74, where a low-flying airplane frightened mink and loss of kittens resulted, recovery was allowed upon a showing that the airplanes were flown at an unlawfully low elevation.

In *Madsen v. East Jordan Irrigation Co.*, 101 Utah 552, 125 P. 2d 794, recovery was denied under facts very similar to those of the instant case, on the ground that the mother mink's intervention broke the chain of causation.

It is our conclusion that the risk of causing harm of the kind here experienced, as a result of the relatively minor vibration, concussion, and noise from distant blasting, is not the kind of risk which makes the activity of blasting ultrahazardous. The doctrine of absolute liability is therefore inapplicable under the facts of this case, and respondent is not entitled to recover damages.

The judgment is *reversed*.

sanction 批准

warrant 保证

fur farm 毛皮兽养殖场
commercial hatchery 商业孵化场

6.3.7 Siegler *v.* Kuhlman — Adoption of the Rylands Rule

While the strict liability rule had been established by the British judges for many decades, the American judges were still very cautious in applying this rule. This time, a young school girl was killed in a gasoline explosion owing to the ignition of the gasoline poured out from an overturned trailer tank. Is the owner, also the operator, of the trailer who was proved without negligence liable for the young girl's death? The Supreme Court of Washington reviewed this case in 1972 and decided to apply the strict liability rule to impose liability on the defendant. This is a case "en banc," meaning that all members of the supreme court reviewed the case. The court does this when the question presented before the court is important or the case is a first impression case. Apparently, there were disagreements among the justices reviewing this case so they wrote separate opinions explaining their views.

en banc 全体出庭法官共同审理案件

Reprinted below are also a concurring opinion and a dissenting opinion. When examining this case, first compare the different opinions drafted by different judges to see how they are different and whether their opinions were justified, then carefully read the discussions on the *Rylands* rule in the opinions and try to consider the line of cases together to see how the rule of precedents and doctrine of *stare decisis* work and what role the common law reasoning plays.

Supreme Court of Washington, *En Banc*
Siegler *v*. Kuhlman
81 Wash.2d 448, 502 P.2d 1181
Nov. 15, 1972

Hale, Associate Justice

Seventeen-year-old Carol J. House died in the flames of a gasoline explosion when her car encountered a pool of thousands of gallons of spilled gasoline. She was driving home from her after-school job in the early evening of November 22, 1967, along Capitol Lake Drive in Olympia; it was dark but dry; her car's headlamps were burning. There was a slight impact with some object, a muffled explosion, and then searing flames from gasoline pouring out of an overturned trailer tank engulfed her car. The result of the explosion is clear, but the real causes of what happened will remain something of an eternal mystery.

Aaron L. Kuhlman had been a truck driver for nearly 11 years after he completed the tenth grade in high school and after he had worked at other jobs for a few years. He had been driving for Pacific Intermountain Express for about 4 months, usually the night shift out of the Texaco bulk plant in Tumwater. That evening of November 22nd, he was scheduled to drive a gasoline truck and trailer unit, fully loaded with gasoline, from Tumwater to Port Angeles. Before leaving the Texaco plant, he inspected the trailer, checking the lights, hitch, air hoses and tires. Finding nothing wrong, he then set out, driving the fully loaded truck tank and trailer tank, stopping briefly at the Trail's End Cafe for a cup of coffee. It was just a few minutes after 6 p.m., and dark, but the roads were dry when he started the drive to deliver his cargo — 3,800 gallons of gasoline in the truck tank and 4,800 gallons of gasoline in the trailer tank. With all vehicle and trailer running lights on, he drove the truck and trailer onto Interstate Highway 5, proceeded north on that freeway at about 50 miles per hour, he said, and took the offramp about 1 mile later to enter Highway 101 at the Capitol Lake interchange. Running downgrade on the offramp, he felt a jerk, looked into his left-hand mirror and then his right-hand mirror to see that the trailer lights were not in place. The trailer was still moving but leaning over hard, he observed, onto its right side. The trailer then came loose. Realizing that the tank trailer had disengaged from his tank truck, he stopped the truck without skidding its tires. He got out and ran back to see that the tank trailer had crashed through a chain-link highway fence and had come to rest upside down on Capitol Lake Drive below. He heard a sound, he said, "like somebody kicking an empty fifty-gallon drum and that is when the fire started." The fire spread, he thought, about 100 feet down the road.

The trailer was owned by defendant Pacific Intermountain Express. It had traveled about 329,000 miles prior to November 22, 1967, and had been driven by Mr. Kuhlman without incident down the particular underpass above Capitol Lake Drive about 50 times. When the trailer landed upside down on Capitol Lake Drive, its lights were out, and it was unilluminated when Carol House's car in one way or another ignited the spilled gasoline.

Carol House was burned to death in the flames. There was no evidence of impact on the vehicle she had driven, Kuhlman said, except that the left front headlight was broken.

Why the tank trailer disengaged and catapulted off the freeway down through a chain-link fence to land upside down on Capitol Lake Drive below remains a mystery. What caused it to separate from the truck towing it, despite many theories offered in explanation, is still an enigma. Various theories as to the facts and cause were advanced in the trial. Plaintiff sought to prove both negligence on the part of the driver and owner of the vehicle and to bring the proven circumstances within the res ipsa loquitur doctrine. Defendants sought to obviate all inferences of negligence and the circumstances leading to the application of res ipsa loquitur by showing due care in inspection, maintenance and operation. Plaintiff argued negligence per se and requested a directed verdict

offramp 匝道

interchange 交换道

jerk 猛然一动

disengage 分开

chain-link 铁丝网

underpass 地下通道

unilluminated 不发光的

catapult 猛投

enigma 谜

res ipsa loquitur 不证自明
obviate 避免

per se 本身

on liability. On appeal, plaintiff relied in part on *RCW* 46.44.070 and *RCW* 46.61.655, relating to the drawbar connecting trailer to truck, and provisions prohibiting a load from dropping, shifting, leaking or escaping from the vehicle.

[*RCW* 46.44.070 reads in part as follows:
The drawbar or other Connection between vehicles in combination Shall be of sufficient strength to hold the weight of the towed vehicle on any grade where operated. No trailer shall whip, weave or oscillate or Fail to follow substantially in the course of the towing vehicle.

RCW 46.61.655 reads in part as follows:
No vehicle shall be driven or moved on any public highway unless such vehicle is so Constructed or loaded as to prevent any of its load from dropping, sifting, leaking or otherwise Escaping therefrom, except that sand may be dropped for the purpose of securing traction, or water or other substance may be sprinkled on a roadway in the cleaning or maintaining of such roadway by public authority having jurisdiction.]

The jury apparently found that defendants had met and overcome the charges of negligence. Defendants presented proof that both the truck, manufactured by Peterbilt, a division of Pacific Car and Foundry Company, and the tank and trailer, built by Fruehauf Company, had been constructed by experienced companies, and that the fifth wheel, connecting the two units and built by Silver Eagle Company, was the type of connecting unit used by 95 percent of the truck-trailer units. Defendants presented evidence that a most careful inspection would not have revealed the defects or fatigue in the metal connections between truck and trailer; that the trailer would not collapse unless both main springs failed; there was evidence that, when fully loaded, the tank could not touch the wheels of the tank trailer without breaking the springs because the maximum flexion of the springs was less than 1 inch. Defendants presented evidence that the drawbar was secure and firmly attached; that the tanks were built of aluminum to prevent sparks; and that, when fully loaded with 4,800 gallons of cargo, there would be 2 or 3 inches of space between the cargo and top of the tank; that two safety cables connected the two units; that the truck and trailer were regularly serviced and repaired, and records of this preserved and put in evidence; that the unit had been subject to Interstate Commerce Commission spot checks and conformed to ICC standards; and that, at the time of the accident, the unit had traveled less than one-third of the average service life of that kind of unit. There was evidence obtained at the site of the fire that both of the mainsprings above the tank trailer's front wheels had broken as a result of stress, not fatigue — from a kind of stress that could not be predicated by inspection — and finally that there was no negligence on the driver's part.

    Defendants also presented some evidence of contributory negligence on the basis that Carol House, driving on a 35-mile-per-hour road, passed another vehicle at about 45 miles per hour and although she slacked speed somewhat before the explosion, she was traveling at the time of the impact in excess of the 35-mile-per-hour limit. The trial court submitted both contributory negligence and negligence to the jury, declared the maximum speed limit on Capitol Lake Drive to be 35 miles per hour, and told the jury that, although violation of a positive statute is negligence as a matter of law, it would not engender liability unless the violation proximately contributed to the injury. From a judgment entered upon a verdict for defendants, plaintiff appealed to the Court of Appeals which affirmed. 3 Wash. App. 231, 473 P. 2d 445 (1970). We granted review (78 Wash. 2d 991 (1970)), and reverse.

    In the Court of Appeals, the principal claim of error was directed to the trial court's refusal to give an instruction on *res ipsa loquitur*, and we think that claim of error well taken. Our reasons for ruling that an instruction on *res ipsa loquitur* should have been given and that an inference of negligence could have been drawn from the event are found, we believe, in our statement on the subject: *ZeBarth v. Swedish Hosp. Medical Center*, 81 Wash. 2d 12, 499 P. 2d 1 (1972); *Miles v. St. Regis Paper Co.*, 77 Wash. 2d 828, 467 P. 2d 307 (1970); *Douglas v. Bussabarger*, 73 Wash. 2d 476, 438 P. 2d 829 (1968); *Pederson v. Dumouchel*, 72 Wash. 2d 73, 431 P. 2d 973 (1967). We think, therefore, that plaintiff was entitled to an instruction permitting the jury to infer negligence from the occurrence.

But there exists here an even more impelling basis for liability in this case than its derivation by allowable inference of fact under the *res ipsa loquitur* doctrine, and that is the proposition of strict liability arising as a matter of law from all of the circumstances of the event.

Strict liability is not a novel concept; it is at least as old as *Fletcher v. Rylands*, L.R. 1 Ex. 265, 278 (1866), affirmed, House of Lords, 3 H.L. 330 (1868). In that famous case, where water impounded in a reservoir on defendant's property escaped and damaged neighboring coal mines, the landowner who had impounded the water was held liable without proof of fault or negligence. Acknowledging a distinction between the natural and nonnatural use of land, and holding the maintenance of a reservoir to be a nonnatural use, the Court of Exchequer Chamber imposed a rule of strict liability on the landowner. The *ratio decidendi* included adoption of what is now called strict liability, and at page 278 announced, we think, principles which should be applied in the instant case:

> [T]he person who for his own purposes brings on his lands and collects and keeps there anything likely to do mischief if it escapes, must keep it in at his peril, and, if he does not do so, is *prima facie* answerable for all the damage which is the natural consequence of its escape.

All of the Justices in *Fletcher v. Rylands*, *supra*, did not draw a distinction between the natural and nonnatural use of land, but such a distinction would, we think, be irrelevant to the transportation of gasoline. The basic principles supporting the *Fletcher* doctrine, we think, control the transportation of gasoline as freight along the public highways the same as it does the impounding of waters and for largely the same reasons. *See* Prosser, *Torts*, s 78 (4th ed. 1971).

In many respects, hauling gasoline as freight is no more unusual, but more dangerous, than collecting water. When gasoline is carried as cargo — as distinguished from fuel for the carrier vehicle — it takes on uniquely hazardous characteristics, as does water impounded in large quantities. Dangerous in itself, gasoline develops even greater potential for harm when carried as freight —

extraordinary dangers deriving from sheer quantity, bulk and weight, which enormously multiply its hazardous properties. And the very hazards inhering from the size of the load, its bulk or quantity and its movement along the highways presents another reason for application of the *Fletcher v. Rylands, supra,* rule not present in the impounding of large quantities of water — the likely destruction of cogent evidence from which negligence or want of it may be proved or disproved. It is quite probable that the most important ingredients of proof will be lost in a gasoline explosion and fire. Gasoline is always dangerous whether kept in large or small quantities because of its volatility, inflammability and explosiveness. But when several thousand gallons of it are allowed to spill across a public highway — that is, if, while in transit as freight, it is not kept impounded — the hazards to third persons are so great as to be almost beyond calculation. As a consequence of its escape from impoundment and subsequent explosion and ignition, the evidence in a very high percentage of instances will be destroyed, and the reasons for and causes contributing to its escape will quite likely be lost in the searing flames and explosions.

That this is a sound case for the imposition of a rule of strict liability finds strong support in Professor Cornelius J. Peck's analysis in *Negligence and Liability Without Fault in Tort Law*, 46 Wash. L. Rev. 225 (1971). Pointing out that strict liability was imposed at common law prior to *Fletcher v. Ryland, supra,* that study shows the application of a rule of strict liability in a number of instances, *i.e.*, for harm done by trespassing animals; on a *bona fide* purchaser of stolen goods to their true owner; on a bailee for the misdelivery of bailed property regardless of his good faith or negligence; and on innkeepers and hotels at common law. But there are other examples of strict liability: The Supreme Court of Minnesota, for example, imposed liability without fault for damage to a dock inflicted by a ship moored there during a storm. *Vincent v. Lake Erie Transp. Co.*, 109 Minn. 456, 124 N.W. 221 (1910).

The rule of strict liability rests not only upon the ultimate idea of rectifying a wrong and putting the burden where it should belong as a matter of abstract justice, that is, upon the one of the two innocent parties whose acts instigated or made the harm possible, but it also rests on problems of proof:

sheer quantity 绝对数量
bulk 体积

cogent evidence 确凿的证据

volatility 挥发性
inflammability 易燃性

impoundment 储水量

bona fide purchaser 善意第三人
bailee 指根据寄托合同接受并保管寄托财产的人
misdelivery 错误交付
good faith 善意

moor 系住,停泊

rectify 校正

instigate 教唆

One of these common features is that the person harmed would encounter a difficult problem of proof if some other standard of liability were applied. For example, the disasters caused by those who engage in abnormally dangerous or extra-hazardous activities frequently destroy all evidence of what in fact occurred, other than that the activity was being carried on. Certainly, this is true with explosions of dynamite, large quantities of gasoline, or other explosives. It frequently is the case with falling aircraft. Tracing the course followed by gases or other poisons used by exterminators may be difficult if not impossible. The explosion of an atomic reactor may leave little evidence of the circumstances which caused it. Moreover, application of such a standard of liability to activities which are not matters of common experience is well-adapted to a jury's limited ability to judge whether proper precautions were observed with such activities.

Problems of proof which might otherwise have been faced by shippers, bailors, or guests at hotels and inns certainly played a significant role in shaping the strict liabilities of carriers, bailees, and innkeepers. Problems of proof in suits against manufacturers for harm done by defective products became more severe as the composition and design of products and the techniques of manufacture became less and less matters of common experience; this was certainly a factor bringing about adoption of a strict liability standard. (*Footnote omitted.*)

C. Peck, Negligence and Liability Without Fault in Tort Law, 46 *Wash. L. Rev.* 225, 240 (1971). See, also, G. P. Fletcher, Fairness and Utility in Tort Theory, 85 *Harv. L. Rev.* 537 (1972), for an analysis of the judicial philosophy relating to tort liability as affecting or affected by concepts of fault and negligence; and Comment, Liability Without Fault: Logic and Potential of a Developing Concept, 1970 *Wis. L. Rev.* 1201.

Thus, the reasons for applying a rule of strict liability obtain in this case. We have a situation where a highly flammable, volatile and explosive substance is being carried at a comparatively high rate of speed, in great and dangerous quantities as cargo upon the public highways, subject to all of the hazards of high-speed traffic, multiplied by the great dangers inherent in the volatile and explosive nature of the substance, and multiplied again by the quantity and size of the load. Then we have the added dangers of ignition and explosion generated when a load of this size, that is, about 5,000 gallons of gasoline, breaks its container and, <u>cascading</u> from it, spreads over the highway so as to release an invisible but highly volatile and explosive vapor above it.

  Danger from great quantities of gasoline spilled upon the public highway is extreme and extraordinary, for any spark, flame or appreciable heat is likely to ignite it. The <u>incandescent filaments</u> from a broken automobile headlight, a spark from the heat of a <u>tailpipe</u>, a lighted cigarette in the hands of a driver or passenger, the hot coals from a smoker's pipe or cigar, and the many hot and sparking spots and units of an automobile motor from <u>exhaust</u> to <u>generator</u> could readily ignite the vapor cloud gathered above a highway from 5,000 gallons of spilled gasoline. Any automobile passing through the vapors could readily have produced the flames and explosions which killed the young woman in this case and without the provable intervening negligence of those who loaded and serviced the carrier and the driver who operated it. Even the most prudent and careful motorist, coming unexpectedly and without warning upon this gasoline pool and vapor, could have driven into it and ignited a <u>holocaust</u> without knowledge of the danger and without leaving a trace of what happened to set off the explosion and light the searing flames.

  Stored in commercial quantities, gasoline has been recognized to be a substance of such dangerous characteristics that it invites a rule of strict liability — even where the hazard is <u>contamination</u> to underground water supply and not its more dangerous properties such as its explosiveness and flammability. *See Yommer v. McKenzie*, 255 Md. 220, 257 A.2d 138 (1969). It is even more appropriate, therefore, to apply this principle to the more highly hazardous act of transporting it as freight upon the freeways and public thoroughfares.

  Recently this court, while declining to apply strict liability in a particular case, did acknowledge the suitability of the rule in a proper case. In *Pacific Northwest Bell Tel. Co. v. Port of Seattle*, 80 Wash. 2d 59, 491 P.2d 1037 (1971), we observed that strict liability had its beginning in *Fletcher v. Rylands*, *supra*, but said

cascade 大量落下

incandescent 白炽的
filament 灯丝
tailpipe 排气管

exhaust 排气装置
generator 发电机

holocaust 浩劫

contamination 污染

that it ought not be applied in a situation where a bursting water main, installed and maintained by the defendant Port of Seattle, damaged plaintiff telephone company's underground wires. There the court divided — not on the basic justice of a rule of strict liability in some cases — but in its application in a particular case to what on its face was a situation of comparatively minor hazards. Both majority and dissenting justices held, however, that the strict liability principles of *Fletcher v. Rylands*, *supra*, should be given effect in some cases; but the court divided on the question of whether underground water mains there constituted such a case.

The rule of strict liability, when applied to an abnormally dangerous activity, as stated in the *Restatement* (*Second*) *of Torts* s 519 (Tent. Draft No. 10, 1964), was adopted as the rule of decision in this state in *Pacific Northwest Bell Tel. Co. v. Port of Seattle*, *supra*, at 64, 491 P. 2d, at 1039, 1040, as follows:

> (1) One who carries on an abnormally dangerous activity is subject to liability for harm to the person, land or chattels of another resulting from the activity, although he has exercised the utmost care to prevent such harm.
>
> (2) Such strict liability is limited to the kind of harm, the risk of which makes the activity abnormally dangerous.

As to what constitutes an abnormal activity, s 520 states:

> In determining whether an activity is abnormally dangerous, the following factors are to be considered:
>
> (a) Whether the activity involves a high degree of risk of some harm to the person, land or chattels of others;
>
> (b) Whether the gravity of the harm which may result from it is likely to be great;
>
> (c) Whether the risk cannot be eliminated by the exercise of reasonable care;
>
> (d) Whether the activity is not a matter of common usage;
>
> (e) Whether the activity is inappropriate to the

place where it is carried on; and
(f) The value of the activity to the community.

Applying these factors to this system, we do not find the activity to be abnormally dangerous. There has never been a break in the system before, absent an earthquake, and the pipe could have been expected to last many more years. It is a system commonly used for fire protection, and its placement under ground is, of course, appropriate. We do not find s 519 of the *Restatement*, (Tent. Draft No. 10, 1964), or *Rylands v. Fletcher*, *supra*, applicable.

It should be noted from the above language that we rejected the application of strict liability in *Pacific Northwest Bell Tel. Co. v. Port of Seattle*, *supra*, solely because the installation of underground water mains by a municipality was not, under the circumstances shown, an abnormally dangerous activity. Had the activity been found abnormally dangerous, this court would have applied in that case the rule of strict liability.

Contrast, however, the quiet, relatively safe, routine procedure of installing and maintaining and using underground water mains as described in *Pacific Northwest Bell v. Port of Seattle*, *supra*, with the activity of carrying gasoline as freight in quantities of thousands of gallons at freeway speeds along the public highway and even at lawful lesser speeds through cities and towns and on secondary roads in rural districts. In comparing the quiescence and passive job of maintaining underground water mains with the extremely heightened activity of carrying nearly 5,000 gallons of gasoline by truck, one cannot escape the conclusion that hauling gasoline as cargo is undeniably an abnormally dangerous activity and on its face possesses all of the factors necessary for imposition of strict liability as set forth in the *Restatement (Second) of Torts* s 519 (Tent. Draft No. 10, 1964), above.

Transporting gasoline as freight by truck along the public highways and streets is obviously an activity involving a high degree of risk; it is a risk of great harm and injury; it creates dangers that cannot be eliminated by the exercise of reasonable care. That gasoline cannot be practicably transported except upon the public highways does not decrease the abnormally high risk arising from its transportation. Nor will the exercise of due and reasonable care assure protection to the public from the

quiescence 沉寂的
heightened 繁重的

disastrous consequences of concealed or latent mechanical or metallurgical defects in the carrier's equipment, from the negligence of third parties, from latent defects in the highways and streets, and from all of the other hazards not generally disclosed or guarded against by reasonable care, prudence and foresight. Hauling gasoline in great quantities as freight, we think, is an activity that calls for the application of principles of strict liability.

The case is therefore *reversed* and *remanded* to the trial court for trial to the jury on the sole issue of damages.

Rosellini, Associate Justice (concurring).

I agree with the majority that the transporting of highly volatile and flammable substances upon the public highways in commercial quantities and for commercial purposes is an activity which carries with it such a great risk of harm to defenseless users of the highway, if it is not kept contained, that the common-law principles of strict liability should apply. In my opinion, a good reason to apply these principles, which is not mentioned in the majority opinion, is that the commercial transporter can spread the loss among his customers — who benefit from this extrahazardous use of the highways. Also, if the defect which caused the substance to escape was one of manufacture, the owner is in the best position to hold the manufacturer to account.

I think the opinion should make clear, however, that the owner of the vehicle will be held strictly liable only for damages caused when the flammable or explosive substance is allowed to escape without the apparent intervention of any outside force beyond the control of the manufacturer, the owner, or the operator of the vehicle hauling it. I do not think the majority means to suggest that if another vehicle, negligently driven, collided with the truck in question, the truck owner would be held liable for the damage. But where, as here, there was no outside force which caused the trailer to become detached from the truck, the rule of strict liability should apply.

It also is my opinion that the legislature has expressed an intent that owners and operators of vehicles carrying trailers should be required to keep them under control, and that intent can be found in the statutes cited in the majority opinion. Thus the application of the common-law principles of strict liability is in accord with the manifest legislative view of the matter.

It also should be remarked, I think, that there was in this case no evidence that the alleged negligence of the deceased, in driving faster than the posted speed, was in any sense a proximate cause of the tragedy which befell her. There was no showing that, had she been proceeding at the legal rate of speed, she could have stopped her vehicle in time to avoid being enveloped in the flames or that the gasoline would not have ignited. Thus we are not confronted in this case with a question whether contributory negligence might under some circumstances be a defense to an action of this kind. It should be understood that the court does not pass upon that question at this time.

Neill, Associate Justice (dissenting).

The application of the doctrine of strict liability to the facts of this case is warranted, at least as the applicability is qualified by the concurring opinion of Justice Rosellini. However, to decide this case on that theory violates our established rules of appellate review. *National Indemnity Co. v. Smith-Gandy, Inc.*, 50 Wash.2d 124, 309 P.2d 742 (1957); *State v. McDonald*, 74 Wash.2d 474, 445 P.2d 345 (1968).

Plaintiff seeks money redress for the death of an exemplary young woman whose life was horribly terminated in a tragic accident. A jury absolved the defendants from culpability. Irrespective of our sympathy, that jury verdict must stand unless error was committed at the trial. On appeal, the Court of Appeals affirmed the verdict and judgment. *Siegler v. Kuhlman*, 3 Wash. App. 231, 473 P.2d 445 (1970). We granted review. 78 Wn.2d 991 (1970).

The only issue brought to this court by the appeal is the procedural effect of *res ipsa loquitur*. Before discussing that issue, I will address other portions of the majority and concurring opinions with which I am in disagreement.

The injection of the issue of the applicability and construction of *RCW* 46.44.070 is improper. The issue was not raised at trial, not in the Court of Appeals. Following the granting of a petition for review, this court, *sua sponte*, requested counsel to submit supplemental briefs as to the statute. This is an appellate procedure to which I have previously expressed by dissent.

the deceased 死者
befall 降临于,发生在

money redress 金钱补偿

culpability 有罪

injection 加入
applicability 适用性
construction 阐释

sua sponte 出于自愿

Maynard Inv. Co. v. McCann, 77 Wash. 2d 616, 625, 465 P. 2d 657 (1970). [Both the majority and dissenting opinion in *Maynard Inv. Co. v. McCann*, 77 Wash. 2d 616, 625, 465 P. 2d 657 (1970), recognize several exceptions to the general rule that appellate courts will not consider a theory or issue which was not presented by the litigants. *See generally* 5 *Am. Jur. 2d* Appeal and Error ss 545-552. However, none of these exceptions justify the injection of these issues by this court in this case.] My disagreement with such judicial usurpation of an adversary function is even stronger here, where the meaning ascribed to the statute in focus depends upon an interpretation which that statute has not heretofore received. The majority opinion assumes that the language of *RCW* 46.44.070 requiring the trailer "connection ... (to) be of sufficient strength to hold the weight of the towed vehicle on any grade where operated" applies to situations where the trailer breaks away to the side of the towing vehicle. Whether or not that interpretation should be applied to the statute is a question that should await a case where the issue is timely and properly presented.

Further, *RCW* 46.44.070, even as read by the majority, cannot be applied here without first assuming as fact that the connection was not secure. In this case that assumption is an inappropriate trespass on the jury's function. As the majority notes, the question of whether the connection came loose because improperly secured is raised by circumstantial evidence. In fact, much of the trial was directed to expert testimony as to whether the trailer connection first became loose or whether the breaking of a supporting spring caused the ultimate separation of the connection. Thus any answer to that question is properly the subject of the jury's consideration from the evidence and reasonable inference from the circumstantial evidence. Unless we are prepared to hold that the statute makes the operator of a truck and tractor rig a guarantor of the security of the connection under all circumstances, we cannot state that the answer is a matter of certitude.

The jury was instructed on contributory negligence. No exception was taken nor has error been assigned to the instruction. Yet, the concurring opinion, *sua sponte*, questions the giving of the instruction. It has been my understanding that an instruction to which error is not assigned becomes the law of the case. *E.g.*, *Kindelspire v. Lawrence*, 44 Wash. 2d 722, 270 P. 2d 477 (1954); *Ralston v. Vessey*, 43 Wash. 2d 76, 260 P. 2d 324 (1953). I think it beyond the proper scope of appellate review to "try the case" for the parties.

I turn to the sole and only assignment of error presented to us: that the jury should have been given one of two *res ipsa loquitur* instructions proposed by plaintiff. The applicability of that doctrine to the facts of this case is not contested and is not in issue here. The question is the procedural effect to be given that doctrine in the case at hand. I disagree with the treatment that the majority has given to this question and adhere to the lead opinion in *Zukowsky v. Brown*, 79 Wash. 2d 586, 488 P. 2d 269 (1971). First, the majority opinion chooses to ignore, rather than grapple with, the serious and difficult problems associated with the question of the procedural effect to be given *res ipsa loquitur*. See *Zukowsky v. Brown*, supra, and authorities therein cited. Also see *Siegler v. Kuhlman*, 3 Wash. App. 231, 473 P. 2d 445 (1970). In consequence, the majority decision, as to this point, contributes nothing to the body of law, and yields only a *sui generis* result. Having refused to meet the problem, the majority cannot be read as either enhancing, diminishing or altering answers arrived at in cases where the issue has been met. [In this respect, the Court of Appeals commendably met and discussed the problem. *Siegler v. Kuhlman*, 3 Wash. App. 231, 240-244, 473 P. 2d 445 (1970).]

In addition, plaintiff's proposed instructions on *res ipsa* were defective. Each proposed instruction contains language criticized in *Clark v. Icicle Irrigation Dist.*, 72 Wash. 2d 201, 203, 432 P. 2d 541 (1967):

We particularly disagree with the statement that "the happening of the accident alone affords reasonable evidence ... that the accident arose from the want of reasonable care." We have been at some pains to make it clear that the happening does not afford "reasonable evidence"; that it does no more than permit the jury to infer, though it is not required to so infer, that the defendant or its agents were at some point negligent. See recent discussion in *Pederson v. Dumouchel* (72 Wn. 2d 73), 431 P. 2d 973 (1967).

Plaintiff's first assignment of error is the trial court's failure to give a requested instruction stating:

grapple with 努力解决困境

sui generis 自成一类的；独特的
enhance 增强
diminish 使……削弱
alter 改变

commendably 很好地

at some pains 处于痛苦中

You are instructed that when a thing which causes an injury to another is shown to be under the management and control of the person charged with negligence in operation or maintenance of such thing, or in the failure to keep it in a reasonably safe condition, and if it [is] shown that an accident happened which, in the ordinary course of things, does not happen if those in charge of the management and maintenance of the thing exercised reasonable care, then The happening of the accident alone affords reasonable evidence in the absence of explanation by the person charged with negligence That the accident arose from the want of reasonable care on the part of such person.

Plaintiff's second, and only other, assignment of error is the failure to give an instruction stating:

You are instructed that when an object which causes an injury to another is shown to be under the management and control of a person charged with negligence in the operation of such thing, or in the failure to keep it in a reasonably safe condition and if it is shown that the incident happened which in the ordinary course of things does not happen, if those in charge of this management and control exercise reasonable care, then The happening of said occurrence affords reasonable evidence, in the absence of an explanation by the person charged with negligence, That the occurrence arose from the want of reasonable care on the part of such person.

Thus plaintiff's proposed *res ipsa* instructions were defective by including the "affords reasonable evidence" language criticized in Clark. [This distinction between evidence and inference is supported by eminent writers in the field. *E. g.*, *Wigmore*, *Evidence* (3d ed. 1940) s 1 (b), "Argument and Evidence, distinguished," and s 30.] A trial court need not give an erroneous instruction. *State v. Wilson*, 26 Wash. 2d 468, 174 P. 2d 553 (1946).

I would *affirm* the trial court and the Court of Appeals.

6.3.8 Clay *v.* Missouri Highway & Transportation Commission — New Development

In the case below, a property owner brought action

against Missouri Highway and Transportation Commission (MHTC), and contractor hired by MHTC to perform work on highway project, to recover for damage allegedly caused by blasting for project. The trial court held against contractor under strict liability theory, and the Court of Appeals held that evidence of problems with water supply was sufficient to state claim for strict liability for blasting. Read the relevant excerpt of the opinion below.

Missouri Court of Appeals, Western District
Clay v. Missouri Highway & Transp. Com'n
951 S.W. 2d 617
June 30, 1997

Laura Denvir Stith, Judge

After a civil jury trial, plaintiffs Leslie and Alma Clay were awarded $22,340 from contractor Max Rieke & Brothers, Inc. (Rieke) under a theory of strict liability for blasting, for property damage caused by the blasting of rock during construction of a nearby road. The Clays alleged that the blasting damaged their property by damaging an <u>aquifer</u> that had been supplying unusually high quality water to their property.

aquifer 地下蓄水层

The Clays appeal the trial court's refusal to submit a strict liability for blasting claim against MHTC. Rieke <u>cross-appeals</u> the trial court's decision to allow the Clays to submit a strict liability for blasting claim against it, alleging that Plaintiffs failed to prove that the blasting caused their damage or trespassed on their property. We find that the trial court properly submitted only a strict liability for blasting claim against Rieke.

cross-appeal 交叉上诉

I. Factual and Procedural Background

Leslie R. Clay, Jr. and his wife Alma Clay are residents of Tiffany Springs, Missouri. Their residence in Tiffany Springs sits above an aquifer. This aquifer had supplied a well on their property with unusually high-quality drinking water since 1945.

In November 1989, roadwork began on Highway 152 in the Tiffany Springs area. MHTC hired Rieke to cut <u>the right of way</u> for the new highway down to a grade specified by MHTC. Rieke used explosives to break up and remove rock from the roadway site. MHTC had anticipated that Rieke would use explosives to blast away rock, but had not specifically required the use of

the right of way 通行权

explosives in its contract.

Rieke tried to blast in a controlled fashion. Specially-placed explosive charges cut the rock and left smooth walls of rock for the sides of the highway. At trial, some experts testified that this controlled blasting only caused shock waves to move about twenty feet into the rock. The Clays alleged, however, that the blasting caused vibrations at their home some .85 miles away and that it affected the quality and quantity of the water coming from the aquifer. More specifically, they alleged that due to cracks in the aquifer caused by the blasting, sediment such as sand and oil contaminated the aquifer and, ultimately, their well-water, that the water level of their well dropped, and that the water flow in their well was drastically reduced.

The Clays brought suit against the MHTC and Rieke. They sought recovery against both defendants under the theory that both defendants were strictly liable for blasting for any damage to the common aquifer and percolating waters, and the resulting damage to the Clays' property. The Clays sought damages ... for the loss of value to their real property, the cost and future cost of purchasing and hauling water, and the loss of the future intended use of their real property for agricultural purposes (as a vegetable farm) because of the pollution and diminished supply of their well water. Mr. Clay testified that the inability to start a farm on the land cost him $250,000 in profits. Defendants presented evidence that the alleged damage to the land caused a maximum of $12,700 in damages. Each party attacked the credibility of the other's figures.

The court eventually found that ... the Clays could not submit a strict liability ... claim against MHTC because it is a public entity and no exception permitting suit applied.

...

The court also allowed the Clays to submit a claim against Rieke for strict liability for blasting. The damage instruction for this claim was modeled on *MAI* 4.02 and included the optional loss of use tail:

If you find in favor of plaintiffs, then you must award plaintiffs such sum as you may find from the evidence to be the difference between the fair market value before it was damaged and its fair market value after it was damaged, plus such sum as you may find from the evidence will fairly and justly compensate plaintiffs for the loss of use thereof during the time reasonably necessary for the property to be repaired or replaced.

The Clays had also sought to submit loss of use damages against MHTC and to present lost profits and the lost value of the water itself. The court found evidence of the lost value of the water itself was not recoverable as a separate item of damage, but rather was a part of the submission for loss of fair market value of the property. It also found that lost profits from the proposed vegetable farm were too speculative to be admitted. The Clays made an offer of proof in which they described the water quality they had enjoyed before the blasting, the decline in water quality after the blasting, Mr. Clay's plans to start a vegetable farm after he retired, how his plans were ruined by the decline in the well water's quality, and his damage estimate of $250,000.

offer of proof 提出证据

The jury returned a verdict in favor of the Clays and awarded them damages of ... $22,340 against Rieke. The Clays appeal the trial court's refusal to let them offer evidence of the other items of damage listed above ... The defendants cross-appeal the verdicts, arguing that they are duplicative of each other and that the damage awards are not supported by the evidence. Rieke also argues that the Clays failed to make a submissible case of strict liability for blasting because they failed to show an actual trespass on their land and failed to prove there was a diminution in the fair market value of their property.

diminution 减损

II. Claims Submissible against Rieke

As noted above, the court allowed the Clays to submit a strict liability for blasting claim against Rieke ... Each party appeals the rulings contrary to its position.

A. Submissibility of Strict Liability for Blasting

Rieke claims that the trial court erred in submitting the Clays' strict liability for blasting claim against it because they failed to plead facts showing that vibrations or concussions from the blasting entered their property and caused the alleged damage to their well. Rieke argues that proof of trespass is a necessary element of a claim of strict liability for blasting. Second, Rieke argues that the Clays failed to set forth sufficient evidence that its actions caused any damage — whether or not in the form of trespass — to the Clays' property. In response, the Clays argue that they presented a submissible strict liability for blasting claim because they presented testimony that vibrations were felt and concussions heard that coincided with the physical damage to their well, thus proving both damage and trespass, and further that separate and apart from this evidence their land was damaged by the blasting because the blasting damaged their well and their water supply.

To the extent that Rieke is arguing that a claim of strict liability for blasting is necessarily based on trespass, or that trespass must be submitted as a separate element of the cause of action, we disagree. As noted in *Bennett v. Mallinckrodt, Inc.*, 698 S. W. 2d 854 (Mo. App. 1985), *certiorari denied*, 476 U. S. 1176, 106 S. Ct. 2903 (1986), "[i]n blasting cases, ... a claim for strict liability is as valid a claim as a claim based upon nuisance or trespass." *Id*. at 868.

What Rieke really appears to be arguing, and what it asserted at the instruction conference below, is that indirect or consequential damage from blasting is not enough to support a strict liability for blasting claim. It asserts that in order to prove the element of damage from blasting one must prove direct damage by showing that the blasting caused either rocks or vibrations to enter the property, and the latter caused the damage. In keeping with this argument, Rieke offered an instruction that required the jury to find not only that Rieke engaged in blasting and that the Clays were damaged as a direct result of the blasting, but also that "vibrations or concussions resulting from the explosion entered plaintiffs' property" and that "the vibrations or concussions directly caused damage to plaintiffs' property."

We note that there was evidence to support the submission that vibrations or concussions resulting from the explosion entered the plaintiffs' property, for there was testimony that the Clays and their neighbors felt and heard the blasting. They also testified that they began to have problems with their water supply after the blasting. Thus, they do claim a trespass, and they do claim their damage resulted from the blast. What they do not claim, however, is that the vibrations or concussions which they felt directly caused their damage. Rather, they claim that the same blasting that caused the vibrations also, but separately, split and cracked rock outside their property, and that as a result, it caused a lowering of the water level in the entire aquifer, including that on their property, and polluted the aquifer that supplied their well.

We think that the trial court properly refused to require the Clays to prove that it was the vibrations or concussions from the blasting that directly caused their damage; they were required to submit only that it was the blasting that caused their damage. We so rule because we conclude from a review of the history of the doctrine of strict liability for blasting that, while such a claim may be established by proof of vibration and concussion, see Wiley v. Pittsburg & Midway Coal. Mining Co., 729 S. W. 2d 228, 232 (Mo. App. 1987), it may also be established by other methods of proof.

The doctrine of strict liability for abnormally dangerous activities such as blasting originated in the English case Rylands v. Fletcher, 1 L. R.-Ex. 265 (1866), aff'd, 3 L. R.-E. & I App. 330 (1868). Missouri applies the "true rule," or <u>narrow rule</u>, of Rylands v. Fletcher. As Rylands v. Fletcher is narrowly applied in Missouri, a person is strictly liable "when he damages another by a thing or activity unduly dangerous and inappropriate to the place where it is maintained, in the light of the character of that place and its surroundings." Bennett, 698 S. W. 2d at 867 (quoting Prosser, Law of Torts § 78, at 508 (4th ed. 1971)); Richardson v. Holland, 741 S. W. 2d 751, 755 (Mo. App. 1987). The narrow application of the rule means that the activity (1) must be an activity relating to land or other <u>immovables</u> and (2) must itself cause the injury and the defendant must have been engaged directly in the <u>injury-producing activity</u>. Richardson, 741 S. W. 2d at 755 (explaining the imposition of strict liability on abnormally dangerous activities in Missouri). Sections 519 and 520 of the Restatement (Second) of Torts (1977) also reflect this narrow application of Rylands v. Fletcher. See Bennett, 698 S. W. 2d at 867. The Restatement limits strict liability for abnormally dangerous activities "to the kind of harm, the possibility of which makes the activity abnormally dangerous." Restatement (Second) of Torts § 519.

The potential that blasting might cause widespread damage to other people's property is precisely the reason that liability is imposed on users of explosives without regard to their negligence. As a general rule, under a

narrow rule 适用范围较窄的规则

immovable 不动产

injury-producing activity 可能对他人产生伤害的行为

theory of strict liability for blasting defendants are liable for any damage caused by the blasting, irrespective of their negligence. *Wiley.*, 729 S. W. 2d at 232; *Donnell v. Vigus Quarries, Inc.*, 526 S. W. 2d 314, 316 (Mo. App. 1975); *Summers v. Tavern Rock Sand Co.*, 315 S. W. 2d 201, 203 (Mo. 1958); *Richards v. C. B. Contracting Co.*, 395 S. W. 2d 737, 739-40 (Mo. App. 1965). Plaintiffs must present evidence that the blasting was of sufficient capacity to have caused the damage. This evidence may be circumstantial. *Wiley*, 729 S. W. 2d at 232; *Donnell*, 526 S. W. 2d at 316.

Certainly, in most cases involving damage from blasting, plaintiffs will make their case for damages by presenting testimony that rocks landed or vibrations or concussions were felt coincidentally with the blasting and that physical damage was observed thereafter as a result of the vibrations or concussions. *Wiley*, 729 S. W. 2d at 232. But Rieke cites no cases that state that these are the only ways to show that blasting caused physical damage to the property. In contrast, our own research has identified a number of cases from other jurisdictions which have permitted submission of a strict liability for blasting theory based on damage to water supply in plaintiff's property without regard to trespass.

The most analogous case is *Bumbarger v. Walker*, 193 Pa. Super. 301, 164 A. 2d 144, 149 (1960). In *Bumbarger*, landowners brought a trespass action against defendants who were conducting a strip mining operation. The defendants' strip mine was approximately 2,250 feet from, and at a higher elevation than, a spring used by the landowners for their water supply. The plaintiffs alleged that water with a high sulphur content that the defendants used in the mine had flowed into their spring and rendered it unfit for use. They presented testimony that there had been blasting and drilling at the mine, that water disappeared from the bottom of the mine after the blasting, that the ground and underground rock strata sloped downward from the mine to the spring, that local home owners felt concussions and suffered some direct damages from the blasting, and that their spring was fed by subterranean percolating water.

The Superior Court of Pennsylvania found that the plaintiffs' evidence was sufficient for a jury to find that the defendants' blasting and removal of the water from the mine altered underground geological structures in a manner that damaged the plaintiffs' spring. *Bumbarger*, 164 A. 2d at 147. It relied on Section 519 of the *Restatement of Torts* (1938), which did not limit recovery for ultrahazardous activities to direct damages. As a general rule, it provided that:

> one who carries on an ultrahazardous activity is liable to another whose person, land or chattels the actor should recognize as likely to be harmed by the unpreventable miscarriage of the activity for harm resulting thereto from that which makes the activity ultrahazardous, although the utmost care is exercised to prevent the harm.

Restatement of Torts § 519 (quoted in *Bumbarger*, 164 A.2d at 148). See also *Opal v. Material Serv. Corp.*, 9 Ill. App. 2d 433, 133 N. E. 2d 733 (1956) (rejecting requirement of proof of trespass in blasting cases and extending strict liability for direct and consequential damages that are the natural and probable result of blasting); *Atlas Chem. Indus., Inc. v. Anderson*, 514 S. W. 2d 309 (Tex. Civ. App. 1974) (imposing strict liability where defendant <u>intentionally</u> discharged pollutant into stream and holding defendant liable for all foreseeable damages resulting from the pollutant), <u>*aff'd in part and rev'd on other grounds*</u>, 524 S. W. 2d 681 (Tex. 1975); *Branch v. Western Petroleum, Inc.*, 657 P. 2d 267 (Utah 1982) (applying strict liability to nontrespassory injuries to plaintiff's wells caused by the defendant's pumping of polluted water into its own oil wells and the subsequent percolation of the polluted water into the subterranean water supply).

<u>Policy considerations</u> support such imposition of strict liability for blasting even though no <u>physical invasion</u> of the premises has taken place. Neither an industry nor the State should be allowed to use its property in an abnormally dangerous way that injures the property of its neighbors with <u>impunity</u>, because to do so is effectively an appropriation of the neighbor's property for the industry or State's use. The <u>blaster</u>, and not the wholly innocent party, should <u>assume the costs</u> of its blasting. See *Atlas Chem. Indus.*, 514 S. W. 2d at 316 (characterizing the damage inflicted on other people's property as <u>inverse condemnation</u>); *Branch*, 657 P. 2d at 275.

We think these principles have application here,

intentionally 故意地

aff'd in part and rev'd on other grounds 原判中的一部分被维持,另一部分基于其他理由被推翻。

policy consideration 政策考量
physical invasion 实质入侵

impunity 免受惩罚

blaster 爆破方
assume the costs 承担费用

inverse condemnation 逆向征用。国家征用土地而使邻近地块价值大减,该地块虽未被正式征用而应推定为已征用,其所有人有权要求政府合理补偿。

where the Clays similarly claim that the blasting caused physical damage to their property by damaging the rock formations underlying nearby property, thereby causing injury to the aquifer or to other subterranean aspects of the property in question. They presented expert testimony by Dr. Paul Hilpman, a Professor Emeritus of Geology at the University of Missouri and the Director of the Center for Underground Studies, to support this theory. He testified that the blasting damaged geological structures that resulted in the contamination of the Clays' well. Dr. Hilpman testified that the blasting fractured rock and sandstone layers in the aquifer and that these fractures in turn caused the water table to drop and allowed oil to migrate up into the water-producing area of the rock strata. This resulted in a lower water level in the Clays' well and in pollution of their well water. This type of damage is equally serious and equally likely to affect the value of property as is damage caused by vibrations or concussions on the property. We find the Clays' proof of damage was sufficient to support their strict liability for blasting and inverse condemnation claims.

B. Proof of Causation

Rieke also argues that any damage to the aquifer was not caused by the blasting, but rather by the fact that the road had to be dug to a level which required penetration of numerous layers of rock and sediment. It argues that even if it had dug the road by hand, it eventually would have had to break through the same layers of rock, and the same lowering and contamination of the aquifer would have occurred. Thus, it argues, the injury (if any) was not from the blasting but from the design and location of the road, matters which were in MHTC's control, and as to which Rieke had no input or discretion.

While the jury might have agreed with this interpretation of the evidence, there was also evidence that the blasting itself caused more severe fracturing of the rock strata than would have been caused by other methods of digging. Dr. Hilpman testified that some of the rock had to be blasted and that the blasting would cause more subterranean fracturing than simple cutting. He also testified that the oil showed up in the Clays' well because it was able to migrate up into the water zone through fractures in a limestone layer that were caused by blasting. While the evidence on this point was not extensive, the jury apparently accepted it and it was adequate to support the jury's verdict.

C. Diminution of value

Rieke also argues that the Clays failed to make a submissible case because they failed to offer sufficient evidence that there was a diminution in fair market value of their property, and further that the evidence did not support the amount of the jury's verdict.

We disagree. Rieke's position is based on its argument that the only evidence of fair market value was (1) its own appraiser's testimony that the difference in fair market value of the Clays' property before and after the blasting was $12,700, and (2) Mr. Clay's testimony that his property did not have any fair market value prior to the blasting because of its zoning and proximity to Kansas City International Airport. Rieke argues that Mr. Clay's testimony necessarily implied that the water problems did not affect the fair market value of the property and so that defeated the Clays' own claim.

appraiser 评定者

While Mr. Clay's testimony did not help his position, he clarified that he meant that the home had little or no value as a residence due to its location near the airport, but that it would have considerable value as a farm. In addition, on cross-examination Rieke's appraiser admitted that his appraisal was incomplete in that he had not considered some relevant facts in reaching his $12,700 figure.

(Original footnote: The Clays claim that the appraiser's report should not have been admitted at all because it was hearsay. We do not reach this issue, because the Clays have failed to include the appraiser's report in the record on appeal. As Rieke notes, an appellant's failure to make exhibits that are claimed to have been improperly admitted a part of the appellate record precludes review of the propriety of the trial court's ruling. *State ex rel. Missouri Highway & Transp. Comm'n v. Gannon*, 898 S.W.2d 141, 144 (Mo.App.1995). But were we to reach the merits of the Clays' argument, we would find that its admission was harmless because the report was merely cumulative of other similar evidence admitted without objection. *Dunn v. St. Louis-San Francisco Ry. Co.*, 621 S.W.2d 245, 252 (Mo. banc 1981), *cert. denied sub nom. Burlington N. R. R. Co. v. Dunn*, 454 U.S. 1145, 102 S.Ct. 1007 (1982); *State*

hearsay 传闻证据

propriety 正当

ex rel. Missouri Highway & Transp. Comm'n v. McDonald's Corp., 896 S. W. 2d 652, 655 (Mo. App. 1995).

More specifically, the appraiser testified that because fair market value is based on the "highest and best use" of the "next most likely buyer," and because he had determined that the "highest and best use" of the "next most likely buyer" to be as a "suburban residence with small acreage," he did not determine whether the property had any incidental agricultural use that should be reflected in its value. He admitted that if the well water had some unique characteristics it might enhance the property value. He also admitted that he had not given the well water any special value because of its favorable chemical balance, had not specifically checked a water bill for the property, had not considered the $2,800 cost to hook-up to the city water line once the well was polluted, had not considered the "storm water charge" on the water bill, and had not considered that such factors could affect the property value.

The evidence was sufficient to support the jury's determination that the blasting caused a decrease in fair market value of the Clay's property in the $19,640 amount found by the jury.

...

Affirmed as to liability and *remanded* for modification of the damage award in accordance with this opinion.

All concur.

The above line of cases illustrates how different courts decided cases under the doctrine of *stare decisis*. They also give us a general idea on the establishment, development, and application of a common law rule. Although the case *Rylands* does not bind the U.S. courts, most jurisdictions in the United States have adopted, or at least respected and analyzed the *Rylands* rule. Actually, the *Rylands* rule is articulated in the *Restatement Second*, *Torts* § 519. It says: One who carries on an abnormally dangerous activity is subject to liability for harm to the person, land, or chattels of another resulting from the activity, although he has exercised the utmost care to prevent the harm. It further provides that "this strict liability is limited to the kind of harm, the possibility of which makes the activity abnormally dangerous." There is at least one court in the United States committed to broader application of the *Rylands* rule than is reflected in the *Restatement*. *National Steel Service Center, Inc. v. Gibbons*, 319 N.W. 2d 269 (Iowa 1982). Other authority applies what it terms the "true rule," or the narrow rule, of *Rylands*. Under the narrow rule, in order for a person to be held strictly liable for the damage caused by an abnormally dangerous activity, the activity must be an activity relating to the land or other immovables, and must itself cause the injury, and the defendant must have been engaged directly in the injury-producing activity.

However, a number of jurisdictions reject the doctrine. Specifically, some authority holds that the liability of the defendant must be determined according to the law of negligence in cases involving injuries caused by the keeping of dangerous instrumentalities, agencies, or substances which <u>imperil</u> other property or persons in the neighborhood, by the use of explosives in blasting, or storage of explosives, by keeping wild animals, and by transmitting electricity. For instance, in *Kennedy Building Associates v. Viacom, Inc.*, 375 F. 3d 731 (8th Cir. 2004), the Court of Appeals held that under Minnesota law, owner of land whose soil and groundwater were contaminated by prior owner did not have strict liability cause of action against prior owner's corporate successor pursuant to Minnesota's version of *Rylands* rule, which provided plaintiff with strict liability claim against landowner based on harmful release of substance not naturally occurring on landowner's property, inasmuch as rule required "escape" of instrumentality causing plaintiff's harm beyond landowner's own property, and thus did not apply to situations in which harm was done to landowner's own property.

imperil 危及;使陷于危险中

Review Questions

1. Summarize the arguments and methods of reasoning that a common law attorney may use when representing their clients.
2. What techniques used in common law reasoning have you learned from the line of cases decided after *Fletcher v. Rylands*?
3. What is a favorable authority and what is an adverse authority?
4. What is the difference between strict liability and absolute liability?
5. Write a short essay describing the development of the strict liability rule at common law.

Chapter 7
CASE REPORTING SYSTEMS

Case law is an important source of law in common law system. In Chapter 5, we discussed the fundamental notion of common law, i.e., the doctrine of *stare decisis* from which we know how case law functions based on this doctrine. Basically when a common law court decides a case, it must follow precedents, which are the prior judicial decisions made by the court itself or a court superior to it. Each judicial opinion contains various parts and only the *ratio decidendi* or holding is binding whereas the *dicta* is not, although the *dicta* may be suggestive to some extent. Where there are multiple opinions published on one case, only the majority opinion represents the disposition of the case by the court. However, the dissenting and concurring opinions are also helpful for lawyers to better understand the majority's reasoning as well as the weak points of the majority's opinion. These are not part of the precedent and thus not binding. Nevertheless, they are worth reading because when a court decides a case of first impression, these opinions will be examined and some of the rules contained in the dissenting or concurring opinions may become law in the future.

Since prior judicial decisions are essential for common law judges and lawyers to perform their functions, an accurate and efficient system of reporting judicial decisions is very necessary. This Chapter will give a brief introduction to the case reporting system and provide a guidance on where and how to find those precedents. Although England and the United States are both common law countries, they have different law reporting systems.

7.1 Law Reports in England

7.1.1 Law Reports

The earliest case reports in England was the *Year*

Books starting from the fourteenth century. For a long time in the English history, there had been no official case reports and thus there was no case reporting system at all until 1865. At that time, all case reports were compiled by private companies or institutions. Since the sixteenth century, a wide variety of reports have emerged in England, which are referred to by the initials of the reporter. For instance, *the Reports of Lord Coke* is referred to as Co. Rep., and *the English Reports* is referred to as E. R. The doctrine of precedent and *stare decisis* was developed at about mid-1860s, which required an accurate and systematic reporting system. In 1865, *the Incorporated Council of Law Reporting for England and Wales* was established under professional control to ensure more systematic and economic reporting. Since then, a unified law reporting system has been established in England. There are various series of law reports. Each volume covers the work of a particular court. For instance, *Young v. Lopez* [1978] Ch. 254 refers to the case determined by Chancery. While "Ch." Refers to the Chancery, the reference "A. C." signifies Appeal Cases, which are reports of House of Lords and Privy Council cases. Several other series are commonly used, such as the *All England Law Reports* (All E. R.) and *Weekly Law Reports* (W. L. R.). Others again are in professional periodicals, notably the *Solicitors Journal* (S. J.) and *Estates Gazette* (E. G.).

7.1.2 Format of a Case in the Law Reports

The format of a case in the law reports is generally the same, although there are slight variations in each series of reports. However, since the publisher of the case reports may add some information on the court opinion to aid the readers, it is very important to distinguish between the actual opinion of the court and the additional information provided by the publisher when examining a case in the law reports. It is the opinion of the court that has authority as precedent, not the information provided by the publisher. Cases in casebooks will usually contain only an edited version of the actual opinion. It is useful, however, to know what other information may be contained in the law reports.

A. Headnotes

The headnote is a summary of a case at the beginning of the report of the case immediately after the case name which is prepared by the publisher. It usually includes a

headnote 判决提要,判例汇编中对案件主要事实所作的简要概括。

statement of the rule of law pronounced in the case, a summary of the facts of the case, and the ruling or decision of the court as to the respective rights of the parties. The headnote is intended to provide the readers with a capsule summary of the case but it is not part of the opinion made by the court; therefore it is not part of the precedent. The publishers try to summarize the headnotes accurately, but one should not rely on them because they just reflect the publisher's point of view and sometimes inaccurate or misleading. The right way is to read and summarize the case by yourself.

B. Summary and Counsel's Arguments

Many series of law reports include at the very beginning of the case a paragraph in italics containing a series of key words or phrases. This paragraph is intended to indicate the key words or issues in dispute in the case. It is sometimes helpful to the extent that it can give the reader a general idea of what the case is about. In addition, the publishers often provide a summary of the facts and procedure in the lower courts and a summary of the arguments made in the hearing before the appellate court. The only series of law reports which contains a fairly complete summary of the arguments made by counsel for each party at the hearing is the semi-official series known as the *Law Reports*.

C. Cross-References and Notes

Cases in the *All England Reports* include cross-references to the relevant sections of the leading legal encyclopedia of English law, *Halsbury's Laws of England*, where you will find a general discussion of the points of law at issue in the case. It also includes cross-references to the leading legal digest. The *Digest* is a collection of all case summaries based on different issues. It will help you find summaries of other cases where the same points of law were considered. Sometimes the *All England Reports* contain editorial notes which are useful to the readers because they put the case in perspective. In the *All England Reports Reprints* series, the reprints of the older cases include *Notes* listing subsequent cases which have considered the reported case. This is very helpful for one to find out how subsequent cases have treated the reported case as a precedent.

D. Names and Titles of Judges

The name of the judge who actually delivered the opinion in the case always appears after the <u>aforementioned preliminary information</u>. Starting from here, the court opinion begins. Usually the judge's surname and an <u>abbreviation</u> indicating his or her title will be shown. If the judge who delivered the opinion was speaking on behalf of all of the judges who heard the case, it will indicate that he "delivered the judgment of the court." In cases from the House of Lords, the usual practice is to write "Lord" before the name of the Law Lord, followed by any special title. For example, "Lord Cairns L. C." would indicate that he is the Lord Chancellor, the head of the judicial system. The other most important abbreviations for the titles of English judges include: "M. R. ," Master of the Rolls, member of the Court of Appeal and for practical purposes its head; "L. J. ," Lord Justice, a member of the Court of Appeal; "C. J. ," Chief Justice, head of the Queen's Bench Division ("L. C. J." if a Law Lord); "C. B. ," Chief Baron, the head of the former Court of Exchequer; "B. ," Baron of the Exchequer, a member of the former Court of Exchequer.

aforementioned 前面提到的，上述的

preliminary information 初步资料

abbreviation 摘要

E. Date of the Opinion

The date a judgment was delivered often appears with the judge's name. The abbreviation "*Cur. Ad. Vult.*" (<u>*curia advisari vult*</u>) may also appear just above the judge's name. This abbreviation means "the court wishes to be advised." When used in a law report just above the judge's name it means that the judgment was not delivered immediately after it was heard by the court, but that time was taken for consideration.

curia advisari vult 法庭将考虑，指当案件涉及新的或疑难问题时，法庭决定推迟作出判决直至对该问题考虑成熟。

F. The Opinion

The actual opinion of the court begins immediately after the name of the judge. It generally contains a description of the procedural history of the case, a summary of the facts of the case, the legal issues presented before the court, the decisions made by the court, and the reasons for the decision. This is the part which lawyers should read carefully in order to find the binding rules.

G. Names of Counsels

The names of the lawyers in the case and the names of their law firms are often found at the end of the report. If a Queen's Counsel had argued the case the initials "Q. C." will appear after his or her name. Queen's Counsels are barristers "learned in the law" who have been appointed Counsel to Her Majesty on the recommendation of the Lord Chancellor. A Queen's Counsel may have chambers in London. If retained to conduct a case in court they are referred to as "leader" and the person instructed to appear with them is referred to as "junior."

7.2 Case Reporters in the United States

Case reporters in the United States are compiled by different institutions and in different systems, but the function of them is essentially similar to that of the law reports in England. Usually the court decisions are collected chronologically in volumes called case reporters, and summarized by subject matters in reference works called case digests.

7.2.1 Case Reporters

Since there is a federal court system and fifty state court systems in the United States, each system has a different case reporting system or practice.

A. Cases from Federal Courts

Each level of the federal courts has at least one case reporter for its decisions. Cases decided by the United States Supreme Court are collected and published in a series of books called *United States Reports* (abbreviated "U. S."), which is the government-approved official reporter of these decisions. In addition, there are two unofficial reporters: West Publishing Company publishes *the Supreme Court Reporter* ("S. Ct."), and Lawyers Cooperative Publishing Company publishes *the United States Supreme Court Reports, Lawyers' Edition* ("L. Ed." and "L. Ed. 2d"). "L. Ed. 2d" refers to the second series of this Lawyers' Cooperative Publication. Legal publishers frequently divide continuing lines of publications into consecutively numbered series, simply to break them into more manageable sets of books. These unofficial reporters contain everything in the official reporter, plus some helpful editorial features added by the publishers' in-house staffs. Strictly speaking, *United States Reports* is the only official, authoritative reporter of U. S. Supreme Court opinions; the unofficial reporters, however, are highly

case digest 案件摘要

reliable and widely used by lawyers and judges. In addition to these reporters, the full texts of U.S. Supreme Court decisions are reprinted in *United States Law Week* and *Supreme Court Bulletin*, both of which are a type of publication known as "looseleaf service."

looseleaf service 活页版

United States Court of Appeals decisions from all circuits are found in *the Federal Reporter*, published by the West Publishing Company (hereinafter "West"). The first series of this reporter contains opinions issued from 1880 to 1924 and is abbreviated as "F." The second series covers the period starting from 1924. From 1880 to 1932, United States District Court opinions were reported along with U.S. Court of Appeals decisions in the first and second series of *Federal Reporter*. Since 1932, U.S. District Court opinions have been collected in a reporter known as *Federal Supplement* ("F. Supp."). In addition, since 1938, certain kinds of District Court opinions which dealt with procedural rules that apply in the United States District Courts have been published in *Federal Rules Decisions* ("F. R. D.") instead of *Federal Supplement*.

hereinafter 以下,在下文中

In 1894, West published *Federal Cases* ("F. Cas.") as a retrospective supplement to *Federal Reporter*. *Federal Cases* collects opinions of the United States Court of Appeals and District Courts issued between 1789 and 1880, when West began publishing *Federal Reporter*. Editorial exigencies compelled West to arrange the opinions in *Federal Cases* alphabetically by plaintiffs' names rather than by the date of a decision's issuance.

In addition, the opinions made by other specialized federal courts, such as the United States Court of International Trade are also reported in the federal reporters. But the District Courts, Courts of Appeals, and the Supreme Court are the federal courts whose opinions the majority of lawyers and judges rely on most frequently. For easy reference, a list appears at the beginning of each volume of the federal reporters indicating all the courts whose decisions are reported in that volume.

B. Cases from State Courts

Decisions of state courts are collected in state case reporters. Each state has at least one official reporter for its highest court. Some states also have separate reporters for their intermediate appellate courts, and a few states have reporters for trial level courts. In general, the larger a state's population, the greater the number of reporters that state has. For example, as a highly populous state, New York has reporters all the way down to its trial level courts. Less populous Nevada and New Hampshire, on the other hand, have reporters only for their highest courts.

Many state court opinions are also published by West Publishing Company in a series of reporters called regional reporters, each of which reprints the full text of opinions from courts in a specific geographical region of the country. Some states have designated as official reporters for their jurisdictions the regional reporters containing their courts' opinions.

7.2.2 Case Digests

Case reporters at both the federal and state levels compile court decisions chronologically, *i.e.*, by date of the decisions' issuance. When lawyers do legal research, they need to find out the cases dealing with the same issues. In order to meet their needs, the publishers arrange the court decisions based on their topics and publish the multi-volume compilations known as case digests. In effect, the digests serve as grand indexes to the case reporters. Each digest collection breaks the law into hundreds of legal topics. Because any given court opinion typically deals with several different legal topics, a court opinion usually cannot be classified under only one topic. Moreover, reprinting the full opinion under each appropriate legal topic in a digest would be unmanageable. Therefore, each digest publisher's editorial staff analyzes published opinions, determines which legal issues each opinion deals with, and summarizes in a one-paragraph digest along with the citation to the case from which it is drawn, is assigned to and published under an appropriate topical heading in the digest. As a result, a single case may appear digested under several topics.

For federal courts, there are several digests. *United States Supreme Court Digest* (published by West) and *United States Supreme Court Digest, Lawyers' Edition* (published by Lawyers Cooperative) contain digests of only U.S. Supreme Court cases. West also publishes a series of digests containing summaries of decisions of all federal courts: *Federal Digest* covers cases decided during the period from 1789 to 1939; *Modern Federal Practice Digest* covers from 1939 to 1961; *West's Federal Practice Digest 2d* covers 1961 to 1975; and *West's Federal Practice Digest 3d* covers 1975 to the present.

For state courts, West publishes separate digests for nearly every state plus the District of Columbia, as well as digests tied to five of West's seven regional case reporters. In some states, there are also case digests available from publishers other than West.

In addition, West publishes a continuing series of digests collecting all the one-paragraph case summaries contained in both its state and federal digests during <u>consecutive</u> ten-year periods. Known as *Decennial Digests*, these multi-volume publications follow the format of West's individual federal and state digests, arranging each ten-year collection of summaries according to West's digest topics. *Decennial Digests* are supplemented by a series of periodically issued non-cumulative paperbound and hardbound volumes called *General Digests*. In effect, the *Decennial Digests* (and *General Digests*) use chronological criteria in selecting which summaries to include, whereas state and federal digests use jurisdictional or geographical standards for selection. For most research purposes, using a federal digest or the digest for just the state whose law you are researching will be sufficient, but the *Decennial Digests* permit researchers to compare how federal and state courts throughout the country have ruled on particular points of law.

consecutive 连续的,连贯的
decennial 十年一度的

7.2.3 Format of a Case in the Case Reporters

The format of a case collected in a U.S. case reporter is essentially the same as that of a case contained in an English law reports, with a few variations. For example, the counsel's names are provided preceding the main body of the opinion. Commercial publishers also put additional information before the opinion in order to aid their readers. Again, these are not part of the opinion and thus not part of the precedent. Since there is no unified format for case reporters, each jurisdiction or publisher may determine its own way to publish these cases.

Below is an example:

Barnes, et al., Appellants, *v.* Treece, et al., Respondents
Court of Appeals of Washington, Division One
15 Wn. App. 437; 549 P.2d 1152
May 10, 1976

PRIOR HISTORY:
Appeal from a judgment of the Superior Court for

King County, No. 769424, Robert E. Dixon, J. Pro Tem., entered June 3, 1974.

DISPOSITION:
Affirmed.

LexisNexis (TM) HEADNOTES — Core Concepts:
HEADNOTES: [1] Contracts — Formation — Mutual Assent — Unexpressed Intention. Whether a person's statements or actions constitute an enforceable expression of contractual intent is a question of fact to be determined from that person's objective manifestations as seen within the context of the surrounding circumstances; unexpressed intentions may not be considered.

[2] Contracts — Unilateral Contract — Offer and Acceptance. A promise to do something upon another person's performance of a requested act is an offer for a unilateral contract. A contract results when the other person does the specified act with the intention of accepting the offer.

[3] Contracts — Consideration — Adequacy — In General. Consideration is not inadequate to support a contract unless it is constructively fraudulent.

[4] Corporations — Officers — Vice-President — Authority. A corporate vice-president does not have actual authority to bind the corporation by virtue of his office, but may be clothed with apparent authority by the corporation.

[5] Principal and Agent — Apparent Authority — Justifiable Reliance. An agent has apparent authority when his principal acts in such a way as would lead a reasonable person to believe the agent possesses such authority, deter him from further inquiry, and cause him to rely on the agent's authority. Whether an agent possesses such apparent authority is a question of fact to be determined in light of the surrounding circumstances.

[6] Contracts — Corporations — Officers — Implied Ratification of Contract. A corporation impliedly ratifies a contract which was entered into by one of its officers when it has full knowledge of the contract and it receives benefits thereunder, it acts in a manner which demonstrates its adoption and recognition of the contract

as binding, or its failure to repudiate or disaffirm the contract causes the other party to change his position and suffer a resulting loss. Whether there has been an implied ratification is a question of fact.

SYLLABUS:

Action for breach of contract. The plaintiffs appeal from a judgment in favor of one of the defendants.

COUNSEL:

Oberquell & Ahlf and *Kenneth R. Ahlf*, for appellants.

Warner, Pierce & Peden and *Leo J. Peden*, for respondents.

JUDGES:

Callow, J., James and Andersen, JJ., concur.

OPINION BY:

CALLOW

OPINION:

The plaintiffs Barnes appeal, and the defendant Warren Treece cross-appeals, from a judgment entered in plaintiffs' breach of contract action against Treece and the defendant Vend-A-Win, Inc. The plaintiffs appeal from the portion of the judgment dismissing Vend-A-Win from the action with prejudice and assert that Vend-A-Win either clothed Treece with apparent authority or ratified the contract made by him. ...

This is part of a case published by Lexis-Nexis, a commercial publisher competing with West in the United States. The first line of the case indicates the name of the case, including both parties' names and status. *Barnes* is the appellant and *Treece* is the respondent, or appellee. Apparently there is more than one appellant and respondent; therefore "*et al.*" follows the parties' names. Between the parties' names is the abbreviation of "*versus*." When lawyers cite this case, they do not need to cite the complete names of the parties; instead, they just need to cite the last name of the first person of each party. In this case, it could be "*Barnes v. Treece.*"

The second line tells us which court reviewed this case. It is Division One of the Court of Appeals of

syllabus 判决摘要

et al. 以及其他人

versus 诉

Washington, a state appellate court. Next line is the citation of the case. "Wn. App." refers to the case reporter *Washington Appellate Court Case Reporter*, the number "15" preceding it refers to the volume number of the reporter, while the number "437" following it indicates the beginning page of this case in that volume. There is also a parallel citation which refers to a regional reporter *Pacific Reporter*, *Second Series*, i.e., "P. 2d." Similarly, the number "549" preceding the reporter's name is the volume number of the reporter where you can find the volume containing this case, and the number "1152" following the name of the reporter is the first page on which the case is reprinted. Following the citation comes the date when the decision was made by the court. Thus from the first part of the case, readers will know the parties to the case, the court decided the case, the citation (s) of the case, and the date when the case was decided.

Following the first part is the additional information provided by the publisher in order to aid readers to better understand the case. This is not part of the precedent, therefore they are not binding. The information here includes the prior history, disposition, and headnotes of the case. The actual opinion starts from "syllabus," where a simple introduction as to the cause of action of the case is given. This case is an action for breach of contract. From the sentence we also know that one of the defendants won the case in the lower court therefore the plaintiffs appeal to the appellate court.

Then the counsel's names are listed. The practice of England and the United States is different as to where to put counsel's names. In England the counsel's names are listed at the end of the opinion but in a U.S. case, they are normally listed before the main body of the opinion. First, the appellants retain the law firm named "*Oberquell & Ahlf*," which designated one of its attorneys (most probably a partner guessing from his last name) to represent before the court. The respondents are represented by the law firm of "*Warner, Pierce & Peden*," which also assigned the case to one of their attorneys named Leo J. Peden.

The judges who reviewed this case are then listed. This is a regular appellate review and a penal of three judges discussed the case. Judge Callow is the one who wrote the opinion. The other two judges are Judge James and Judge Andersen. Finally, before the actual opinion, the author of the opinion is indicated.

The main body of the opinion follows. The structure of an opinion is similar to that of an opinion made by an English judge as described above. Details about the format of a case opinion will be discussed in Chapter 8.

7.3 Case Names and Citations

The above introduction tells us how to identify and where to find a precedent. In a law report or case reporter, people can locate the title of a case. However, how will a case be addressed in speaking or cited in writing?

7.3.1 Case Names

Most of the cases are referred to by the names of the parties. When there is more than one plaintiff or defendant in a case, the names of all of the parties will not appear in the case name. Instead the name of the first plaintiff or defendant will be followed by an abbreviation of "*et al.*" meaning "and others."

When a case name is written, the abbreviation "*v.*" of "*versus*" appears between the names of the parties; but in speaking, "*versus*" may be read in different ways by British and U.S. lawyers. In the United States, lawyers simply read "*v.*" as "*versus*," regardless of the nature of the case. However, in England, lawyers understand and read them differently depending on whether it is a civil case or a criminal case. If it is a civil case, when speaking it, the English convention is to say "and" between the surname of the parties rather than "*versus*." The names of criminal cases in England usually begin with <u>Rex</u> or <u>Regina</u> (both abbreviated as "*R.*"), which stands for the King or Queen, respectively. For example, the name of a criminal case which has been brought against a person named Smith might be written as *Regina v. Smith*. The convention of referring to the name of the case in court, however, would be to say "the Queen against Smith." In criminal cases the "*v.*" is never pronounced "and" as it is in civil cases. In certain criminal cases the actual or official name of the prosecutor may be used in the case name instead of *Rex* or *Regina*. For example, the practice in the House of Lords prior to 1979 in criminal cases was usually to use the name of the official prosecutor, the Director of Public Prosecutions, rather than *Rex* or *Regina*, in the case

Rex 国王
Regina 女王

name.

When a case is appealed to an appellate court, the case name may sometimes be changed because the appellant before the appellate court may be the defendant in the trial court. In that case, the names of the parties will be reversed because the convention in some appellate courts is to place the name of the appellant first, rather than the name of the plaintiff. However, in other courts, the names of the parties will not be changed. In that case, you cannot identify who is the appellant and who is the appellee simply from the case name unless you read through the procedural history of the case.

Case names are also different in certain types of cases. For example, special proceedings in civil cases relating to property or estates will have special names. The name of a case concerning the estate of a deceased person named Jones may be *In re Jones*. The abbreviation "*in re*" means "in the matter of." Another common abbreviation used in certain special cases is "*ex parte*," which means "on the application of." The name of a case in a special proceeding which was brought on the application of a person named Smith might be *Ex parte Smith*.

7.3.2 Case Citations

When attorneys write a pleading for the court, or legal scholars write a paper or article of law, they need to cite cases because cases are the law. We have discussed the way for lawyers to understand a case name and to address a case when speaking; the topic of this sub-section is about how to cite a case in writing.

The first thing we should keep in mind is that the purpose of citing a case is to provide the readers with sufficient information so that they will be able to find the published form of that case if they want to check and examine the case to see whether the case (the law) really supports the author's point. An accurately cited case may also enable the readers to get more information about the case if they are interested in or simply curious about it. Therefore, a case citation must include the information necessary to locate a report of the case in one of the series of law reports or case reporters. Accordingly, a case citation must include the name of the case, the law report or reporter in which it is published (normally an abbreviation of the name of the law report), the number of the relevant volume of the report, and the page at which the case begins. In addition, case citations also commonly include the date or year of the decision and an abbreviation indicating the name or level of the court which decided the case.

The citation system of England and the United States are different although they basically contain the similar information. The citation of an English case is illustrated as following. For instance, the citation to the report decision of the Court of Exchequer Chamber in *Fletcher v. Rylands* in *the Law Journal Reports* is 35 L.J. Ex. 154 (1866). In this citation the year is in round brackets because it is not essential to locating the correct volume of the report series. A citation to the report of the case in *All England Reports Reprints* is [1861-73] All E.R. Rep. 1 (Exch. Cham.). In this citation the year is in square brackets because the year is essential to locating the correct volume. The three series of law reports containing modern English cases are the *Law Reports*, *Weekly Law Reports* and *All England Reports*. The following are citations to the case *Hedley Byrne & Co. v. Heller & Partners Ltd.* in those reports: [1964] A.C. 465; [1963] 3 W.L.R. 101; and [1963] 2 All E.R. 575. Note that in *the Law Reports* the abbreviations refer to the relevant division of that series, such as A.C. for Appeal Cases and Q.B. for Queen's Bench.

Below is an example and explanation of a typical citation of a state case in the United States. State cases are cited to the regional reporter, in this case *the Pacific Reporter, Second Series*, abbreviated P.2d: *Alaska State Housing Authority v. Walsh & Co., Inc.*, 625 P.2d 831 (Alaska 1980). "*Alaska State Housing Authority v. Walsh & Co., Inc.*" is the name of the case, italicized, or achieved by underlining if typed or written. Apparently both parties to this case are companies. If the parties are individuals, however, the last name of the parties will be used. If there are more than one person within each party, use only the name of the first person from each party. As explained above, "P.2d" is the name of the case reporter and the number "625" preceding the name of the reporter is the number of the volume containing the case. The number "831" following the name of the case reporter is the page number at which the case begins. The parenthetical following the beginning page number identifies the jurisdiction and court, and the year the case was decided. Because *the Pacific Reporter* includes cases from many states, you must identify the jurisdiction of the case. Identification by the abbreviation of the state means that the case was decided by the highest court in that state. If the case was not decided by the highest court, then identify the court if it is not otherwise identified. For example, if a case was decided by the Court of Appeals of Washington in 1976, cite it as *Barnes v. Treece*, 549 P.2d 1152 (Wash. Ct. App. 1976).

A case decided by the Supreme Court of the United States is cited to the official reporter, *United States Reports*, abbreviated "U.S." For example, *Nathanson v. Victor*, 300 U. S. 52 (1980). There are no official reporters for decisions from the United States District Courts or Courts of Appeals; cases are cited only to West reporters and you must always identify the court, by district or by circuit, in the parentheses. For instance, *John v. Marshall*, 400 F. Supp. 12 (W. D. Va. 1976). This case is from the United States District Court for the Western District of Virginia. *John v. Marshall*, 400 F.2d 12 (2d Cir. 1976). This case is from the United States Court of Appeals for the Second Circuit.

Understanding the common law citations is important for lawyers in civil law countries to do legal research on common law. The above brief introduction may give you a general idea about what citations mean and where you can find the published cases based on their citations. If you want to learn more about citation, there are several books, among others, *A Uniform System of Citation* compiled by the editors of *the Columbia Law Review*, *the Harvard Law Review*, *the University of Pennsylvania Law Review*, and *the Yale Law Journal*.

Review Questions

1. Why is the case reporting system important in the common law countries?
2. Why do people need to cite cases?
3. Should there be a unified format for judicial opinions?

PART III
CASE ANALYSIS

HAVING discussed the basic common law concept and the case law approach, this Part and the following one will further discuss how a common law lawyer analyzes precedents and applies precedents to his own cases when doing legal work. It is essential to keep it in mind that cases, in form of judicial decisions or opinions, are the law in common law countries and the common law courts record their decisions in opinions, which describe what the dispute was about and why the court decided the case as it did. In analyzing cases, common law lawyers are actually analyzing the law, just as the civil law lawyers apply the written statutes to their cases. Since the doctrine of precedent and *stare decisis* require common law courts to follow the *ratio decidendi* of prior binding cases in resolving disputes, cases have enormous value in predicting what a court might do in a specific situation and in persuading a court to reach a particular conclusion. It is thus very important for common law lawyers to research prior precedents to see whether a precedent will be applied for or against their own cases by the court. The ability to understand what these cases mean is thus a necessary skill in analyzing or writing about any legal problem.

Chapter 8
CASE ANALYSIS

Chapter 7 has introduced the various parts of a case as published in a law report or case reporter, this section will examine the opinion of a case, without considering the other additional information provided by the publishers of law reports or case reporters. "Cases," "decisions," "judicial opinions," or "opinions" in this Chapter are thus used interchangeably meaning the main body of the court opinion, including the *ratio decidendi* and *dicta*. The importance of studying cases lies in that cases demonstrate the basic methods of legal reasoning that judges used in deciding cases and lawyers will use in practicing law. Courts must decide whether a particular law can or cannot apply to a specific factual situation, and must explain their reasoning to support their conclusion. Similarly, the practice of law requires attorneys to decide whether certain laws apply to certain facts. In order to make their conclusion persuasive, attorneys must also explain their reasoning. No doubt, it is important for new attorneys to study legal reasoning through analyzing the ways that courts analyze legal problems.

interchangeably 可交换的,可交替的

8.1 Basic Structure of a Judicial Opinion

Judges write judicial opinions to explain the reasons and policies based on which they decided a particular case in a particular way. Different judges delivered the opinions differently. However, every opinion usually starts with the court's jurisdiction, explaining the power and authority of the court to hear and decide the case. Then it states the procedural history, if the case has already litigated before reaching this court, and the fact of the case. Followed is the discussion part where the court analyzes the case by applying the rules of law to the particular facts of the case and stating the reasons and policies behind the conclusion. The last part of the opinion contains the proposition of law and the disposition of the case. This section will introduce the different types of judicial opinion attorneys may encounter in their practices, the common actions made by the courts, and the basic elements of a judicial opinions which is helpful for lawyers to draft a case brief.

8.1.1 Different Types of Opinions

As discussed in earlier Chapters and seen from the cases decided by English and American judges, there may be more than one opinion on a particular case reviewed by an appellate court. There are various types of opinions you may find in case reporters. When reading, analyzing, discussing, or briefing an opinion, you need to know what type of opinion it is because the different type of opinion will affect its precedential value and the weight of its authority. The various types of opinions that may be given by appellate court judges are introduced below.

A. Majority Opinion

If all of the appellate court judges agree on the disposition of a case, one of the judges will be assigned to write the opinion on it. If this is the case, there is only one opinion. Sometimes, however, the majority judges agree on the disposition of the case and write the opinion, while one or more judges disagree with the majority's disposition or the reasoning. The disagreeing judges may write separate opinion or opinions expressing their own thoughts on the case. If that happens, the opinion written by the majority judges is referred to as the "majority opinion." Even though there are concurring or dissenting opinions on it, a majority opinion is the disposition of the case by the appellate court, and it is the opinion lawyers need to study because it represents the principles of law and reasoning supported by a majority of the members of the court. When lawyers talk about "opinion" of a case, they refer to the majority opinion.

B. Concurring Opinion

A judge who agrees with the disposition of law contained in the majority opinion but disagrees with the reasoning that leads to that disposition may write a separate opinion. This opinion is called concurring opinion. A concurring opinion is not the disposition of

---

concurring opinion 协同意见,指一名或少数法官的单独意见,同意多数法官作出的判决,但对判决依据提出不同理由。

the case and thus not binding. It sometimes limits the majority opinion to some extent. Although a concurring opinion is not binding, lawyers often find instructive values in the concurring opinion when analyzing future cases.

C. Dissenting Opinion

A judge who disagrees with the disposition of law contained in the majority opinion may write a separate opinion. This opinion is called dissenting opinion, which may express disagreement with the reasoning, principles of law or social policy discussed in the majority opinion. It is not binding but it may acutely point out the weak points of the majority opinion. Thus the losing party may find many supports out of a dissenting opinion. It is also possible that in the future the rules stated in a dissenting opinion will be accepted by the majority of the court when dealing with new cases and will thus become binding. Therefore, studying dissenting opinions will help lawyers predict the trend of development of the law.

dissenting opinion 异议意见，指一名或几名法官持有的不同意根据多数法官意见所达成的判决结果的意见。

D. Plurality Opinion

A judicial opinion is composed of the disposition of law and the reasoning behind it. When voting for the decision, the judges may agree or disagree on both the disposition of law and the reasoning, or, the judges may agree on either the disposition or the reasoning, while disagree on the other. If a majority of the judges agrees on the disposition of the case, but less than a majority agrees with the reasoning of the decision, the opinion published by the court is called a plurality opinion. A portion of a plurality opinion may represent the majority view if that portion is also supported in the separate opinions of enough judges to constitute a majority of the court, but "the holding of the court may be viewed as that position taken by those Justices who concurred in the judgment on the narrowest grounds." 5 Am. Jur. 2d § 602 (2004). Normally, plurality decisions of a state supreme court are not binding under the doctrine of *stare decisis*. If a majority merely agrees to a particular result, without agreeing as to the grounds for a decision, the parties are bound by the decision but the case provides no binding authority beyond the immediate parties. Such an opinion may be easily overruled in appeal.

E. *Per Curiam* Opinion

When "*per curiam*" is written in the beginning of an opinion, it means that this opinion has been made by the whole court while the author of the opinion is not identified. The reason for having such an opinion is because the case is an easy one without much controversy, *i.e.*, the issue in the case is simple and the facts are without disputes so that the whole court reach a unanimous opinion. Occasionally, if the issue is sensitive and no single judge would like to be named as the author of the opinion, the court would also publish a *per curiam* opinion.

F. Memorandum Opinion

When a case is simple and without much controversy, the court will write a concise opinion called memorandum opinion expressing the holding of the whole court. Accordingly, a memorandum opinion normally does not contain lengthy comparison or reasoning.

8.1.2 Common Actions of a Court

When reading and briefing a judicial opinion, lawyers will have to describe the action that the court took, *e.g.*, the court held something, said something, or found something. Different verbs refer to different court actions. For example, if a court "held" something, it means that the following statement is the holding, *i.e.*, the disposition of law of the case which is binding. If a court "said" something, "stated" something, or "explained" something, it means the following statement is *dicta*, *i.e.*, although it is not binding, it expresses the court's opinion on an issue not presented in this case but may be instructive for future cases. If a court "found" something, it means that the statement is about the facts determined by the court. You must be very careful to use the correct verb. It is not simply an art of wording. The common actions of a court include the following.

A. Affirm *v.* Reverse

When an appellate court reviews a lower court's decision and determines to agree with all or part of the disposition of law made by the lower court, the appellate court will "affirm" all or part of the lower court's decision. If an appellate court disagrees with all or part of a lower court's decision, it can "reverse" that part. An appellate court may affirm or reverse a lower court decision only if the appeal was based on the disposition of law contained in that lower court's decision.

B. Follow v. Distinguish v. Overrule

The doctrine of *stare decisis* requires a court to follow a precedent if it determines the facts of the present case and the facts of the precedent case are similar and that justice requires them to be treated alike. When a court applies the rules contained in a precedent, it follows the precedent. Sometimes a court may also follow a decision in another case that is not binding but required to be followed under the rule of precedent when the facts of that case are sufficiently similar for justice to require similar treatment.

As a limitation of the doctrine of *stare decisis*, a court may distinguish a precedent for reason that the facts of the precedent are sufficiently different from the facts of the case before the court so that it is more fair and just not to apply the rules contained in the precedent; instead, they should be treated differently.

A court may overrule a decision in another case that was issued by itself or a lower court in the same jurisdiction. A court can never overrule a decision from another jurisdiction, a higher court in the same jurisdiction, or an equal court in the same jurisdiction. A decision that has been overruled has no authority as precedent.

overrule 推翻

C. Find v. Hold

If a court makes determination of facts based on the evidence presented before it, the court "finds" or "found" the facts. A court cannot "find" conclusions of law or non-factual matters. When a court states the disposition of the case in its opinion, it usually uses the word "hold." As we learned, this part is the holding of the case which has binding authority. Some other times, a court may use other verbs, such as conclude, determine, decide, reason, define, etc. to state the holding of the case. The holding of a court refers only to its decision on a question of law (*i.e.*, *ratio decidendi*) and not to other portions of its decision such as findings of fact or *dicta*.

find 查明

D. Dismiss v. Remand

When a court determines an action, motion, or

dismiss 驳回

prosecution that is before it has no legal basis, the court will dismiss it; as a result, the matter is discontinued, quashed, or removed from consideration by the court. For example, in the case *Barnes v. Treece*, 549 P. 2d 1152 (Wash. App. Ct. 1976) reprinted later, the plaintiffs Barnes sued Treece and Vend-A-Win, Inc. before the lower court. The lower court dismissed the action against Vend-A-Win, Inc., therefore no further actions were proceeded against this defendant in the trial.

If an appellate court does not agree with the lower court's decision, it may remand a case, i.e., remit or return the case to the lower court from which it came from for further proceedings.

E. Rule *v.* Say

A court rules when it makes findings of fact, draws conclusions of law, or enters an order. It is incorrect to state that a court "ruled" when you are referring to *dicta* in its opinion. A court "says" only those things which are *dicta*. "Say" is not an appropriate verb if you are referring to a court's holding or ruling.

F. Argue *v.* Stipulate

Attorneys argue or stipulate, not judges. Judges may argue in their concurring or dissenting opinions. If you find the word "argue" or "argument" in a judicial opinion, you must make it clear who is arguing. A court never stipulates or makes stipulations, but it may refer to a stipulation made by the parties. Only the parties to a lawsuit may stipulate by agreement, admission, or concession to a matter incident to a judicial proceeding.

8.1.3 Essential Elements of an Opinion

Being familiarized with the common actions a court may take, we will discuss the essential elements of a judicial opinion. When analyzing a case, you may need to summarize the opinion since each opinion could be lengthy and may contain many issues. Such a summary is called "a case summary" by English lawyers and "a case brief" by American attorneys. Basically, a case summary is an organized, written summary of the important elements of a case. Although judicial opinions can contain many things, several components are critical. These are the procedural history of the case, a description of the legally relevant facts, a statement of the legal issue or issues presented for decision, the holding of the case, the rule of law established by the case, the policies and reasons that support the holding, and the judgment.

The following example describes the basic elements of a judicial opinion:

State *v.* Jones

(1) Jones appeals his conviction for possession of marijuana. (2) When the police stopped and searched Jones' van, they found an ounce of marijuana in a backpack in the far rear of the vehicle. (3) Although Jones admitted he knew the marijuana was there, he defended against the charge by claiming that the backpack and drugs belonged to a hitchhiker who had been riding with him and who had accidentally left them in the van. (4) In this state, it is presumed that drugs are in the possession of the person who controls them. (5) The issue in this case is whether the marijuana was within Jones' control even though it was in a backpack in the rear of his van. (6) That the backpack and drugs may have been owned by someone else is irrelevant. (7) Public policy dictates that possession should not be synonymous with ownership because the difficulty of proving ownership would permit too many drug offenders to evade prosecution. (8) It is sensible to assume that anything inside a vehicle is within the control of the driver. (9) We hold that Jones possessed marijuana because the backpack was within Jones' van and thus under his control. (10) Affirmed.

synonymous 同义的

Dernbach, A PRACTICAL GUIDE 19-20.

All of the essential elements of a case are included in the above example. Sentence (1) sets out the procedural history. Sentences (2) and (3) give the legally relevant facts. Sentence (5) is the issue presented for decision by the appellate court. Sentence (9) is the court's holding. Sentence (4) gives the rule of law applicable to this factual situation. Sentences (6), (7), and (8) are reasons and policies that support the holding. Sentence (10) is the judgment of the case. This is a good example of a case opinion which contains all of the basic elements, but not every case has been written in such a clear and organized way. However, each case should contain these elements.

legally relevant facts 对判定案件结果起决定作用的事实

In order to completely understand a case, you need to read the case opinion for several times. During your initial reading you will gain a general understanding of who the parties were, how the dispute originated, and what effect the court's decision had on the parties. You will also form <u>tentative</u> theories concerning the basic components of the opinion, which you will test and clarify during later readings. After you have acquired a basic understanding of the facts of the case and the "real world" implications of the court's decision, you can figure out what the court decided. Only after you have understood the basic structure of the court's opinions will you be able to write a "case summary" or "case brief" covering the main aspects of the case. After having located the essential parts of a judicial opinion, the lawyers then start to frame the case brief.

Before further discussing each part individually, see an example of a case brief. When reading it, try to see how much information you may get out of it.

Brief of Carlill *v*. Carbolic Smoke Ball Co.
Ct. of App., 1892, 1 Q. B. 256 (1893)

Procedural History: Carlill brought an action against Carbolic Smoke Ball Co. to recover damages for breach of contract. The trial court awarded damages in the amount of the original advertised reward to Carlill. Carbolic Smoke Ball Co. appealed.

Facts: Carbolic Smoke Ball Co. advertised in various newspapers a reward to any person who contracted influenza, colds, or any disease caused by taking cold after having used the Carbolic Smoke Ball three times daily for two weeks according to printed directions on each ball. Carlill used the ball as directed but still caught influenza.

Issue: When a company advertises a reward to anyone who performs certain conditions and someone performs such conditions, has a valid contract been formed?

Holding: Yes, when a company advertises a reward to anyone who performs certain conditions and someone performs such conditions, a valid contract has been formed.

Rule of Law: An advertised reward to anyone who performs certain conditions specified in the advertisement is an offer, and the performance of such conditions is an acceptance which creates a valid contract.

Reasons: The advertisement clearly offered a reward to anyone who performed certain specified conditions. Since

tentative 试探性的,试验的

such an advertisement requests deeds, not words, an offeree need not give notice that he is going to perform the required deeds. As such, when Carlill performed these conditions she was entitled to the reward. Furthermore, there is no basis for Carbolic Smoke Ball Co.'s to contend that there was no consideration for its promise. Any acceptance of the Company's offer benefited it by stimulating sales of the smoke ball, and Carlill was inconvenienced by using the ball.
Judgment: The trial court's decision is affirmed.

The original opinion of this case is much longer. You may have understood the rule of law or the reasoning behind it through your first reading; however, when you need to use those information, you find that you have totally forgot it, or your memory only reveals a vague impression of it. Then you have to read the long opinion again. But if you have drafted a case brief as above, it is concise but includes all essential parts of the case. Reviewing the case brief that is less than one page will save your time. You write case brief not only for your own use. Sometimes you need to present it to your colleagues or supervisors who are too busy to read the original opinion. Therefore briefing cases is one of the important lawyering skills.

Now, after discussing the basic structure and elements of a judicial opinion and with the specific court actions in mind, we will deconstruct a judicial opinion and study each of its elements.

8.2 Procedural History

When briefing a case, attorneys should first understand the procedural history of the case and then write it down as the first part of the case brief. The purpose of spotting the procedural history is to pinpoint the current procedural status of the case. The procedural history firstly identifies the relevant background for the case. For example, who are the parties to the case and what are their roles in the case both at trial and on appeal, plaintiff-defendant, or appellant-appellee? What is the plaintiff's cause of action or the basis for the plaintiff's suit? It is important since the court's decision determines the legal rights and duties of the parties arising from that claim. What is the disposition of the case and which party won at the trial level and which party is appealing now in which appellate court for what relief? Usually the party appealing is the losing party in the trial court.

Procedural history of a case is not always clearly stated in an opinion. Sometimes you need to find it here and there from the opinion. The following example describes the procedural history of a Washington case.

Court of Appeals of Washington, Division One
Barnes *v.* **Treece**
549 P. 2d 1152
May 10, 1976

Opinion:

(1) The plaintiffs Barnes appeal, and the defendant Warren Treece cross-appeals, from a judgment entered in plaintiffs' breach of contract action against Treece and the defendant Vend-A-Win, Inc. (2) The plaintiffs appeal from the portion of the judgment dismissing Vend-A-Win from the action with prejudice and assert that Vend-A-Win either clothed Treece with apparent authority or ratified the contract made by him. (3) Treece cross-appeals from the portion awarding plaintiffs a $100,000 judgment against him personally and claims that no contract was ever formed. (4) We affirm the trial court's holding that Treece was personally liable on a valid, enforceable contract, but that he did not have apparent authority to enter into the contract on behalf of the corporation and Vend-A-Win did not ratify the contract.

This is the first paragraph of the opinion. The judge described the procedural history of the case right in the beginning of the opinion. Sentence (1) tells us the parties of the case and their roles. The Barnes were plaintiffs before the trial court, and appellants and cross-respondents before the appellate court; Treece and Vend-A-Win, Inc. were defendants before the trial court, and respondents and cross-appellants before the appellate court. It also indicates that the cause of action brought by the plaintiffs was breach of contract. Sentences (2) and (3) further explain the disposition of the case by the trial court: the action by plaintiffs against one of the defendants Vend-A-Win was dismissed by the trial court with prejudice; however, the plaintiffs won the action against the other defendant Treece and the trial court granted the plaintiffs $100,000 compensation. Sentence (4) continues to tell us the legal grounds for the trial court's decision. The plaintiffs won the breach of contract action against the individual defendants Treece because there was a valid and enforceable contract for which Treece was personally liable. However, the action against the corporate defendant Vend-A-Win was dismissed because Treece did not have apparent authority to enter into the contract on behalf of Vend-A-Win and the latter did not ratify the contract. It also tells us the appellate court's position, i.e., the appellate court affirmed the trial court's holding.

8.3 Statement of Facts

The doctrine of *stare decisis* requires that a precedent be applied to subsequent similar cases. Accordingly, only when the fact of the present case is similar to that of the precedent will the *ratio decidendi* of the precedent be applied to the present case. Therefore, the common law decisions often involve lengthy comparison of facts between the present case and the precedent case.

The facts describe the events occurred between the parties that resulted in the litigation and tell how the case came before the court that is now deciding it. There may be many facts relating to the litigated matter, but not all of them are relevant. The facts that should be identified in your case brief are the legally relevant facts or key facts, i.e., the facts relevant to the issue the court must decide. Since many cases on appeal concern a conflict over the existence of a particular element or elements necessary to establish the plaintiff's cause of action, the factual summary presented in an appellate opinion generally focuses on a particular segment of the facts detailed in the trial court record. For example, in a cause of action for breach of contract, the only element in dispute may be the element of offer (as in *Barnes v. Treece*), which is one of the elements necessary to form a contract. The facts about this alleged offer are legally relevant facts. These facts affected the court's decision. Because facts are <u>inextricably</u> tied to legal issues and rules, it is impossible to know which facts are relevant without first knowing what the court decided. Sometimes a court will state

inextricably 分不开地

precisely those facts it thought significant in deciding the case. At other times you will have to guess those facts from the court's holding and reasons. There is no rule that indicates which facts are outcome determinative, and no single fact is necessarily legally significant.

You can often tell from how an appellate court organizes its written opinion and from the language it uses what the court considers to be the legally relevant facts. For example, a court may emphasize the legally relevant facts by mentioning them first; however, some judges distribute those facts throughout the opinion and others present facts in chronological order so that the facts mentioned first are simply the earliest occurring facts in a series of events and may or may not be the most relevant ones. Sometimes, the court explicitly characterizes the facts it considers most significant; e.g., "it is important …;" or "what is decisive here …" or "the Court determines …." However, sometimes an appellate court simply summarizes the allegations of facts by the plaintiff or by the defendant at trial, beginning with "the plaintiff contended …" or "the defendant maintained. …" This summary is not the legally relevant facts recognized by the court, although the court may adopt it by saying that the court determined the facts are correct or without disputes.

Now look at another part of the case *Barnes v. Treece* and identify the legally relevant facts.

Barnes *v.* Treece
549 P.2d 1152（Wash. App. Ct. 1976）

Vend-A-Win is a Washington corporation engaged primarily in the business of distributing punchboards. Warren Treece served as vice-president, was a member of the board of directors, and owned 50 percent of the stock of Vend-A-Win. On July 24, 1973, Treece spoke before the Washington State Gambling Commission in support of punchboard legitimacy and Vend-A-Win's particular application for a temporary license to distribute punchboards. During the testimony, as stated by the trial judge, Treece made a statement to the following effect:

I'll put a hundred thousand dollars to anyone to find a crooked board. If they find it, I'll pay it.

The statement brought laughter from the audience.

The next morning, July 25, 1973, the plaintiff Barnes was watching a television news report of the proceedings before the gambling commission and heard Treece's previous statement that $100,000 would be paid to anyone who could produce a crooked punchboard. Barnes also read a newspaper report of the hearings that quoted Treece's statement. A number of years earlier, while employed as a bartender, Barnes had purchased two fraudulent punchboards. After learning of Treece's statement, Barnes searched for and located his two punchboards. On July 26, 1973, Barnes telephoned Treece, announced that he had two crooked punchboards, and asked Treece if his earlier statement had been made seriously. Treece assured Barnes that the statement had been made seriously, advised Barnes that the statement was firm, and further informed Barnes that the $100,000 was safely being held in escrow. Treece also specifically directed Barnes to bring the punchboard to the Seattle office of Vend-A-Win for inspection.

On July 28, 1973, Barnes traveled to Seattle, met Treece and Vend-A-Win's secretary-treasurer in Vend-A-Win's offices, produced one punchboard, and received a receipt for presentation of the board written on Vend-A-Win stationery, signed by Treece and witnessed by Vend-A-Win's secretary-treasurer. Barnes was informed that the punchboard would be taken to Chicago for inspection. The parties next met on August 3, 1973, before the Washington State Gambling Commission. Barnes produced his second punchboard during the meeting before the commission.

Both Treece and Vend-A-Win refused to pay Barnes $100,000. Barnes then initiated this breach of contract action against both defendants. The trial court found that the two punchboards were rigged and dishonest, that Treece's statements before the gambling commission and reiterated to Barnes personally on the telephone constituted a valid offer for a unilateral contract, and that Barnes' production of two dishonest punchboards constituted an acceptance of the offer. The trial court also found that Vend-A-Win had not manifested any apparent authority in Treece to make the offer, had not impliedly ratified the contract, and therefore was not liable on the contract.

8.4 Issue

Issue is the question presented before the court that must be resolved by it. Such a question should identify the legally relevant facts of the case and the apparently applicable rules of law. In order to find the applicable rules of law, you should first identify the cause of action asserted by plaintiff against defendant in the trial court and the elements necessary to establish that cause of action. These elements constitute the rule of law that governs the dispute, and are often mentioned in the court's opinion. A case can contain more than one issue because there may have been several disagreements about the law that the appellate court was asked to resolve. When this is the case, you should describe each issue according to above requirement and analyze each separately.

The issue in a case can be express or implied. Many times the court will tell you the issue directly. For example: "The first issue is whether the statement of Treece was the manifestation of an offer which could be accepted by the offeree and bind the offeror to perform his promise." The court may also indicate the issue by stating "the question presented in this case is . . ." It seems easy to spot the issue if the court explicitly states the issue in this way. However, sometimes a court just states an incomplete issue; for example, the "issue" may only contain purely legal rules, or does not spell out the elements of the rule. Sometimes the court may tell you the issue is one thing but your close reading of the case demonstrates that it is something else. Other times the court will not expressly tell you the issue at all. When this happens, you must read the case carefully and identify the issue based on the holding and the reasons that support the holding. The holding helps identify the issue because the holding is the answer to the issue. Once you have identified the holding in a case, you should have little trouble spotting the issue.

After you have located the issue, you need to formulate the issue for your case brief. Usually an issue in a case brief is formed as a question that combines the rule of law with the material facts of the case. Suppose the cause of action of a case is breach of contract. If you formulate the issue as "Was there a binding contract?" it fails to incorporate any legally relevant facts. Since all cases determine liability about particular facts, there is no issue and no liability without such facts. Hence, a formulation of an issue must include at least some of the legally relevant facts. If you formulate the issue as "Did A tell B about the advertisement?" it fails to raise a question about the legal significance of these facts. This sentence is purely factual. Cases, however, not only inquire about facts. They also inquire about their legal significance. Hence, a formulation of an issue must also raise a question about liability.

The correct way to formulate an issue is to incorporate the legally relevant facts and the elements of the applicable rules of law in a one-sentence question. An example of a statement of the issue in controversy in a one sentence question is: "Did A's statement, which was made to the public that he promised to pay anyone who presented to him a qualified product a specified amount of money, constitute an offer which created power in the offeree to accept it and, upon its acceptance, form a binding contract?" This example illustrates the three components of an issue. "A promised to pay anyone who presented to him a qualified product a specified amount of money" is the legally relevant fact; "an offer" is the particular element of contract; and "a binding contract" refers to the applicable rule.

Please locate and formulate the issue in the following case:

Barnes v. Treece
549 P. 2d 1152 (Wash. App. Ct. 1976)

The last question presented is whether Vend-A-Win is also liable on the contract either because of the claim that the contract was made within an apparent authority given Treece or because of an implied ratification of the contract by Vend-A-Win.

Treece, as a corporate vice-president, was an agent of Vend-A-Win and <u>agency</u> principles apply to his acts. Vend-A-Win, therefore, may be bound to a contract made by Treece if the contract was within the scope of his apparent authority as a corporate vice-president. Vice-presidents do not have authority to bind their corporations by virtue of their office. Apparent authority to bind a corporation in contract exists only if the corporation, as the principal, knowingly permits the agent to act or <u>holds</u>

agency 代理

hold ... out 声称

the agent <u>out</u> as having authority. In order for a corporation to be bound by the apparent authority of its officers, it must have acted or conducted itself in a manner that manifested to third persons that the agent had authority. To constitute a manifestation of an agent's apparent authority by the principal, the circumstances must be such that a prudent person would have believed that the agent possessed the authority to do the particular act in question. The manifestation must be sufficient to mislead a reasonable person, to deter further inquiry, and to cause reliance on the manifestation of apparent authority.

8.5 Holding

Holding is the court's direct response to the issue in controversy presented before the court. It is the part of the opinion that is binding. As discussed earlier, the holding of a case is also called the "*ratio decidendi*." The doctrine of *stare decisis* requires the *ratio decidendi* of a precedent be followed by the courts in deciding similar cases. Therefore, holding is the most important part of an opinion and it is crucial to locate the holding of a case in order to apply the precedent rule.

The court may explicitly or impliedly state the holding in the opinion. Sometimes the court will expressly and clearly announce its holding. However, as in issue-spotting, sometimes the holding is implicit rather than explicit; or, the explicit holding by the court is not precise or correct. Sometimes the court may use the term "holding" saying that the holding is something; however, this may not be the true holding and after careful examination, you may find the actual holding is something else. Also the holding <u>articulated</u> by the courts may be too broad or narrow. In these situations, you have to locate the holding through your own examining of the opinion. For example, the court may make a number of legal statements which seem to be the holding of the case. However, if they do not relate to the issue actually presented before it, they are but *dicta* instead of holding.

articulate 言语表达

Locating the holding of a case is also important for finding the issue of the case and the reasons behind the court's decision. If there is more than one issue raised in the case, there should be more than one holding.

After you identify the holding of an opinion, you

must formulate it in your own language. Since the holding of a case is the rule of law that comes from that decision, it must include the court's decision as to the question that was actually before the court. Therefore, an accurate holding should include both the important facts of that litigated case and the reasons that the court gave for deciding the issue as it did based on those facts. Thus, a holding is different from a general principle of law. A principle of law tells you the legal rule while a holding tells you both the facts and the rule applicable specifically to these facts. If a court in a contract case says "a contract requires an offer and an acceptance," that is a pure legal principle that has come from many years of contract litigation, but it is not necessarily a statement of the holding of the case because it does not specifically mention the facts of the case.

The way of formulating holdings is similar to that of formulating issues. Since the holding provides an answer to the question, the structure of a holding is much similar to that of an issue. A holding is usually one declarative sentence which identifies the legally relevant facts, the cause of action, and the particular elements of the rules of law that the court applied to the facts in order to resolve the dispute. "The defendant is liable for breach of contract" is not a correct statement of a holding because it does not contain any facts of the case. A holding is not a pure legal conclusion either. "A did tell the public that he would pay to anyone who presented the qualified product" is not a correct statement of a holding because it is purely factual. A correct statement of a holding should be: "A's statement made before the public in which he promised to pay a certain amount of money to anyone who presented the qualified product constituted an offer, which created power in the offeree to accept it and, upon its acceptance, a binding contract was formed." Or: "When B produced a fraudulent punchboard as required by the advertisement, he accepted the offer and a contract had been formed."

The formulation of a holding could be <u>tailored</u> according to the purpose of your writing. When you are considering the relationship between a precedent case and your problem case, you might formulate a court's holding differently from the way you would if you were simply briefing the case. How you formulate the holding depends on how many facts you include as essential and how you characterize those facts. If you describe the facts exactly

tailor 专门制作,定做

as they were in the case, then the holding you state will be very narrow. If you think the precedent is unfavorable to your client's case and you would rather not to apply that precedent, you may state the holding of the precedent case in a narrow way thus limiting it to its facts. If, however, you would like to apply the holding of a precedent, you would omit some particular facts, generalize the facts, and describe them more broadly. In doing so, the holding will apply to your case whose facts may not be exactly the same as the facts of the precedent case; however, the facts come within the broader description. To this end, the way you formulate the holding may depend on the result you want to reach in applying that case, the purpose of the document you are writing, and its intended readers. Of course, there are limits to formulating the holding broadly or narrowly. If you manipulate the facts to violate the sense of the case, you will be engaging in unethical behavior and faulty analysis.

Please read another part of the case *Barnes v. Treece* and try to formulate the holding of it.

Barnes *v.* Treece
549 P. 2d 1152 (Wash. App. Ct. 1976)

jest 笑话,俏皮话

When expressions are intended as a joke and are understood or would be understood by a reasonable person as being so intended, they cannot be construed as an offer and accepted to form a contract. However, if the jest is not apparent and a reasonable hearer would believe that an offer was being made, then the speaker risks the formation of a contract which was not intended. It is the objective manifestations of the offeror that count and not secret, unexpressed intentions. 1 A. Corbin, *Corbin on Contracts* § 34 (1963); 1 S. Williston, *A Treatise on the Law of Contracts* § 21, at 43 (3d ed. 1957). As stated in *Wesco Realty, Inc. v. Drewry*, 9 Wn. App. 734, 735, 515 P. 2d 513 (1973):

If a party's words or acts, judged by a reasonable standard, manifest an intention to agree in regard to the matter in question, that agreement is established, and it is immaterial what may be the real but unexpressed state of the party's mind on the subject.

The trial court found that there was an objective manifestation of mutual assent to form a contract. This was a matter to be evaluated by the trier of fact. *In re Estate of Richardson*, 11 Wn. App. 758, 525 P. 2d 816 (1974). The record includes substantial evidence of the required mutual assent to support the finding of the trial court. Although the original statement of Treece drew laughter from the audience, the subsequent statements, conduct, and the circumstances show an intent to lead any hearer to believe the statements were made seriously. There was testimony, though contradicted, that Treece specifically restated the offer over the telephone in response to an inquiry concerning whether the offer was serious. Treece, when given the opportunity to state that an offer was not intended, not only reaffirmed the offer but also asserted that $100,000 had been placed in escrow and directed Barnes to bring the punchboard to Seattle for inspection. The parties met, Barnes was given a receipt for the board, and he was told that the board would be taken to Chicago for inspection. In present day society it is known that gambling generates a great deal of income and that large sums are spent on its advertising and promotion. In that prevailing atmosphere, it was a credible statement that $100,000 would be paid to promote punchboards. The statements of the defendant and the surrounding circumstances reflect an objective manifestation of a contractual intent by Treece and support the finding of the trial court.

The trial court properly categorized Treece's promise of $100,000 as a valid offer for a unilateral contract. The offer made promised that a contract would result upon performance of the act requested. Performance of the act with the intent to accept the offer constituted acceptance. The trial judge entered a specific finding that Barnes performed the requested act of acceptance when he produced a rigged and fraudulent punchboard. We concur with the trial court's holding that a binding unilateral contract was formed between Barnes and Treece and uphold the conclusions of the trial court in that regard.

Treece also contends that an oral contract would be unenforceable pursuant to two statute of frauds provisions of the Uniform Commercial Code, RCW 62A.1-206 and RCW 62A.2-201. However, both provisions apply only to contracts for the sale of personal property or goods. Since the contract involved is not a sales transaction, the

mutual assent 双方意思表示一致,合意

uphold 维持

statute of frauds 防欺诈法,即要求某些合同必须为书面形式的法律规定

U.C.C. statute of frauds provisionsare inapplicable.

In addition, Treece asserts that the contract is unenforceable due to an unconscionable discrepancy in consideration. However, it is only when consideration is so inadequate as to be constructively fraudulent that a court should inquire into the comparative value of an act performed in response to a promise. *Browning v. Johnson*, 70 Wn.2d 145, 422 P.2d 314 (1967); *Rogich v. Dressel*, 45 Wn.2d 829, 278 P.2d 367 (1954). The record does not suggest constructive fraud, and therefore the adequacy of the consideration cannot be weighed.

8.6 Reasons and Policies

As the doctrine of *stare decisis* requires, a court's reasoning in a precedent case must apply equally well to the facts in your problem case when the facts are similar. Thus, the reasoning of an opinion is often scrutinized by judges and lawyers who may apply it in future cases. When studying a case, you should determine the exact reasoning process the court employed and the policies the court considered to arrive at its holding on an issue. Only through understanding the reasons behind a court's decision can you understand what the decision actually means or how broadly or narrowly the case might be interpreted. While courts need not explain and justify their holdings, there is a powerful tradition which usually leads to such explanation and justification by appellate courts. Now after we have discussed how to locate and formulate the procedural history, facts, issue, and holding of an opinion, it is time to dissect the reasoning and policy, which is the court's explanation and justification for its holding and resolution of the issue in controversy.

Reasons are explanations of a court regarding how it arrives at its holding. Through the reasoning part, a court tries to demonstrate that its decision is justified by precedent, principle, or policy. Policies are the underlying purposes of the legal rules which will determine the future direction of the law. They are similar to but broader than reasons. The reasons and policies are often confusingly similar so that it is difficult to tell the two from each other. Actually, the reasons indicate how the court arrived at its holding while policies tell you why this holding is socially desirable. An opinion can make sense without any policy justifications, but it cannot make sense without reasons explaining how the court arrived at its conclusion. In order to identify the reasons and policies supporting the holding of the case, you should start from identifying the holding first. Once you have located the holding, it is easier for you to look for the explanations and social justifications supporting that holding. When you brief a judicial decision, you need to identify the types of reasoning, the various arguments, and techniques the court used in reaching the opinion.

8.7 Judgment

Judgment is the result or disposition of the case made by a court which announces who won what and who lost what. Sometimes judgment is mentioned in the beginning of an opinion, or in the middle of it; however, it is almost always specified at the end of an opinion and is therefore easy to identify. Judgments should be distinguished from holdings. While holdings answer the questions presented before the court, judgments determine the result of the case by taking the form of an incomplete sentence, *e.g.*, "judgment for the plaintiff affirmed" or simply "reversed."

8.8 Summary

A case brief is a short summary of a case that may be useful when you are resolving a new problem. It is brief and concise, giving you a ready reference so that you do not have to reread a long opinion to refresh what it was about. Once you have located the procedural history, facts, issue, holding, reasons and polices, and judgment of the case, your work is almost done. However, before you complete your case brief, you should check these elements against one another to make sure they are <u>conciliated</u> with each other. There is an interplay among them that should be obvious by now. The court's holding will be a combination of the relevant rule of law and the legally relevant facts. The issue is the holding stated in the form of a question which includes all of the elements contained in a holding. The answer to the issue will be the holding. Policies and reasons form a basis for the holding which explains and justifies how and why the court reached the decision of the case. Such interaction makes

conciliate 抚慰,安抚

the case an interlocking whole and underscores why you cannot understand any one element without reference to the others.

8.9 Case Brief Exercises

Read the following cases and brief them according to the elements discussed above.

8.9.1 Exercise 1: Katko v. Briney

Supreme Court of Iowa
Katko v. Briney
183 N.W. 2d 657
Feb. 9, 1971

Moore, Chief Justice

The primary issue presented here is whether an owner may protect personal property in an unoccupied boarded-up farm house against trespassers and thieves by a spring gun capable of inflicting death or serious injury.

We are not here concerned with a man's right to protect his home and members of his family. Defendants' home was several miles from the scene of the incident to which we refer *infra*.

Plaintiff's action is for damages resulting from serious injury caused by a shot from a 20-gauge spring shotgun set by defendants in a bedroom of an old farm house which had been uninhabited for several years. Plaintiff and his companion, Marvin McDonough, had broken and entered the house to find and steal old bottles and dated fruit jars which they considered antiques.

At defendants' request plaintiff's action was tried to a jury consisting of residents of the community where defendants' property was located. The jury returned a verdict for plaintiff and against defendants for $20,000 actual and $10,000 punitive damages.

After careful consideration of defendants' motions for judgment notwithstanding the verdict and for new trial, the experienced and capable trial judge overruled them and entered judgment on the verdict. Thus we have this appeal by defendants.

I. In this action our review of the record as made by the parties in the lower court is for the correction of errors at law. We do not review actions at law *de novo*. Rule

334, Rules of Civil Procedure. Findings of fact by the jury are binding upon this court if supported by substantial evidence. Rule 344(f), par. 1, R.C.P.

II. Most of the facts are not disputed. In 1957 defendant Bertha L. Briney <u>inherited</u> her parents' farm land in Mahaska and Monroe Counties. Included was an 80-acre tract in southwest Mahaska County where her grandparents and parents had lived. No one occupied the house thereafter. Her husband, Edward, attempted to care for the land. He kept no farm machinery thereon. The outbuildings became <u>dilapidated</u>.

For about 10 years, 1957 to 1967, there occurred a series of trespassing and housebreaking events with loss of some household items, the breaking of windows and "messing up of the property in general." The latest occurred June 8, 1967, prior to the event on July 16, 1967 herein involved.

Defendants through the years boarded up the windows and doors in an attempt to stop the <u>intrusions</u>. They had posted "no trespass" signs on the land several years before 1967. The nearest one was 35 feet from the house. On June 11, 1967 defendants set "a shotgun trap" in the north bedroom. After Mr. Briney cleaned and oiled his 20-gauge shotgun, the power of which he was well aware, defendants took it to the old house where they secured it to an iron bed with the <u>barrel</u> pointed at the bedroom door. It was <u>rigged with wire</u> from the doorknob to the gun's trigger so it would fire when the door was opened. Briney first pointed the gun so an intruder would be hit in the stomach but at Mrs. Briney's suggestion it was lowered to hit the legs. He admitted he did so "because I was mad and tired of being <u>tormented</u>" but "he did not intend to injure anyone." He gave to explanation of why he used a loaded shell and set it to hit a person already in the house. <u>Tin</u> was nailed over the bedroom window. The spring gun could not be seen from the outside. No warning of its presence was posted.

Plaintiff lived with his wife and worked regularly as a gasoline station attendant in Eddyville, seven miles from the old house. He had observed it for several years while hunting in the area and considered it as being abandoned. He knew it had long been uninhabited. In 1967 the area around the house was covered with high weeds. Prior to July 16, 1967 plaintiff and McDonough had been to the premises and found several old bottles and fruit jars which

inherit 继承

dilapidated 破旧的

intrusion 闯入

barrel 桶
rigged with wire 用铁丝扎起来

torment 折磨

tin 锡

they took and added to their collection of antiques. On the latter date about 9:30 p.m. they made a second trip to the Briney property. They entered the old house by removing a board from a porch window which was without glass. While McDonough was looking around the kitchen area plaintiff went to another part of the house. As he started to open the north bedroom door the shotgun went off striking him in the right leg above the ankle bone. Much of his leg, including part of the tibia, was blown away. Only by McDonough's assistance was plaintiff able to get out of the house and after crawling some distance was put in his vehicle and rushed to a doctor and then to a hospital. He remained in the hospital 40 days.

Plaintiff's doctor testified he seriously considered amputation but eventually the healing process was successful. Some weeks after his release from the hospital plaintiff returned to work on crutches. He was required to keep the injured leg in a cast for approximately a year and wear a special brace for another year. He continued to suffer pain during this period.

There was undenied medical testimony plaintiff had a permanent deformity, a loss of tissue, and a shortening of the leg.

The record discloses plaintiff to trial time had incurred $710 medical expense, $2056.85 for hospital service, $61.80 for orthopedic service and $750 as loss of earnings. In addition thereto the trial court submitted to the jury the question of damages for pain and suffering and for future disability.

III. Plaintiff testified he knew he had no right to break and enter the house with intent to steal bottles and fruit jars therefrom. He further testified he had entered a plea of guilty to larceny in the nighttime of property of less than $20 value from a private building. He stated he had been fined $50 and costs and paroled during good behavior from a 60-day jail sentence. Other than minor traffic charges this was plaintiff's first brush with the law. On this civil case appeal it is not our prerogative to review the disposition made of the criminal charge against him.

IV. The main thrust of defendants' defense in the trial court and on this appeal is that "the law permits use of a spring gun in a dwelling or warehouse for the purpose of preventing the unlawful entry of a burglar or thief." They repeated this contention in their exceptions to the trial court's instructions 2, 5 and 6. They took no exception to the trial court's statement of the issues or to other instructions.

In the statement of issues the trial court stated plaintiff and his companion committed a <u>felony</u> when they broke and entered defendants' house. In instruction 2 the court referred to the early case history of the use of spring guns and stated under the law their use was prohibited except to prevent the commission of felonies of violence and where human life is in danger. The instruction included a statement breaking and entering is not a felony of violence.

felony 重罪

Instruction 5 stated: "You are hereby instructed that one may use reasonable force in the protection of his property, but such right is subject to the <u>qualification</u> that one may not use such means of force as will take human life or inflict great bodily injury. Such is the rule even though the injured party is a trespasser and is in violation of the law himself."

qualification 限制

Instruction 6 stated: "An owner of premises is prohibited from <u>willfully</u> or intentionally injuring a trespasser by means of force that either takes life or inflicts great bodily injury; and therefore a person owning a premise is prohibited from setting out 'spring guns' and like dangerous devices which will likely take life or inflict great bodily injury, for the purpose of harming trespassers. The fact that the trespasser may be acting in violation of the law does not change the rule. The only time when such conduct of setting a 'spring gun' or a like dangerous device is justified would be when the trespasser was committing a felony of violence or a felony punishable by death, or where the trespasser was <u>endangering</u> human life by his act."

willfully 明知地

endanger 危及

Instruction 7, to which defendants made no objection or exception, stated: "To entitle the plaintiff to recover for <u>compensatory damages</u>, the <u>burden of proof</u> is upon him to establish by <u>a preponderance of the evidence</u> each and all of the following propositions:

compensatory damages 补偿性损害赔偿金
burden of proof 举证责任
a preponderance of the evidence 大量证据

1. That defendants erected a shotgun trap in a vacant house on land owned by defendant, Bertha L. Briney, on or about June 11, 1967, which fact was known only by them, to protect household goods from trespassers and thieves.

2. That the force used by defendants was in excess of that force reasonably necessary and which persons are entitled to use in the protection of their property.

3. That plaintiff was injured and damaged and the amount thereof.

4. That plaintiff's injuries and damages resulted directly from the discharge of the shotgun trap which was set and used by defendants."

The overwhelming weight of authority, both textbook and case law, supports the trial court's statement of the applicable principles of law.

Prosser on Torts, Third Edition, pages 116-118, states:

... the law has always placed a higher value upon human safety than upon mere rights in property, it is the accepted rule that there is no privilege to use any force calculated to cause death or serious bodily injury to repel the threat to land or chattels, unless there is also such a threat to the defendant's personal safety as to justify a self-defense. * * * spring guns and other mankilling devices are not justifiable against a mere trespasser, or even a petty thief. They are privileged only against those upon whom the landowner, if he were present in person would be free to inflict injury of the same kind.

Restatement of Torts, section 85, page 180, states:

The value of human life and limb, not only to the individual concerned but also to society, so outweighs the interest of a possessor of land in excluding from it those whom he is not willing to admit thereto that a possessor of land has, as is stated in s 79, no privilege to use force intended or likely to cause death or serious harm against another whom the possessor sees about to enter his premises or meddle with his chattel, unless the intrusion threatens death or serious bodily harm to the occupiers or users of the premises ... A possessor of land cannot do indirectly and by a mechanical device that which, were he present, he could not do immediately and in person. Therefore, he cannot gain a privilege to install, for the purpose of protecting his land from intrusions harmless to the lives and limbs of the occupiers or users of it, a mechanical device whose only purpose is to inflict death or serious harm upon such as may intrude, by giving notice of his intention to inflict, by mechanical means and indirectly, harm which he could not, even after request, inflict directly were he present.

In Volume 2, Harper and James, *The Law of Torts*, section 27.3, pages 1440, 1441, this is found:

> The possessor of land may not arrange his premises intentionally so as to cause death or serious bodily harm to a trespasser. The possessor may of course take some steps to repel a trespass. If he is present he may use force to do so, but only that amount which is reasonably necessary to effect the repulse. Moreover if the trespass threatens harm to property only — even a theft of property — the possessor would not be privileged to use deadly force, he may not arrange his premises so that such force will be inflicted by mechanical means. If he does, he will be liable even to a thief who is injured by such device.

repulse 击败

Similar statements are found in 38 *Am. Jur.*, *Negligence*, section 114, pages 776, 777, and 65 *C.J.S. Negligence* s 62(23), pages 678, 679; Anno. 44 A.L.R.2d 383, entitled "*Trap to protect property.*"

In *Hooker v. Miller*, 37 Iowa 613, we held defendant vineyard owner liable for damages resulting from a spring gun shot although plaintiff was a trespasser and there to steal grapes. At pages 614, 615, this statement is made: "This court has held that a mere trespass against property other than a dwelling is not a sufficient justification to authorize the use of a deadly weapon by the owner in its defense; and that if death results in such a case it will be murder, though the killing be actually necessary to prevent the trespass. The *State v. Vance*, 17 Iowa 138." At page 617 this court said: "[T]respassers and other inconsiderable violators of the law are not to be visited by barbarous punishments or prevented by inhuman inflictions of bodily injuries."

barbarous 残暴的
inhuman 野蛮的

The facts in *Allison v. Fiscus*, 156 Ohio 120, 110 N.E.2d 237, 44 A.L.R.2d 369, decided in 1951, are very similar to the case at bar. There plaintiff's right to damages was recognized for injuries received when he feloniously broke a door latch and started to enter defendant's warehouse with intent to steal. As he entered

dynamite 炸药

exemplary damages 惩罚性赔偿金

pitfall 陷阱
mantrap（私人领地里的）捕人陷阱
contrivance 装置

homicide 杀人；谋杀

a trap of two sticks of dynamite buried under the doorway by defendant owner was set off and plaintiff seriously injured. The court held the question whether a particular trap was justified as a use of reasonable and necessary force against a trespasser engaged in the commission of a felony should have been submitted to the jury. The Ohio Supreme Court recognized plaintiff's right to recover punitive or exemplary damages in addition to compensatory damages.

In *Starkey v. Dameron*, 96 Colo. 459, 45 P. 2d 172, plaintiff was allowed to recover compensatory and punitive damages for injuries received from a spring gun which defendant filling station operator had concealed in an automatic gasoline pump as protection against thieves.

In *Wilder v. Gardner*, 39 Ga. App. 608, 147 S. E. 911, judgment for plaintiff for injuries received from a spring gun which defendant had set, the court said: "A person in control of premises may be responsible even to a trespasser for injuries caused by pitfalls, mantraps, or other like contrivances so dangerous in character as to imply a disregard of consequences or a willingness to inflict injury."

In *Phelps v. Hamlett*, Tex. Civ. App., 207 S. W. 425, defendant rigged a bomb inside his outdoor theater so that if anyone came through the door the bomb would explode. The court reversed plaintiff's recovery because of an incorrect instruction but at page 426 said: "While the law authorizes an owner to protect his property by such reasonable means as he may find to be necessary, yet considerations of humanity preclude him from setting out, even on his own property, traps and devices dangerous to the life and limb of those whose appearance and presence may be reasonably anticipated, even though they may be trespassers."

In *United Zinc & Chemical Co. v. Britt*, 258 U. S. 268, 275, 42 S. Ct. 299, the court states: "The liability for spring guns and mantraps arises from the fact that the defendant has ... expected the trespasser and prepared an injury that is no more justified than if he had held the gun and fired it."

In addition to civil liability many jurisdictions hold a land owner criminally liable for serious injuries or homicide caused by spring guns or other set devices. See *State v. Childers*, 133 Ohio 508, 14 N. E. 2d 767 (melon thief shot by spring gun); *Pierce v. Commonwealth*, 135

Va. 635, 115 S. E. 686 (policeman killed by spring gun when he opened unlocked front door of defendant's shoe repair shop); *State v. Marfaudille*, 48 Wash. 117, 92 P. 939 (murder conviction for death from spring gun set in a trunk); *State v. Beckham*, 306 Mo. 566, 267 S. W. 817 (boy killed by spring gun attached to window of defendant's chili stand); *State v. Green*, 118 S. C. 279, 110 S. E. 145, 19 A. L. R. 1431 (intruder shot by spring gun when he broke and entered vacant house. Manslaughter conviction of owner-affirmed); *State v. Barr*, 11 Wash. 481, 39 P. 1080 (murder conviction affirmed for death of an intruder into a boarded up cabin in which owner had set a spring gun).

In Wisconsin, Oregon and England the use of spring guns and similar devices is specifically made unlawful by statute. 44 A. L. R., section 3, pages 386, 388.

The legal principles stated by the trial court in instructions 2, 5 and 6 are well established and supported by the authorities cited and quoted *supra*. There is no merit in defendants' objections and exceptions thereto. Defendants' various motions based on the same reasons stated in exceptions to instructions were properly overruled.

V. Plaintiff's claim and the jury's allowance of punitive damages, under the trial court's instructions relating thereto, were not at any time or in any manner challenged by defendants in the trial court as not allowable. We therefore are not presented with the problem of whether the $10,000 award should be allowed to stand.

We express no opinion as to whether punitive damages are allowable in this type of case. If defendants' attorneys wanted that issue decided it was their duty to raise it in the trial court.

The rule is well established that we will not consider a contention not raised in the trial court. In other words we are a court of review and will not consider a contention raised for the first time in this court. *Ke-Wash Company v. Stauffer Chemical Company*, Iowa, 177 N. W. 2d 5, 9; *In re Adoption of Moriarty*, 260 Iowa 1279, 1288, 152 N. W. 2d 218, 223.

court of review 复审法院

In our most recent reference to the rule we say in *Cole v. City of Osceola*, Iowa, 179 N. W. 2d 524, 527: "Of course, questions not presented to and not passed upon by the trial court cannot be raised or reviewed on appeal."

Under our law punitive damages are not allowed as a matter of right. *Sebastian v. Wood*, 246 Iowa 94, 100, 101, 66 N.W.2d 841, 844. When malice is shown or when a defendant acted with wanton and reckless disregard of the rights of others, punitive damages may be allowed as punishment to the defendant and as a deterrent to others. Although not meant to compensate a plaintiff, the result is to increase his recovery. He is the fortuitous beneficiary of such an award simply because there is no one else to receive it.

The jury's findings of fact including a finding defendants acted with malice and with wanton and reckless disregard, as required for an allowance of punitive or exemplary damages, are supported by substantial evidence. We are bound thereby.

This opinion is not to be taken or construed as authority that the allowance of punitive damages is or is not proper under circumstances such as exist here. We hold only that question of law not having been properly raised cannot in this case be resolved.

Study and careful consideration of defendants' contentions on appeal reveal no reversible error.

Affirmed.

All Justices concur except Larson, J., who dissents.

8.9.2 Exercise 2: Palsgraf v. Long Island Railroad Co.

Brief another case for practice. Note that this is a case with a dissenting opinion. Brief both the majority opinion and the dissenting opinion. Pay attention to the reasons and policies contained in both.

Court of Appeals of New York
Palsgraf v. The Long Island Railroad Co.
16 N.E. 99
May 29, 1928

Cardozo, Ch. J.

Plaintiff was standing on a platform of defendant's railroad after buying a ticket to go to Rockaway Beach. A train stopped at the station, bound for another place. Two men ran forward to catch it. One of the men reached the platform of the car without mishap, though the train was already moving. The other man, carrying a package, jumped aboard the car, but seemed unsteady as if about to fall. A guard on the car, who had held the door open, reached forward to help him in, and another guard on the platform pushed him from behind. In this act, the package was dislodged, and fell upon the rails. It was a package of small size, about fifteen inches long, and was covered by a newspaper. In fact it contained fireworks, but there was nothing in its appearance to give notice of its contents. The fireworks when they fell exploded. The shock of the explosion threw down some scales at the other end of the platform, many feet away. The scales struck the plaintiff, causing injuries for which she sues.

  The conduct of the defendant's guard, if a wrong in its relation to the holder of the package, was not a wrong in its relation to the plaintiff, standing far away. Relatively to her it was not negligence at all. Nothing in the situation gave notice that the falling package had in it the potency of peril to persons thus removed. Negligence is not actionable unless it involves the invasion of a legally protected interest, the violation of a right. "Proof of negligence in the air, so to speak, will not do" (Pollock, *Torts* [11th ed.], p. 455; *Martin v. Herzog*, 228 N.Y. 164, 170; cf. Salmond, *Torts* [6th ed.], p. 24). "Negligence is the absence of care, according to the circumstances" (Willes, J., in *Vaughan v. Taff Vale Ry. Co.*, 5 H. & N. 679, 688; 1 Beven, *Negligence* [4th ed.], 7; *Paul v. Consol. Fireworks Co.*, 212 N.Y. 117; *Adams v. Bullock*, 227 N.Y. 208, 211). The plaintiff as she stood upon the platform of the station might claim to be protected against intentional invasion of her bodily security. Such invasion is not charged. She might claim to be protected against unintentional invasion by conduct involving in the thought of reasonable men an unreasonable hazard that such invasion would ensue. These, from the point of view of the law, were the bounds of her immunity, with perhaps some rare exceptions, survivals for the most part of ancient forms of liability, where conduct is held to be at the peril of the actor (*Sullivan v. Dunham*, 161 N.Y. 290). If no hazard was apparent to the eye of ordinary vigilance, an act innocent and harmless, at least to outward seeming, with reference to her, did not take to itself the quality of a tort because it happened to be a wrong, though apparently not one involving the risk of bodily insecurity, with reference to someone else. "In every instance, before negligence can be predicated of a given act, back of the act must be

dislodge 移走

scale 瓦片

sue 控告

potency 力量，潜力

ensue 接踵发生

immunity 豁免

actor 行为人
vigilance 警觉

sought and found a duty to the individual complaining, the observance of which would have averted or avoided the injury" (McSherry, C. J., in *W. Va. Central R. Co. v. State*, 96 Md. 652, 666; cf. *Norfolk & Western Ry. Co. v. Wood*, 99 Va. 156, 158, 159; *Hughes v. Boston & Maine R. R. Co.*, 71 N. H. 279, 284; *U. S. Express Co. v. Everest*, 72 Kan. 517; *Emry v. Roanoke Nav. Co.*, 111 N. C. 94, 95; *Vaughan v. Transit Dev. Co.*, 222 N. Y. 79; *Losee v. Clute*, 51 N. Y. 494; *DiCaprio v. N. Y. C. R. R. Co.*, 231 N. Y. 94; 1 *Shearman & Redfield on Negligence*, § 8, and cases cited; *Cooley on Torts* [3d ed.], p. 1411; *Jaggard on Torts*, vol. 2, p. 826; Wharton, *Negligence*, § 24; Bohlen, *Studies in the Law of Torts*, p. 601). "The ideas of negligence and duty are strictly correlative" (Bowen, L. J., in *Thomas v. Quartermaine*, 18 Q. B. D. 685, 694). The plaintiff sues in her own right for a wrong personal to her, and not as the vicarious beneficiary of a breach of duty to another.

A different conclusion will involve us, and swiftly too, in a maze of contradictions. A guard stumbles over a package which has been left upon a platform. It seems to be a bundle of newspapers. It turns out to be a can of dynamite. To the eye of ordinary vigilance, the bundle is abandoned waste, which may be kicked or trod on with impunity. Is a passenger at the other end of the platform protected by the law against the unsuspected hazard concealed beneath the waste? If not, is the result to be any different, so far as the distant passenger is concerned, when the guard stumbles over a valise which a truckman or a porter has left upon the walk? The passenger far away, if the victim of a wrong at all, has a cause of action, not derivative, but original and primary. His claim to be protected against invasion of his bodily security is neither greater nor less because the act resulting in the invasion is a wrong to another far removed. In this case, the rights that are said to have been violated, the interests said to have been invaded, are not even of the same order. The man was not injured in his person nor even put in danger. The purpose of the act, as well as its effect, was to make his person safe. If there was a wrong to him at all, which may very well be doubted, it was a wrong to a property interest only, the safety of his package. Out of this wrong to property, which threatened injury to nothing else, there has passed, we are told, to the plaintiff by

avert 防止

vicarious 替代的

trod 踩

valise 旅行袋

victim 受害者
derivative 衍生的

derivation or succession a right of action for the invasion of an interest of another order, the right to bodily security. The <u>diversity</u> of interests emphasizes the <u>futility</u> of the effort to build the plaintiff's right upon the basis of a wrong to someone else. The gain is one of emphasis, for a like result would follow if the interests were the same. Even then, the <u>orbit</u> of the danger as disclosed to the eye of <u>reasonable vigilance</u> would be the orbit of the duty. One who <u>jostles</u> one's neighbor in a crowd does not invade the rights of others standing at the outer <u>fringe</u> when the <u>unintended</u> contact casts a bomb upon the ground. The wrongdoer as to them is the man who carries the bomb, not the one who explodes it without suspicion of the danger. Life will have to be made over, and human nature transformed, before <u>prevision</u> so <u>extravagant</u> can be accepted as the norm of conduct, the customary standard to which behavior must conform.

The argument for the plaintiff is built upon the shifting meanings of such words as "wrong" and "wrongful," and shares their instability. What the plaintiff must show is "a wrong" to herself, *i. e.*, a violation of her own right, and not merely a wrong to someone else, nor conduct "wrongful" because unsocial, but not "a wrong" to anyone. We are told that one who drives at reckless speed through a crowded city street is guilty of a <u>negligent</u> act and, therefore, of a wrongful one irrespective of the consequences. Negligent the act is, and wrongful in the sense that it is unsocial, but wrongful and unsocial in relation to other travelers, only because the eye of vigilance perceives the risk of damage. If the same act were to be committed on a speedway or a race course, it would lose its wrongful quality. The risk reasonably to be perceived defines the duty to be obeyed, and risk imports relation; it is risk to another or to others within the range of apprehension (Seavey, *Negligence, Subjective or Objective*, 41 H. L. Rv. 6; *Boronkay v. Robinson & Carpenter*, 247 N. Y. 365). This does not mean, of course, that one who launches a destructive force is always relieved of liability if the force, though known to be destructive, pursues an unexpected path. "It was not necessary that the defendant should have had notice of the particular method in which an accident would occur, if the possibility of an accident was clear to the ordinarily prudent eye" (*Munsey v. Webb*, 231 U. S. 150, 156; *Condran v. Park & Tilford*, 213 N. Y. 341,

diversity 多样性
futility 无益

orbit (影响所及的)范围
reasonable vigilance 合理警惕
jostle 推挤
fringe 边缘
unintended 非故意的

prevision 预知
extravagant 过度的

negligent 疏忽大意的

345; *Robert v. U.S.E.F. Corp.*, 240 N.Y. 474, 477). Some acts, such as shooting, are so imminently dangerous to anyone who may come within reach of the missile, however unexpectedly, as to impose a duty of prevision not far from that of an insurer. Even today, and much oftener in earlier stages of the law, one acts sometimes at one's peril(Jeremiah Smith, *Tort and Absolute Liability*, 30 H. L. Rv. 328; Street, *Foundations of Legal Liability*, vol. 1, pp. 77, 78). Under this head, it may be, fall certain cases of what is known as transferred intent, an act willfully dangerous to A resulting by misadventure in injury to B (*Talmage v. Smith*, 101 Mich. 370, 374). These cases aside, wrong is defined in terms of the natural or probable, at least when unintentional (*Parrot v. Wells-Fargo Co.* [*The Nitro-Glycerine Case*], 15 Wall. [U.S.] 524). The range of reasonable apprehension is at times a question for the court, and at times, if varying inferences are possible, a question for the jury. Here, by concession, there was nothing in the situation to suggest to the most cautious mind that the parcel wrapped in newspaper would spread wreckage through the station. If the guard had thrown it down knowingly and willfully, he would not have threatened the plaintiff's safety, so far as appearances could warn him. His conduct would not have involved, even then, an unreasonable probability of invasion of her bodily security. Liability can be no greater where the act is inadvertent.

Negligence, like risk, is thus a term of relation. Negligence in the abstract, apart from things related, is surely not a tort, if indeed it is understandable at all (Bowen, L.J., in *Thomas v. Quartermaine*, 18 Q.B.D. 685, 694). Negligence is not a tort unless it results in the commission of a wrong, and the commission of a wrong imports the violation of a right, in this case, we are told, the right to be protected against interference with one's bodily security. But bodily security is protected, not against all forms of interference or aggression, but only against some. One who seeks redress at law does not make out a cause of action by showing without more that there has been damage to his person. If the harm was not willful, he must show that the act as to him had possibilities of danger so many and apparent as to entitle him to be protected against the doing of it though the harm was unintended. Affront to personality is still the keynote of the wrong. Confirmation of this view will be found in the history and development of the action on the case. Negligence as a basis of civil liability was unknown to mediaeval law (8 Holdsworth, *History of English Law*, p. 449; Street, *Foundations of Legal Liability*, vol. 1, pp. 189, 190). For damage to the person, the sole remedy was trespass, and trespass did not lie in the absence of aggression, and that direct and personal liability for other damage, as where a servant without orders from the master does or omits something to the damage of another, is a plant of later growth (Wigmore, *Responsibility for Tortious Acts*, vol. 3, *Essays in Anglo-American Legal History*, 520, 523, 526, 533). When it emerged out of the legal soil, it was thought of as a variant of trespass, an offshoot of the parent stock. This appears in the form of action, which was known as trespass on the case. The victim does not sue derivatively, or by right of subrogation, to vindicate an interest invaded in the person of another. Thus to view his cause of action is to ignore the fundamental difference between tort and crime (Holland, *Jurisprudence* [12th ed.], p. 328). He sues for breach of a duty owing to himself.

The law of causation, remote or proximate, is thus foreign to the case before us. The question of liability is always anterior to the question of the measure of the consequences that go with liability. If there is no tort to be redressed, there is no occasion to consider what damage might be recovered if there were a finding of a tort. We may assume, without deciding, that negligence, not at large or in the abstract, but in relation to the plaintiff, would entail liability for any and all consequences, however novel or extraordinary (*Bird v. St. Paul F. & M. Ins. Co.*, 224 N. Y. 47, 54; *Ehrgott v. Mayor, etc., of N. Y.*, 96 N. Y. 264; *Smith v. London & S. W. Ry. Co.*, L. R. 6 C. P. 14; 1 Beven, *Negligence*, 106; Green, *Rationale of Proximate Cause*, pp. 88, 118; cf. *Matter of Polemis*, L.R. 1921, 3 K. B. 560; 44 *Law Quarterly Review*, 142). There is room for argument that a distinction is to be drawn according to the diversity of interests invaded by the act, as where conduct negligent in that it threatens an insignificant invasion of an interest in property results in an unforeseeable invasion of an interest of another order, as, e.g., one of bodily security. Perhaps other distinctions may be necessary. We do not go into the question now. The consequences to be

mediaeval 中世纪的

emerge 出现
variant 变体
offshoot 分枝
trespass on the case 间接侵害之诉,指一方的侵害行为与另一方的损失或伤害之间有间接而非直接的因果关系。
subrogation 代位
vindicate 维护

causation 因果关系

anterior 位于之前的

at large 一般说来
entail 涉及

followed must first be rooted in a wrong.

The judgment of the Appellate Division and that of the Trial Term should be *reversed*, and the complaint *dismissed*, with costs in all courts.

Andrews, J. (dissenting)

Assisting a passenger to board a train, the defendant's servant negligently knocked a package from his arms. It fell between the platform and the cars. Of its contents the servant knew and could know nothing. A violent explosion followed. The concussion broke some scales standing a considerable distance away. In falling they injured the plaintiff, an intending passenger.

Upon these facts may she recover the damages she has suffered in an action brought against the master? The result we shall reach depends upon our theory as to the nature of negligence. Is it a relative concept — the breach of some duty owing to a particular person or to particular persons? Or where there is an act which unreasonably threatens the safety of others, is the doer liable for all its proximate consequences, even where they result in injury to one who would generally be thought to be outside the radius of danger? This is not a mere dispute as to words. We might not believe that to the average mind the dropping of the bundle would seem to involve the probability of harm to the plaintiff standing many feet away whatever might be the case as to the owner or to one so near as to be likely to be struck by its fall. If, however, we adopt the second hypothesis we have to inquire only as to the relation between cause and effect. We deal in terms of proximate cause, not of negligence.

Negligence may be defined roughly as an act or omission which unreasonably does or may affect the rights of others, or which unreasonably fails to protect oneself from the dangers resulting from such acts. Here I confine myself to the first branch of the definition. Nor do I comment on the word "unreasonable." For present purposes it sufficiently describes that average of conduct that society requires of its members.

There must be both the act or the omission, and the right. It is the act itself, not the intent of the actor, that is important. (*Hover v. Barkhoof*, 44 N.Y. 113; *Mertz v. Connecticut Co.*, 217 N.Y. 475.) In criminal law both the intent and the result are to be considered. Intent again is material in tort actions, where punitive damages are sought, dependent on actual malice — not on merely reckless conduct. But here neither insanity nor infancy lessens responsibility. (*Williams v. Hays*, 143 N. Y. 442.)

insanity 精神失常
infancy 未成年
lessen 减少

As has been said, except in cases of contributory negligence, there must be rights which are or may be affected. Often though injury has occurred, no rights of him who suffers have been touched. A licensee or trespasser upon my land has no claim to affirmative care on my part that the land be made safe. (*Meiers v. Koch Brewery*, 229 N. Y. 10.) Where a railroad is required to fence its tracks against cattle, no man's rights are injured should he wander upon the road because such fence is absent. (*Di Caprio v. N. Y. C. R. R.*, 231 N. Y. 94.) An unborn child may not demand immunity from personal harm. (*Drobner v. Peters*, 232 N. Y. 220.)

But we are told that "there is no negligence unless there is in the particular case a legal duty to take care, and this duty must be one which is owed to the plaintiff himself and not merely to others." (Salmond, *Torts* [6th ed.], 24.) This, I think too narrow a conception. Where there is the unreasonable act, and some right that may be affected there is negligence whether damage does or does not result. That is immaterial. Should we drive down Broadway at a reckless speed, we are negligent whether we strike an approaching car or miss it by an inch. The act itself is wrongful. It is a wrong not only to those who happen to be within the radius of danger but to all who might have been there — a wrong to the public at large. Such is the language of the street. Such the language of the courts when speaking of contributory negligence. Such again and again their language in speaking of the duty of some defendant and discussing proximate cause in cases where such a discussion is wholly irrelevant on any other theory. (*Perry v. Rochester Line Co.*, 219 N. Y. 60.) As was said by Mr. Justice Holmes many years ago, "the measure of the defendant's duty in determining whether a wrong has been committed is one thing, the measure of liability when a wrong has been committed is another." (*Spade v. Lynn & Boston R. R. Co.*, 172 Mass. 488.) Due care is a duty imposed on each one of us to protect society from unnecessary danger, not to protect A, B or C alone.

due care 行为准则

It may well be that there is no such thing as negligence in the abstract. "Proof of negligence in the air, so to speak, will not do." In an empty world negligence would not exist. It does involve a relationship between man and his fellows. But not merely a relationship between man and those whom he might reasonably expect his act would injure. Rather, a relationship between him and those whom he does in fact injure. If his act has a tendency to harm someone, it harms him a mile away as surely as it does those on the scene. We now permit children to recover for the negligent killing of the father. It was never prevented on the theory that no duty was owing to them. A husband may be compensated for the loss of his wife's services. To say that the wrongdoer was negligent as to the husband as well as to the wife is merely an attempt to fit facts to theory. An insurance company paying a fire loss recovers its payment of the negligent incendiary. We speak of subrogation — of suing in the right of the insured. Behind the cloud of words is the fact they hide, that the act, wrongful as to the insured, has also injured the company. Even if it be true that the fault of father, wife or insured will prevent recovery, it is because we consider the original negligence not the proximate cause of the injury. (Pollock, *Torts* [12th ed.], 463.)

In the well-known *Polemis Case* (1921, 3 K. B. 560), Scrutton, L. J., said that the dropping of a plank was negligent for it might injure "workman or cargo or ship." Because of either possibility the owner of the vessel was to be made good for his loss. The act being wrongful the doer was liable for its proximate results. Criticized and explained as this statement may have been, I think it states the law as it should be and as it is. (*Smith v. London & Southwestern Ry. Co.*, [1870-71] 6 C. P. 14; *Anthony v. Slaid*, 52 Mass. 290; *Wood v. Penn. R. R. Co.*, 177 Penn. St. 306; *Trashansky v. Hershkovitz*, 239 N. Y. 452.)

The proposition is this. Every one owes to the world at large the duty of refraining from those acts that may unreasonably threaten the safety of others. Such an act occurs. Not only is he wronged to whom harm might reasonably be expected to result, but he also who is in fact injured, even if he be outside what would generally be thought the danger zone. There needs be duty due the one complaining but this is not a duty to a particular individual because as to him harm might be expected. Harm to someone being the natural result of the act, not only that

incendiary 纵火

refrain from 制止

one alone, but all those in fact injured may complain. We have never, I think, held otherwise. Indeed in the *Di Caprio* case we said that a breach of a general ordinance defining the degree of care to be exercised in one's calling is evidence of negligence as to everyone. We did not limit this statement to those who might be expected to be exposed to danger. Unreasonable risk being taken, its consequences are not confined to those who might probably be hurt.

If this be so, we do not have a plaintiff suing by "derivation or succession." Her action is original and primary. Her claim is for a breach of duty to herself — not that she is subrogated to any right of action of the owner of the parcel or of a passenger standing at the scene of the explosion.

The right to recover damages rests on additional considerations. The plaintiff's rights must be injured, and this injury must be caused by the negligence. We build a dam, but are negligent as to its foundations. Breaking, it injures property down stream. We are not liable if all this happened because of some reason other than the insecure foundation. But when injuries do result from our unlawful act we are liable for the consequences. It does not matter that they are unusual, unexpected, unforeseen and unforeseeable. But there is one limitation. The damages must be so connected with the negligence that the latter may be said to be the proximate cause of the former.

These two words have never been given an inclusive definition. What is a cause in a legal sense, still more what is a proximate cause, depend in each case upon many considerations, as does the existence of negligence itself. Any philosophical doctrine of causation does not help us. A boy throws a stone into a pond. The ripples spread. The water level rises. The history of that pond is altered to all eternity. It will be altered by other causes also. Yet it will be forever the resultant of all causes combined. Each one will have an influence. How great only <u>omniscience</u> can say. You may speak of a chain, or if you please, a net. An analogy is of little aid. Each cause brings about future events. Without each the future would not be the same. Each is proximate in the sense it is essential. But that is not what we mean by the word. Nor on the other hand do we mean sole cause. There is no such thing.

Should analogy be thought helpful, however, I prefer that of a <u>stream</u>. The <u>spring</u>, starting on its journey, is

omniscience 上帝

stream 溪流
spring 小溪

joined by tributary after tributary. The river, reaching the ocean, comes from a hundred sources. No man may say whence any drop of water is derived. Yet for a time distinction may be possible. Into the clear creek, brown swamp water flows from the left. Later, from the right comes water stained by its clay bed. The three may remain for a space, sharply divided. But at last, inevitably no trace of separation remains. They are so commingled that all distinction is lost.

As we have said, we cannot trace the effect of an act to the end, if end there is. Again, however, we may trace it part of the way. A murder at Serajevo may be the necessary antecedent to an assassination in London twenty years hence. An overturned lantern may burn all Chicago. We may follow the fire from the shed to the last building. We rightly say the fire started by the lantern caused its destruction.

A cause, but not the proximate cause. What we do mean by the word "proximate" is, that because of convenience, of public policy, of a rough sense of justice, the law arbitrarily declines to trace a series of events beyond a certain point. This is not logic. It is practical politics. Take our rule as to fires. Sparks from my burning haystack set on fire my house and my neighbor's. I may recover from a negligent railroad. He may not. Yet the wrongful act as directly harmed the one as the other. We may regret that the line was drawn just where it was, but drawn somewhere it had to be. We said the act of the railroad was not the proximate cause of our neighbor's fire. Cause it surely was. The words we used were simply indicative of our notions of public policy. Other courts think differently. But somewhere they reach the point where they cannot say the stream comes from any one source.

Take the illustration given in an unpublished manuscript by a distinguished and helpful writer on the law of torts. A chauffeur negligently collides with another car which is filled with dynamite, although he could not know it. An explosion follows. A, walking on the sidewalk nearby, is killed. B, sitting in a window of a building opposite, is cut by flying glass. C, likewise sitting in a window a block away, is similarly injured. And a further illustration. A nursemaid, ten blocks away, startled by the noise, involuntarily drops a baby from her arms to the walk. We are told that C may not recover while A may. As to B it is a question for court or jury. We will all agree that the baby might not. Because, we are again told, the chauffeur had no reason to believe his conduct involved any risk of injuring either C or the baby. As to them he was not negligent.

But the chauffeur, being negligent in risking the collision, his belief that the scope of the harm he might do would be limited is immaterial. His act unreasonably <u>jeopardized</u> the safety of anyone who might be affected by it. C's injury and that of the baby were directly traceable to the <u>collision</u>. Without that, the injury would not have happened. C had the right to sit in his office, secure from such dangers. The baby was entitled to use the sidewalk with reasonable safety.

The true theory is, it seems to me, that the injury to C, if in truth he is to be denied recovery, and the injury to the baby is that their several injuries were not the proximate result of the negligence. And here not what the chauffeur had reason to believe would be the result of his conduct, but what the prudent would foresee, may have a bearing. May have some bearing, for the problem of proximate cause is not to be solved by any one consideration.

It is all a question of <u>expediency</u>. There are no fixed rules to govern our judgment. There are simply matters of which we may take account. We have in a somewhat different connection spoken of "the stream of events." We have asked whether that stream was <u>deflected</u> — whether it was forced into new and unexpected channels. (*Donnelly v. Piercy Contracting Co.*, 222 N. Y. 210). This is rather <u>rhetoric</u> than law. There is in truth little to guide us other than common sense.

There are some <u>hints</u> that may help us. The proximate cause, involved as it may be with many other causes, must be, at the least, something without which the event would not happen. The court must ask itself whether there was a natural and continuous sequence between cause and effect. Was the one a substantial factor in producing the other? Was there a direct connection between them, without too many <u>intervening causes</u>? Is the effect of cause on result not too <u>attenuated</u>? Is the cause likely, in the usual judgment of mankind, to produce the result? Or by the exercise of prudent foresight could the result be foreseen? Is the result too remote from the cause, and here we consider remoteness in time and space. (*Bird v. St. Paul*

jeopardize 危及；使处于危险的境地

collision 碰撞

expediency 适宜，权宜之计

deflect 偏离

rhetoric 修辞学

hint 线索

intervening cause 介入原因；介于最初的过失行为或疏忽与损害之间，改变了侵权行为因果关系的独立原因。它可以是受害者的行为、第三人的行为或自然力。介入原因可能减轻最初侵害人的责任，也可能作为主要原因而取代最初侵害人的责任。

attenuated 微弱的

F. & M. Ins. Co., 224 N.Y. 47, where we passed upon the construction of a contract — but something was also said on this subject.) Clearly we must so consider, for the greater the distance either in time or space, the more surely do other causes intervene to affect the result. When a lantern is overturned the firing of a shed is a fairly direct consequence. Many things contribute to the spread of the conflagration — the force of the wind, the direction and width of streets, the character of intervening structures, other factors. We draw an uncertain and wavering line, but draw it we must as best we can.

Once again, it is all a question of fair judgment, always keeping in mind the fact that we endeavor to make a rule in each case that will be practical and in keeping with the general understanding of mankind.

Here another question must be answered. In the case supposed it is said, and said correctly, that the chauffeur is liable for the direct effect of the explosion although he had no reason to suppose it would follow a collision. "The fact that the injury occurred in a different manner than that which might have been expected does not prevent the chauffeur's negligence from being in law the cause of the injury." But the natural results of a negligent act — the results which a prudent man would or should foresee — do have a bearing upon the decision as to proximate cause. We have said so repeatedly. What should be foreseen? No human foresight would suggest that a collision itself might injure one a block away. On the contrary, given an explosion, such a possibility might be reasonably expected. I think the direct connection, the foresight of which the courts speak, assumes prevision of the explosion, for the immediate results of which, at least, the chauffeur is responsible.

It may be said this is unjust. Why? In fairness he should make good every injury flowing from his negligence. Not because of tenderness toward him we say he need not answer for all that follows his wrong. We look back to the catastrophe, the fire kindled by the spark, or the explosion. We trace the consequences — not indefinitely, but to a certain point. And to aid us in fixing that point we ask what might ordinarily be expected to follow the fire or the explosion.

This last suggestion is the factor which must determine the case before us. The act upon which defendant's liability rests is knocking an apparently harmless package onto the platform. The act was negligent. For its proximate consequences the defendant is liable. If its contents were broken, to the owner; if it fell upon and crushed a passenger's foot, then to him. If it exploded and injured one in the immediate vicinity, to him also as to A in the illustration. Mrs. Palsgraf was standing some distance away. How far cannot be told from the record — apparently twenty-five or thirty feet. Perhaps less. Except for the explosion, she would not have been injured. We are told by the appellant in his brief "it cannot be denied that the explosion was the direct cause of the plaintiff's injuries." So it was a substantial factor in producing the result — there was here a natural and continuous sequence — direct connection. The only intervening cause was that instead of blowing her to the ground the concussion smashed the weighing machine which in turn fell upon her. There was no remoteness in time, little in space. And surely, given such an explosion as here it needed no great foresight to predict that the natural result would be to injure one on the platform at no greater distance from its scene than was the plaintiff. Just how no one might be able to predict. Whether by flying fragments, by broken glass, by wreckage of machines or structures no one could say. But injury in some form was most probable.

immediate vicinity 紧邻

Under these circumstances I cannot say as a matter of law that the plaintiff's injuries were not the proximate result of the negligence. That is all we have before us. The court refused to so charge. No request was made to submit the matter to the jury as a question of fact, even would that have been proper upon the record before us.

The judgment appealed from should be *affirmed*, with costs.

Pound, Lehman, and Kellogg, JJ., concur with Cardozo, Ch. J.; Andrews, J., dissents in opinion in which Crane and O'Brien, JJ., concur.

Judgment *reversed*.

Both the majority opinion and the dissenting opinion of this case are very important because some states in the United States adopted the majority opinion while others adopted the dissenting view.

8.9.3 Exercise 3: Barnes v. Treece

Having done the above exercises, write a complete case brief based on the whole decision of the case *Barnes v. Treece* which is provided below.

Court of Appeals of Washington, Division One
Vernon Barnes, et al., Appellants, *v.*
Warren Treece, et al., Respondents
15 Wn. App. 437; 549 P.2d 1152
May 10, 1976

Opinion:

The plaintiffs Barnes appeal, and the defendant Warren Treece cross-appeals, from a judgment entered in plaintiffs' breach of contract action against Treece and the defendant Vend-A-Win, Inc. The plaintiffs appeal from the portion of the judgment dismissing Vend-A-Win from the action with prejudice and assert that Vend-A-Win either clothed Treece with apparent authority or ratified the contract made by him. Treece cross-appeals from the portion awarding plaintiffs a $100,000 judgment against him personally and claims that no contract was ever formed. We affirm the trial court's holding that Treece was personally liable on a valid, enforceable contract, but that he did not have apparent authority to enter into the contract on behalf of the corporation and Vend-A-Win did not ratify the contract.

Vend-A-Win is a Washington corporation engaged primarily in the business of distributing punchboards. Warren Treece served as vice-president, was a member of the board of directors, and owned 50 percent of the stock of Vend-A-Win. On July 24, 1973, Treece spoke before the Washington State Gambling Commission in support of punchboard legitimacy and Vend-A-Win's particular application for a temporary license to distribute punchboards. During the testimony, as stated by the trial judge, Treece made a statement to the following effect:

I'll put a hundred thousand dollars to anyone to find a crooked board. If they find it, I'll pay it.

The statement brought laughter from the audience.
The next morning, July 25, 1973, the plaintiff Barnes was watching a television news report of the proceedings before the gambling commission and heard Treece's

previous statement that $100,000 would be paid to anyone who could produce a crooked punchboard. Barnes also read a newspaper report of the hearings that quoted Treece's statement. A number of years earlier, while employed as a bartender, Barnes had purchased two fraudulent punchboards. After learning of Treece's statement, Barnes searched for and located his two punchboards. On July 26, 1973, Barnes telephoned Treece, announced that he had two crooked punchboards, and asked Treece if his earlier statement had been made seriously. Treece assured Barnes that the statement had been made seriously, advised Barnes that the statement was firm, and further informed Barnes that the $100,000 was safely being held in escrow. Treece also specifically directed Barnes to bring the punchboard to the Seattle office of Vend-A-Win for inspection.

On July 28, 1973, Barnes traveled to Seattle, met Treece and Vend-A-Win's secretary-treasurer in Vend-A-Win's offices, produced one punchboard, and received a receipt for presentation of the board written on Vend-A-Win stationery, signed by Treece and witnessed by Vend-A-Win's secretary-treasurer. Barnes was informed that the punchboard would be taken to Chicago for inspection. The parties next met on August 3, 1973, before the Washington State Gambling Commission. Barnes produced his second punchboard during the meeting before the commission.

Both Treece and Vend-A-Win refused to pay Barnes $100,000. Barnes then initiated this breach of contract action against both defendants. The trial court found that the two punchboards were rigged and dishonest, that Treece's statements before the gambling commission and reiterated to Barnes personally on the telephone constituted a valid offer for a unilateral contract, and that Barnes' production of two dishonest punchboards constituted an acceptance of the offer. The trial court also found that Vend-A-Win had not manifested any apparent authority in Treece to make the offer, had not impliedly ratified the contract, and therefore was not liable on the contract.

The following questions are presented on appeal: (1) Did Barnes and Treece mutually manifest assent to an agreement that formed an enforceable contract, and if so, (2) was the corporation Vend-A-Win bound under the contract either by having invested Treece with apparent authority to this contract in its behalf or by later ratifying the agreement?

The first issue is whether the statement of Treece was the manifestation of an offer which could be accepted to bind the offeror to performance of the promise. Treece contends that no contract was formed. He maintains that his statement was made in jest and lacks the necessary manifestation of a serious contractual intent.

When expressions are intended as a joke and are understood or would be understood by a reasonable person as being so intended, they cannot be construed as an offer and accepted to form a contract. However, if the jest is not apparent and a reasonable hearer would believe that an offer was being made, then the speaker risks the formation of a contract which was not intended. It is the objective manifestations of the offeror that count and not secret, unexpressed intentions. 1 A. Corbin, *Corbin on Contracts* § 34 (1963); 1 S. Williston, *A Treatise on the Law of Contracts* § 21, at 43 (3d ed. 1957). As stated in *Wesco Realty, Inc. v. Drewry*, 9 Wn. App. 734, 735, 515 P. 2d 513 (1973):

> If a party's words or acts, judged by a reasonable standard, manifest an intention to agree in regard to the matter in question, that agreement is established, and it is immaterial what may be the real but unexpressed state of the party's mind on the subject.

See also Swanson v. Holmquist, 13 Wn. App. 939, 539 P. 2d 104 (1975); *Peoples Mortgage Co. v. Vista View Bldrs.*, 6 Wn. App. 744, 496 P. 2d 354 (1972).

The trial court found that there was an objective manifestation of mutual assent to form a contract. This was a matter to be evaluated by the trier of fact. *In re Estate of Richardson*, 11 Wn. App. 758, 525 P. 2d 816 (1974). The record includes substantial evidence of the required mutual assent to support the finding of the trial court. Although the original statement of Treece drew laughter from the audience, the subsequent statements, conduct, and the circumstances show an intent to lead any hearer to believe the statements were made seriously. There was testimony, though contradicted, that Treece specifically restated the offer over the telephone in response to an inquiry concerning whether the offer was serious. Treece, when given the opportunity to state that an offer was not intended, not only reaffirmed the offer but also asserted that $100,000 had been placed in escrow and directed Barnes to bring the punchboard to Seattle for inspection. The parties met, Barnes was given a receipt for the board, and he was told that the board would be taken to Chicago for inspection. In present day society it is known that gambling generates a great deal of income and that large sums are spent on its advertising and promotion. In that prevailing atmosphere, it was a credible statement that $100,000 would be paid to promote punchboards. The statements of the defendant and the surrounding circumstances reflect an objective manifestation of a contractual intent by Treece and support the finding of the trial court.

The trial court properly categorized Treece's promise of $100,000 as a valid offer for a unilateral contract. The offer made promised that a contract would result upon performance of the act requested. Performance of the act with the intent to accept the offer constituted acceptance. The trial judge entered a specific finding that Barnes performed the requested act of acceptance when he produced a rigged and fraudulent punchboard. We concur with the trial court's holding that a binding unilateral contract was formed between Barnes and Treece and uphold the conclusions of the trial court in that regard.

Treece also contends that an oral contract would be unenforceable pursuant to two statute of frauds provisions of the Uniform Commercial Code, RCW 62A.1-206 and RCW 62A.2-201. However, both provisions apply only to contracts for the sale of personal property or goods. Since the contract involved is not a sales transaction, the U.C.C. statute of frauds provisions are inapplicable.

In addition, Treece asserts that the contract is unenforceable due to an unconscionable discrepancy in consideration. However, it is only when consideration is so inadequate as to be constructively fraudulent that a court should inquire into the comparative value of an act performed in response to a promise. *Browning v. Johnson*, 70 Wn.2d 145, 422 P.2d 314 (1967); *Rogich v. Dressel*, 45 Wn.2d 829, 278 P.2d 367 (1954). The record does not suggest constructive fraud, and therefore the adequacy of the consideration cannot be weighed.

The last question presented is whether Vend-A-Win is also liable on the contract either because of the claim that the contract was made within an apparent authority given

Treece or because of an implied ratification of the contract by Vend-A-Win.

Treece, as a corporate vice-president, was an agent of Vend-A-Win and agency principles apply to his acts. *Sons of Norway v. Boomer*, 10 Wn. App. 618, 519 P. 2d 28 (1974). Vend-A-Win, therefore, may be bound to a contract made by Treece if the contract was within the scope of his apparent authority as a corporate vice-president. *Lumber Mart Co. v. Buchanan*, 69 Wn. 2d 658, 419 P. 2d 1002 (1966); *Taylor v. Smith*, 13 Wn. App. 171, 534 P. 2d 39 (1975); *Deers, Inc. v. DeRuyter*, 9 Wn. App. 240, 511 P. 2d 1379 (1973). Vice-presidents do not have authority to bind their corporations by virtue of their office. H. Henn, *Law of Corporations* § 225 (2d ed. 1970). Apparent authority to bind a corporation in contract exists only if the corporation, as the principal, knowingly permits the agent to act or holds the agent out as having authority. *Ford v. United Bhd. of Carpenters*, 50 Wn. 2d 832, 315 P. 2d 299 (1957). In order for a corporation to be bound by the apparent authority of its officers, it must have acted or conducted itself in a manner that manifested to third persons that the agent had authority. *Lumber Mart Co. v. Buchanan, supra*. To constitute a manifestation of an agent's apparent authority by the principal, the circumstances must be such that a prudent person would have believed that the agent possessed the authority to do the particular act in question. *Walker v. Pacific Mobile Homes, Inc.*, 68 Wn. 2d 347, 413 P. 2d 3 (1966). The manifestation must be sufficient to mislead a reasonable person, to deter further inquiry, and to cause reliance on the manifestation of apparent authority. *Lamb v. General Associates, Inc.*, 60 Wn. 2d 623, 374 P. 2d 677 (1962); *Taylor v. Smith, supra*; *Deers, Inc. v. DeRuyter, supra*.

The corporation did not manifest to Barnes that Treece had authority to offer $100,000 for the production of an illegal punchboard. Barnes, as a reasonable, prudent individual, did contact Treece to ascertain whether the offer was serious, but he never inquired of Vend-A-Win concerning whether Treece had any authority to bind the corporation. Whether an agent has apparent authority to make a contract depends upon the circumstances and is to be decided by the trier of fact. *Sons of Norway v. Boomer, supra*; *Louron Indus., Inc. v. Holman*, 7 Wn. App. 834, 502 P. 2d 1216 (1972); 2

W. Fletcher, *Cyclopedia of the Law of Private Corporations* § 451 (perm. ed. rev. 1969). The finding of the trial court that Treece did not have apparent authority to make the contract is supported by the record.

As asserted by the plaintiff, a corporate principal may impliedly ratify an unauthorized contract of an officer agent. *Rayonier, Inc. v. Polson*, 400 F.2d 909 (9th Cir. 1968); *Poweroil Mfg. Co. v. Carstensen*, 69 Wn.2d 673, 419 P.2d 793 (1966). Whether an implied ratification has occurred is likewise to be decided by the finder of fact. 2 W. Fletcher, *Cyclopedia of the Law of Private Corporations* § 781 (perm. ed. rev. 1969).

An implied ratification can arise if the corporate principal, with full knowledge of the material facts (1) receives, accepts, and retains benefits from the contract, (2) remains silent, acquiesces, and fails to repudiate or disaffirm the contract, or (3) otherwise exhibits conduct demonstrating an adoption and recognition of the contract as binding. 2 W. Fletcher, *Cyclopedia of the Law of Private Corporations* § 752 *et seq*. (perm. ed. rev. 1969). The basic inquiry to determine whether an implied ratification has occurred is whether the facts demonstrate an intent to affirm, to approve, and to act in furtherance of the contract. *Poweroil Mfg. Co. v. Carstensen*, *supra*.

disaffirm 撤销，宣告无效

Barnes asserts that Vend-A-Win impliedly ratified the contract through acquiescence by remaining silent and failing to repudiate or disaffirm the contract. Fletcher comments that:

> Ratification, being purely a voluntary act upon the part of the principal, ordinarily requires some positive act. But the rule that when a principal has not disaffirmed an unauthorized act of his agent within a reasonable time after it came to his knowledge, he will be deemed to have acquiesced in such act, applies to corporate bodies as well as individuals. Ratification may be implied, or the corporation be held estopped to deny ratification, from acquiescence on the part of the corporation. When the officers or agents of a corporation exceed their powers in entering into contracts or doing other acts, the corporation, when it has knowledge thereof, must promptly disaffirm the contract or act and not allow the other party or third persons to act

estop 禁止反言

in the belief that it was authorized or has been ratified. If it acquiesces, with knowledge of the facts, or fails to disaffirm, a ratification will be implied, or else it will be estopped to deny a ratification. In other words, acquiescence with the full knowledge of the facts is equivalent to ratification of unauthorized acts of corporate officers or directors. After knowledge of the unauthorized contract, the corporation must repudiate it within a reasonable time or else consent and approval will be presumed to have been given to the officer's act or contract. But one should be aware of the probability that delay may mislead another before he will be estopped because of delay. Of course there is no acquiescence where the corporate officers promptly repudiate an agreement made without authority by a subordinate officer or agent, or where the circumstances of the case sufficiently account for the silence of the principal without construing it as an acquiescence in the act. Furthermore, acquiescence implies knowledge. If there is no knowledge, there is no acquiescence. A ratification by acquiescence cannot arise where the party supposed to acquiesce has not a full knowledge of the facts, or unless he occupies such a relation that knowledge of it must be imputed to him. Moreover, silence and failure to repudiate which does not harm the opposite party does not constitute ratification by estoppel. Where such a ratification is sought to be established by a third person, it must clearly appear that he has been misled thereby, or induced to forego some advantage he would have otherwise enjoyed. Accordingly, it is held that the duty promptly to disaffirm unauthorized acts, on knowledge thereof being acquired, is less imperative, or does not exist, where the corporation has received no benefit from the acts and no loss is caused to the other party and his position is not in any way changed by the failure to notify him. (*Footnotes omitted.*)

2 W. Fletcher, *Cyclopedia of the Law of Private Corporations* § 769 (perm. ed. rev. 1969).

There is no evidence that Vend-A-Win received and retained benefits from the contract nor that Barnes was misled, changed his position, and suffered loss as a result of either the actions or silence of the corporation. Further, the first mention of $100,000 for a "crooked board" was made on July 24, the plaintiff presented his punchboards to Treece at the corporation's office on July 28, and the plaintiff's complaint was filed on August 7, 1973. Little time existed for the corporation to act to repudiate the offer of its vice-president. This <u>substantiates</u> the finding of the trial court, whose province it was to find whether the corporation adopted the unauthorized act of its agent by its silence. Though we might have evaluated the evidence differently, the <u>ascertainment</u> of the existence of either an intent to ratify or an estoppel because of silent acquiescence was within the province of the trial court.

substantiate 证实

ascertainment 调查

The judgment is *affirmed*.

8.10 Summary

Briefing cases is the very first job a common law lawyer does. Since many judicial opinions are lengthy and complicated, it is impossible for attorneys to reread the opinions when they are working on the problems before them. A good case brief will show its readers the main points and the significant parts of the opinion. Therefore, you need to spot the most essential elements of the opinion and arrange them orderly in your brief. The six basic elements of a case brief are the procedural history of the case, the statement of the facts, the issue and holding of the case, the reasons and policies supporting the holding, and the judgment made by the court. Different people have different writing styles, so you may have your own style for a case brief. However, the above elements should be included in all case briefs.

The following is a format which may be helpful for you to brief a case.

Brief of _____ v. _____ (case name and citation)

Procedural History:
State who sued whom for what cause of action in which court and with what result, and who appealed to this court.
Facts:
Describe the legally relevant facts only.

Issue:
Write a one-sentence question containing the legally relevant facts of the case, the cause of action, and the elements of the applicable rules of law, and in the form of "Does the rule of law apply to the legally relevant facts?" or "Whether the rule of law applies to the legally relevant facts."

Holding:
Write a one-sentence statement answering the issue which contains the legally relevant facts, the cause of action, and the elements of the applicable rules of law, and in the form of "Yes, the rule of law does apply to the legally relevant facts," or, "No, the rule of law does not apply to the legally relevant facts."

Reasons/Policies:
Explain and justify why the rule of law does or does not apply to the legally relevant facts and why the holding is socially desirable.

Judgment:
Write a simple statement of the court's action, in the form of "the judgment is affirmed," or "the judgment is reversed," or "the judgment is vacated and remanded," etc.

Review Questions

1. What are the essential elements of most court opinions?
2. Brief the case *Katko v. Briney* reprinted in section 8.9.1.
3. Brief the case *Palsgraf v. Long Island Railroad Co.* reprinted in section 8.9.2.
4. Brief the case *Barnes v. Treece* reprinted in section 8.9.3.

PART IV
LEGAL DOCUMENT DRAFTING

LAWYERS need to communicate with other lawyers, their clients, and ultimately with the court. Frequently these communications are made in written form. The writings submitted to court include various pleadings. The writings provided to clients are normally in the form of legal opinions or legal advisory letters. The writings communicated to other lawyers are legal analysis reports, frequently called <u>legal memorandum</u>. If briefing cases requires lawyers to have the ability to comprehensively read and analyze court opinions, drafting of legal memoranda requires lawyers to be familiar with the law and be creative in conducting common law analysis. It is an essential step of practicing law, not only for common law lawyers, but also for Chinese lawyers who work in a foreign law firm, or a local law firm dealing with foreign clients, or who will have to litigate in a common law country. Under these situations, a Chinese lawyer needs to draft a legal memorandum in English. When you write a memorandum you will make use of the several analytical skills you have been developing. This PART will focus on how to draft a legal memorandum.

legal memorandum 法律备忘录

Chapter 9
Memoranda Drafting

9.1 Common Law Analyses

A legal memorandum is a piece of writing whereby the writer conducts legal analysis based on which a conclusion will be drawn. Therefore, legal analysis is the core of a legal memorandum, and most common law analyses focus on the analysis of cases. The purpose of common law analyses is to help attorneys find and apply the law to their cases.

When doing legal research for case authorities to help resolve a legal issue, a common law attorney should first search for binding precedents because the rule of precedent and the doctrine of *stare decisis* require that the binding precedents be applied to resolve new problems. In order to predict how a court will dispose a case, lawyers should study the precedent cases to find their impact on their cases. The analysis of a precedent must be thorough in that each precedent may have two aspects; one is favorable to the new dispute, while the other may be unfavorable. If an attorney only knows one aspect of the precedent that is favorable to his or her client, the analysis will be misleading. Only when you fully understand both sides can you accurately assess the strengths and weaknesses of your client's position. Therefore, a sound understanding of both sides of a controversy is the primary goal of common law analysis.

In order to thoroughly analyze a precedent to see how much it will bind your client's case, you need to compare the precedent case with your case, because the doctrine of precedent and *stare decisis* require the precedent to be applied only if your problem case is similar to the precedent. Accordingly, if your problem case is different from the precedent in a significant way, the precedent should not be applied and the result of your case does not need to be the same as the result of the precedent case. If your analysis shows that a precedent case is favorable to your client's case and you would like the court to apply the rules established in the precedent case to your case, you must explain in your memorandum the similarities and the differences between the precedent case and your case, and why the similarities are more important than the differences which warrants application of the precedent. Simply discussing the similarities while disregarding the differences may be misleading and even disastrous. On the contrary, if you determine that a precedent case is unfavorable to your client's case and you would like the court not to apply the rule contained therein, you must explain in your memorandum why the differences between the precedent case and your case are more important than the similarities between them, thus the precedent must not be applied to your case.

Therefore, comparison of the precedent case to your client's case is a very important part of your analysis. It includes different aspects. The issues, factual situations, and the underlying policies should all be considered. You must first look at the issues of the precedent case and compare them with the issues of your client's case. Then you should compare the facts of the precedent with the facts of your case. You must then examine the reasons and policies stated in the precedent case to see whether these reasons and policies apply to your case. If your problem case and a precedent case deal with completely different issues, the precedent case will have no impact on your problem case. If your problem case and the precedent case deal with the same issue and with similar facts, then the precedent should be applied and the result should be the same under the doctrine of precedent and *stare decisis*. If your problem case and the precedent case deal with the same issue but with materially different facts, then the precedent is distinguishable and the result should be different. If your case and the precedent case deal with the same issue but the precedent was based on a policy which is no longer persuasive or has not been accepted by another court, the precedent is not applicable either and you should try to persuade the judge to distinguish or even overrule it.

Sometimes, however, a research result may show that there is no precedent applicable to your client's dispute at all because the issue has never been litigated in the jurisdiction. If such a case goes to the court, it is called a "case of first impression," meaning that it will be the first time for the court to decide a case of this kind. Since there is no precedent providing a binding rule, the court may create a rule based on the rules contained in other persuasive authorities. Therefore, in order to predict how the court will decide the case, you should try to find any cases that may be persuasive.

9.2 Principles of Drafting

A legal memorandum is a written document containing analysis of one or more legal issues which is intended to convey information to other lawyers. Usually it is prepared by an attorney (junior attorney) for other attorneys (usually more senior or experienced attorneys) to analyze the legal rules that govern the issues raised by a new controversy and then apply the rules to the controversy to predict how the court will decide the case. The other attorneys who read the memorandum will then use it to understand the issues and the law. They may advise the client based on the analysis and conclusion contained in the memorandum. They may also prepare other legal documents (e.g., various pleadings submitted to the court) for the case based on the memorandum.

Since the purpose of a legal memorandum is to enable the readers to better understand the various aspects of the controversy and the applicable rules of law so that the readers can make an informed decision, it should be a thorough analysis instead of an <u>advocacy</u> paper. In an advocacy paper you could argue only for your client's side of the case because your purpose is to convince the trier that you should win the case; however, in a legal memorandum, you should describe both sides of the controversy to avoid misleading the readers (other attorneys or your client) to believe that your case does not have any weak points. To some extent, the readers of the legal memorandum are standing on the same side with you. You do not need to argue with them; instead, you should try to convince them that your analysis of the problem is correct. Thus a legal memorandum is a discussion in which you explore the problem, evaluate the strengths and weaknesses of each party's arguments, and reach a conclusion. Some fundamental principles should guide you in researching for, drafting, and writing a legal memorandum.

advocacy 辩护

Since the goal of legal analysis is to fully understand both sides of a legal controversy, the first principle of drafting a memorandum is to be objective and exploratory. After all, a legal memorandum is drafted for an objective evaluation of your client's case. You must be honest about whether certain rules of law would apply to the controversy or not. If you are not honest and only assess the strengths of your case, the readers of the memorandum (usually your colleagues in the law firm who will determine whether and how to pursue the litigation) will be misled by your one-sided wishful advocacy. Only after you have objectively scrutinized your own arguments as well as those you anticipate from your opponent can you honestly assess both the strengths and weaknesses of your client's case.

The second principle is to be thorough. This is also related to the principle of objectivity. Since a legal memorandum provides a basis for senior attorneys or your client to make major decisions, you should make every effort to ensure that these decisions can be made on the basis of sound analysis. In order to provide a good analysis to the readers, you must have solid knowledge of the relevant law. You must also be familiar with the factual situations from which the legal controversy arises. Thoroughness also requires that you have a clear mind when analyzing the case.

The third principle of drafting a legal memorandum is to be communicative. The memorandum is used to convey information and your conclusion must be based on a sound analysis. Your goal is to make the readers understand what you are saying. If they do not understand your analysis, your memorandum fails. In order to achieve this primary goal, a legal memorandum must be well organized and written so that your thoughts are clearly presented and precisely stated.

The fourth principle is to be aware of your readers. Your writing must be tailored to meet their needs and expectations. When your readers are the senior attorneys or other attorneys who will work together with you on the case, your memorandum should contain a core of information about the applicable law and its application to the facts of the problem. You do not need to explain the legal procedure or other general legal knowledge that the attorneys have already known because most attorneys are very busy and do not have time to read the part of the

---

objective 客观的
exploratory 探索性的

scrutinize 仔细检查

communicative 易懂的

memorandum that they have already known. However, the attorneys may not know the specific facts, holding, and reasoning of the case and will expect to get this information from your memorandum. Nevertheless, when your reader is your client or a lay person who may not be familiar with the relevant law, you must explain the relevant law and legal procedures in your memorandum so that they will understand the whole process.

9.3 Writing Techniques

The memorandum is a formal document and a professional writing; when drafting a memorandum, you must follow the rules of good written English. These rules are especially important for Chinese lawyers to write a legal memorandum in English. Since English is not their native language, they learn from the English legal documents written by the people who are native English speakers. Actually, some of these documents were badly drafted but the Chinese lawyers may not be able to tell. To some extent, they may think that is the way a legal document should be drafted. The best way to avoid these pitfalls is to read well-drafted documents and be familiar with the drafting rules. For example, you should use standard written English and avoid slang, other kinds of informal speech, and overuse of contractions. Try to avoid using legalese such as "whereas", "herein", or "herein before".

In addition to knowing the don'ts, you should also know the dos. For example, some legal terms are substantive and cannot be substituted by any other words. In that case, you should use these legal terms to describe the corresponding situation. If you are citing or analyzing a provision of a statute, or a rule of law formulated by a judge, you should use the operative language of the statute or of the rule. Your writing style should also be tailored to meet different audiences' needs. You should always keep in mind that you are a legal professional and you are writing as the client's attorney. You should convey the information objectively, persuasively, and convincingly, not present it as your opinion only, so try not to use the first person pronoun in your analysis. For example, you should say "in *Smith v. Smith*, the court held ...," instead of that "I believe that in *Smith v. Smith* the court held . . . ." There are many other rules and principles on

pitfall 陷阱, 圈套

slang 俚语
contraction 缩减
legalese 法律术语
whereas 然而
herein 在此文中
herein before 在下文中

how to write good English. It is a process of learning and accumulation.

9.4 Elements of a Memorandum

Each writer's writing style is different because writing is basically a personal thing. Therefore, there is no unified format that all lawyers use for a legal memorandum. Most legal memoranda, however, are composed of different sections, with each section performing a particular function and conveying a necessary core of information. They are the heading, the question presented, a brief answer, statement of facts, discussion, and a final conclusion. Each section is labeled by underlining or capitalizing its title on a separate line immediately preceding that section. The following sample memorandum represents the format of a legal memorandum that is widely used in the United States.

MEMORANDUM

To: Joan Roslyn
From: Chris Parker
Re: WOW Insurance Contract Action, File No. 00-166
Date: May 20, 2000

Questions Presented

I. Whether Washington's Original Wafers (WOW)'s insurance policies cover the costs for its voluntary cleanup of the land contaminated as result of WOW's waste storage tank A's leak and tanks B and C's explosion, and the medical bills of its employee resulting from his involuntary exposure to the wastes unleashed from tank A, even though WOW has not become a party to or under threat of a formal legal action.

II. Whether the pollution exclusion clause contained in Policy-II bars recovery for WOW's cleanup of tanks B and C.

III. Whether the exception to the pollution exclusion clause contained in Policy-I re-triggers coverage for WOW's cleanup of tank A and the medical bills of its employee resulting from tank A's spill.

Brief Answers

I. Yes. While the policy language does not specify

unleash 爆发,突然释放

whether the liability must be imposed by formal legal action or threat of such, or by a statute which imposes liability, the policies may provide coverage when WOW's cleanup and payment of its employee's medical bills are required under statutes, unless excluded by other clauses.

II. Yes. The pollution exclusion contained in Policy-II does not violate public policy and thus relieves the insurer from indemnifying WOW for cleanup of tanks B and C.

III. Yes. Tank A's spill was not "sudden and accidental" because it was not intended and expected by WOW. Therefore the exception to the pollution exclusion clause contained in Policy-I re-triggers coverage for WOW's cleanup of tank A and the medical bills of its employee resulting from tank A's spill.

Statement of Facts

Washington's Original Wafers (WOW) places its slightly toxic liquid wastes in three large storage tanks behind the factory. Every six months, Holly's Hazard Haulers (Holly) drains the tanks, inspects the tanks for structural integrity, and removes the waste to a state certified toxin disposal center. In January 1998, Holly identified minor vertical cracking on tanks A and B, and informed WOW. Concluding that Holly had overstated the situation, WOW decided to delay the replacement for three years. On June 1, 1998, a vertical tear ripped open tank A. One of WOW's employees, Nami, through involuntarily contacting the waste unleashed from tank A, sustained massive injuries. The remainder of the waste soaked into the ground. WOW decided to accelerate the tank replacement process by one year. On August 10, 1998, a small fire spontaneously erupted in a large trash bin behind WOW's factory. The heat from the growing fire caused the explosion of tanks B and C, as a result, all of their contents were discharged upon the land.

Upon consultation, the Department of Ecology (DOE) of the State of Washington determined that WOW directly violated Washington's Hazardous Waste Cleanup-Model Toxins Control Act. However, in a letter dated August 24, 1998, DOE said that it "[did] not intend to initiate legal proceedings against WOW and this letter should not be read as a threat of legal action" because WOW "expressly desired to deal with this hazard in a responsible manner." Determined to restore its property,

WOW started the reclamation and assumed that the cleanup costs would be covered by their insurance policies.

Erth-Wise Insurance (EWI) provides WOW's insurance coverage. Policy-I was effective from July 1, 1993 to June 30, 1998 and Policy-II effective from July 1, 1998 to June 30, 2003. The spill of tank A falls within Policy-I while the explosion of tanks B and C within Policy-II. Section I of both policies provides that EWI "agrees ... to indemnify for all sums which the Assured shall be obligated to pay by reason of liability." Section IV of Policy-I provides that "the insurance does not apply to bodily injury or property damage arising out of ... (a) Pollution: Discharge, dispersal, release or escape of ... toxic chemicals, liquids, waste materials or the irritants, contaminants or pollutants into or upon land ... but this exclusion does not apply if such discharge, dispersal, release or escape is sudden and accidental." Policy-II contained this same provision but the last sentence — exception to the pollution exclusion — was removed.

When WOW sought indemnification, EWI denied coverage based on the reason that the two policies explicitly exclude coverage. Additionally, under Section I of both policies, recovery is currently unavailable for environmental reclamation indemnification in that WOW has not become legally liable for damages stemming from the contamination. It was alleged that liability for damages might arise when WOW became a party to or under threat of a formal legal action.

WOW now seeks recovery of $158,417.13 for Nami's medical bills and $500,010 for costs associated with tank A's spill and $1,500,490 for the cleanup of tanks B and C.

Discussion

I. **Whether WOW's insurance policies cover the costs for its voluntary cleanup of the land contaminated as result of its waste storage tank A's leak and tanks B and C's explosion, and the medical bills of its employee resulting from his involuntary exposure to the wastes unleashed from tank A, even though WOW has not become a party to or under threat of a formal legal action.**

Comprehensive General Liability (CGL) insurance policies, which provide coverage for all sums which the insured shall be obligated to pay by reason of the liability imposed by law may provide coverage when an insured engages in the cleanup of pollution damages in cooperation with an environmental agency. Such policies can reasonably be read to provide coverage for cleanup actions required under environmental statutes which impose strict liability for such cleanup. *Weyerhaeuser Co. v. Aetna Cas. & Sur.*, 123 Wash. 2d 891, 896-897, 874 P.2d 142, 145 (1994).

In *Weyerhaeuser*, the appellant Weyerhaeuser Co. was engaged in cleanup which was <u>mandated</u> by state and federal statutes imposing strict, <u>joint and several liability</u> for pollution damage. *Id.* at 895, 874 P.2d at 144. The insurers refused to compensate based on the policy provision which stated that the insurer agreed to indemnify for "all sums which the Assured shall be obligated to pay by reason of the liability," while the government agencies involved had not yet filed legal actions or threatened to do so. *Id.* The court held that as the policy language did not specify whether this liability must be imposed by formal legal action or threat of such or by a statute which imposed liability, in the case where a policyholder was liable pursuant to an environmental statute, coverage was available, if it was not otherwise excluded. *Id.* at 913, 874 P.2d at 154.

The situation of WOW is very similar. WOW violated Washington's Hazardous Waste Cleanup-Model Toxins Control Act which provided that the owner or operator of a facility was strictly liable, jointly and severally, for all <u>remedial</u> action costs resulting from the release of hazardous substances. *Wash. Rev. Code Ann.* § 70.105D.050(1) (1992). While DOE expressly assured that it would not sue or threaten to sue, WOW voluntarily undertook the reclamation project to cleanup the contaminated land. When seeking indemnification, WOW's insurer also refused to compensate because WOW had not become a party to or under threat of a formal legal action. Similar to *Weyerhaeuser*, WOW's insurance policies did not specify whether the liability must be imposed by formal legal action or threat of it, or by a statute which imposed liability, either. Therefore, coverage is available for its costs for voluntary cleanup pursuant to the statute unless excluded by other clauses.

Washington law also provides that "each worker injured in the course of his or her employment ... shall receive compensation." *Wash. Rev. Code Ann.* § 51.32.010 (1990). Nami, as WOW's employee, was injured through

mandate 指示；委任

joint and several liability 连带责任

remedial 补救的

involuntary contacting the toxic wastes spilled from tank A in the course of his employment and thus WOW is liable to pay Nami's medical bills pursuant to the statute. Therefore, coverage is also available for Nami's medical bills, unless excluded by other clauses.

II. Whether the pollution exclusion clause contained in Policy-II bars recovery for WOW's cleanup of tanks B and C.

Washington courts will not enforce limitations in insurance contracts which are contrary to public policy and statute, insurers are otherwise free to limit their contractual liability. *Carry v. Allstate Ins. Co.*, 130 Wash. 2d 335, 339-340, 922 P. 2d 1335, 1338 (1996). Public policy is generally determined by the Legislature and established through statutory provisions. *Id.* The pollution exclusion clause contained in WOW's policies did not violate any public policy because there is no statute prohibiting insurers from contracting away their liabilities in the insurance policies.

The interpretation of insurance policies is a question of law. Where the policy language is ambiguous, it is to be interpreted in accord with the understanding of the average purchaser of insurance, and the terms are to be given their plain, ordinary and popular meaning. *Queen City Farms v. Central Nat. Ins. Co.*, 126 Wash. 2d 50, 77, 882 P. 2d 703, 718 (1994). A policy is ambiguous if the language, on its face, is fairly susceptible to two different reasonable interpretations. *Cook v. Evanson*, 83 Wash. App. 149, 152, 920 P. 2d 1223, 1225, *review denied* (1996).

The pollution exclusion clause contained in WOW's Policy-II states that "the insurance does not apply to bodily injury or property damage arising out of ... (a) Pollution: Discharge, dispersal, release or escape of ... toxic chemicals, liquids or gases, waste materials or other irritants, contaminants or pollutants into or upon land." None of these terms is defined in the policy. The language of the pollution exclusion is ambiguous because "discharge, dispersal, release or escape" may mean the initial deposit of toxic wastes at the wastes storage tanks, or the spill and discharge of the wastes from the tanks upon land. The court in *Queen City Farms* held that where material had been deposited in a place which was believed would contain or safely filter the material, the polluting memorandum is aimed at resolving a question of law only, not involving any facts. In that case, the question presented may disregard the facts. You can write the question presented in a form of a question or as a statement beginning with the word "whether." If the problem contains more than one issue, or, one issue contains sub-issue(s), you should list all of the issues and sub-issues and number them respectively.

In formulating the questions presented, several principles are to be followed. The first principle is to describe the factual situation in an appropriate generality. You must consider the readers' knowledge of the case facts when determining the generality of the questions. When your readers have already known the facts of the problem, you can formulate the question presented in a specific way by identifying people by name and identifying events by reference to them. For example, suppose you have a contract problem and the fact statement includes the fact that Mr. Treece is the vice president of a company who made a public announcement that "anyone who could present a disqualified product would receive a reward from the company," and Mr. Barnes is a person who presented a disqualified product. If the issue is written as "Does Mr. Treece make an offer to Mr. Barnes which binds himself?", a reader who has known the facts will probably understand that the problem in the case is whether a statement made to public is an offer. However, if the reader does not know much about the facts, this formulation will fail to work as the question presented to alert the reader; instead, the reader will feel confused, and cannot get it unless read through the whole memorandum. Many times they may lose their curiosity and become impatient.

To avoid this, the question presented should be written more generally by describing the relevant characteristics or relationships of people and events instead of describing them specifically by name, because the reader does not know who or what they are. This type of question is written generally enough to apply to anyone in the position of the person described in the question. For example, the above question would be written, "Does a person make an offer, which binds him, by making a public announcement promising to pay anyone who could present a disqualified product?" This question does not name the parties to the contract but describes their

From: Name of the writer
Re: Short identification of the matter for which the memo was prepared and the file number of the matter
Date: The date when the memo is written

An example of a heading of a legal memorandum looks like this:

MEMORANDUM
To: Scott Brown
From: Mary Jackson
Re: Breach of Contract, *Barnes v. Treece*, File No. 76-001
Date: January 1, 1976

9.6 Questions Presented

One of the most important purposes of a legal memorandum is to resolve a problem, *i.e.*, the issue or question raised before the writer. Thus, before starting to write, the writer must clarify "what is the legal issue in this problem?" Once the issue has been spotted, the writer should identify the issue in the beginning of the legal memorandum to alert the readers to the specific issues to be addressed in the memorandum. This is the section called "Questions Presented." In order to precisely frame the questions in this section, you should avoid stating the issue or issues too broadly or too narrowly. Doing so will not only mislead the readers, but also misrepresent the scope or focus of your analysis and make your discussion less effective. You may recall that "issue" is also an important section in a case brief. In briefing a case, issue is the question presented before the court based on which the court made the decision. Similarly, issue in a legal memorandum is the question presented before the memorandum writer, which needs to be addressed, discussed in the memorandum, and ultimately be resolved by the court. The components of the question presented in a legal memorandum are thus quite similar to the components of an issue in a case brief.

A question presented in a legal memorandum generally contains three parts: the cause of action of the case, the legally significant facts, and the elements of the legal rules that might apply to the problem. Sometimes a that WOW believed that they could still safely hold the wastes for some time. Applying the subjective standard, the polluting event, *i.e.*, tank A's spill, was neither intended, nor expected by WOW. Thus the exception to the pollution exclusion clause contained in Policy-I re-triggers coverage for WOW's cleanup of tank A as well as the medical bills of its employee Nami.

Conclusion

As WOW's insurance policies did not specify whether the liability must be imposed by formal legal action or threat of such, or by a statute which imposed liability, the policies may provide coverage when WOW's cleanup and payment of its employee's medical bills were required under statutes. However, the pollution exclusion clause contained in Policy-II, which did not violate public policy, effectively relieves the insurer from indemnifying WOW for cleanup of tanks B and C. Nevertheless, the exception to the pollution exclusion clause contained in Policy-I re-triggers recovery for cleanup of tank A's spill and WOW's employee Nami's injury because the polluting event — tank A's spill — was not intended or expected by WOW according to the subjective standard.

Therefore, WOW's previous insurance policy — Policy-I may cover $158,417.13 for Nami's medical bills and $500,010 for costs associated with tank A's spill, while the existing policy — Policy-II does not cover $1,500,490 for the cleanup of tanks B and C. I suggest that we tell WOW about the possible result at this stage if they would like to sue EWI.

Consider whether the conclusion of the above memo is convincing and what flows the analysis have, if any. The following sub-sections introduce each element of a legal memorandum individually.

9.5 Heading

A legal memorandum usually begins with a heading with the information of who wrote it, to whom it was written, what it was about, and the date when it was written.

To: Name of the person for whom the memo is written

event was the discharge, dispersal, release, or escape from that place of containment into or upon the land. *Id.* at 79, 882 P. 2d at 719. The waste storage tanks of WOW were believed to contain the wastes before they were drained and removed to toxin disposal center so that the initial deposit to wastes at the tanks were not polluting events within this clause. Instead, the discharge of wastes from tanks B and C upon land following the explosion were the pollution events. Therefore, the pollution exclusion clause in Policy-II bars WOW from recovery of the costs incurring in cleanup of tanks B and C.

III. Whether the exception to the pollution exclusion clause contained in Policy-I re-triggers coverage for WOW's cleanup of tank A and the medical bills of its employee resulting from tank A's spill.

The first part of the pollution exclusion clause in Policy-I is substantially the same as that in Policy-II. It may also effectively bar WOW from recovery if without further exception to it. However, it does contain an exception, which states that coverage may be provided "if such discharge, dispersal, release or escape is sudden and accidental."

The pollution exclusion is aimed at precluding coverage for damage resulting from intentional pollution or pollution which is expected. *Queen City Farms*, 126 Wash. 2d at 87, 882 P. 2d at 723. The language "sudden and accidental" means "unexpected and unintended." *Key Tronic*, 124 Wash. 2d 618, 630, 881 P. 2d 201, 208 (1994). Thus, reading the exclusion and the exception together, a reasonable construction of such policy language is that damage resulting from one of the named polluting events is not covered, unless that polluting event was unexpected and unintended. *Queen City Farms*, 126 Wash. 2d at 92, 882 P. 2d at 726. A subjective test applies to the determination whether the polluting event is expected or intended. *Id.*

Applying these rules to WOW's case, we find that WOW never intentionally polluted the land by discharging its wastes directly into the land. Instead, it established three wastes storage tanks to hold them before they were removed to toxin disposal center. Neither did WOW expect the escape of wastes from its tanks. The reason why WOW did not replace tank A immediately after being informed that there was minor vertical cracking on it was relationship and the relevant characteristics that raise the issue. Even if your readers do not know what happened in the case, they could understand the issue. In summary, if your reader knows the facts, you can formulate the question specifically. But if your reader does not know the facts, you should formulate the question more generally.

The second principle in formulating the question presented is to isolate the specific issue under the cause of action. The question should not be so broadly stated as to encompass many possible issues under the cause of action. For example, "Was a contract formed between Treece and Barnes?" is a poorly conceived question because formation of contract refers to many different legal issues and the question does not specify the relevant one. A question that adequately isolates the issue is, "Was a contract formed between Treece and Barnes when Treece made a public announcement promising to pay to anyone who could find and present a disqualified product and Barnes did find and present such a disqualified product to Treece?"

The third principle in formulating the question presented is to be objective when describing the facts and stating the rule of law. Objectivity is indeed a principle for drafting every section of a legal memorandum because the purpose of the memorandum is to predict how the court will handle the legal problem before the writer. It does not aim to argue or advocate that your client will win the case. Therefore, when you design the question presented, you must describe the factual situation objectively, covering the part favoring your client and the part favoring the opponent. You must also state and analyze the rule of law objectively. If the legal rule has several reasonable interpretations, you should discuss all of these interpretations no matter whether they are favorable to your case or not.

The fourth principle is not to make conclusions in the question presented. The question presented is the section that poses the question to be discussed and resolved by the memorandum, instead of providing answer to the question, which should be contained in the section of brief answers or conclusions. Furthermore, making conclusions here does not necessarily mean to make conclusions to the issue of the memorandum. Sometimes people make conclusions when describing facts and legal principles. For example, if the case law establishes that a contract is formed upon performance by the offeree of a required act contained in a unilateral offer, the following question contains a conclusion: "Is a contract formed if the offeree performed the required act contained in a unilateral offer?" By saying that the statement made by the offeror is a unilateral contractual offer, the writer has made an initial conclusion as to one element of a contract. Based on this conclusion, the writer further concluded that a contract has been formed. The correct way is to ask whether a contract is formed under the specific facts, as in the question, "Is a contract formed when one person made a public announcement promising to pay to anyone who could find and present a disqualified product and the other person did find and present such a disqualified product?"

Other principles in drafting the question presented include keeping the question to a readable length and understandable. There will be a separate section in your memorandum describing the facts, so you do not need to describe everything in the question presented. Instead, you should address only the most relevant facts that raise the issue. A question which is too long will confuse your reader so that your reader will not be able to understand it. Since your memorandum aims to communicate with and convey information to others, it is very important that it is understandable. A question should be as precise and complete as possible without being so complex that your reader cannot understand it. If the case facts are really complex, you may want to summarize them and only include the most relevant facts into your questions presented. When you do this, you have to be very cautious not to distort the facts; and at the same time, must follow the other principles.

9.7 Brief Answers

As the holding in a case brief answers the issue raised before the court, the function of the section of "Brief Answer" in a legal memorandum is to answer the question presented in your client's case and to summarize the reasons for that answer. If there is more than one question presented, you should have a brief answer for each question and number each to correspond to the number of the question it answers. To write this form of answer, you answer the question presented by making a conclusion and adding a sentence that summarizes the reason for your conclusion or adding a necessary qualification to the answer. Normally a brief answer of one or two sentences is sufficient, such as "Yes, a contract is formed if a person made a public announcement promising to pay anyone who could find and present a disqualified product, and another person did find and present such a disqualified product."

We have determined that a question presented must not be conclusive because the function of that section is to pose a question only, therefore only relevant facts and applicable rules governing the cause of action are required. The brief answer, however, should be conclusory since it is an assertion of your answer to the question you have posed. Generally, the format of a brief answer is quite similar to that of a question presented in that it should also include the cause of action, the relevant facts, and the applicable rules of law. Yet the brief answer should be in a form of declaratory statement instead of a question. When drafting the brief answer, avoid discussing any authorities or strengths and weaknesses of your case because those belong to the section of Discussion in the memorandum.

9.8 Statement of Facts

Right after Questions Presented and Brief Answers in your memorandum, you should describe the facts. This section is very important because the rule of precedent and the doctrine of *stare decisis* require precedents be applied to subsequent cases only when they have substantially similar facts. If the facts are materially different, then the precedent is not binding and has no impact on the present case. Before you decide to apply a rule of law, you should first determine what the facts are and whether the facts of your case are substantially similar to the facts of the precedents. The facts of the problem can be the most important determinant of the outcome of a case. Therefore, the essence of legal analysis in your memorandum is to describe the facts of your case and then apply the rule of law to the facts.

What is the fact? A fact is something that happened to someone or to something which causes the problem. If the question presented describes the question directly, the statement of facts introduces the question by telling what happened. This section should include all legally relevant facts, all facts that you mention in the other sections of the memorandum, and any other facts that give necessary background information. It may also include the procedural history of the case if it has already been litigated. In a word, the statement of facts is a formal and objective description of the relevant facts in the problem. It must be accurate and complete, but it should only include the legally relevant facts, not every single piece of facts.

In drafting the statement of facts, the following principles should be followed. First, identify the facts acutely. Don't confuse your readers by stating all of the numerous extraneous facts which are not relevant to the analysis of the case or not necessary to understand and resolve the legal issues. The facts to be included in the Statement of Facts of your memorandum are legally significant facts and key background facts only. The legally significant facts are those that will affect the legal outcome of your client's case. In order to know which facts are relevant, you will need to know what the issue in the problem is, and what rules of law are applicable to resolve the issues. The relevant facts are those that are used to prove or disprove those elements. Therefore, only after you have identified the issues and the relevant law will you acutely spot the facts legally relevant to the case. Legally significant facts tell part of the story, but these facts alone may not tell the whole story. Background facts are often needed to make the factual situation understandable and to put the legally significant facts in context. Background facts are introductions to the parties, the legal problems arising from the disputes, and the procedural history if the case has already been litigated.

Secondly, organize the facts <u>intelligibly</u>. After you have identified the key background information and the legally relevant facts, you should organize them intelligibly and logically so that your readers will better understand the internal relationship among the factors. You should first set up a framework for the problem so that your readers can conceive the rest of the facts within that framework. Since this is the first section in your memorandum that introduces the case problem to your readers by telling them what happened, you should explain to your readers the key background facts, such as, who the parties are, what your client wants, what the problem is about, and then give any other descriptions that are necessary. In doing so, your readers will get a

intelligibly 清晰地

general picture and be prepared for the rest of the facts.

After setting out the background information, you should put the crucial information first, and use the rest of this section to develop the facts. If some facts are similar or have internal relationship, you should group these facts together. The statement of legally significant and key background facts should tell your client's story completely and coherently. Generally, the best and easiest way to develop the events is chronologically, that is, in the order in which the events occurred. This is both easier for the readers to understand and convenient for the writer to write. For some problems, however, a topical organization in which you structure the facts in terms of the elements you need to establish or by the parties involved, if there are many parties, may work better.

You may end the section by stating what relief your client wants, or what you have been asked to analyze in the memo.

Third, describe the facts objectively. Objectivity is the basic principle of drafting through each and every section of a memorandum because the purpose of the memorandum is not to advocate, but to persuade. Therefore, you should describe the complete facts objectively, not only those favorable to your client, but also those unfavorable to your client. If your memorandum is written for a senior attorney, he or she will rely on the statement of facts to make decisions and to prepare other legal documents for the case. If your statement of facts is not objective, the attorney will be misled to believe that your client will have a better position than the opponent. But later on when he or she learns the other part of the story from other sources, the attorney will be surprised and unprepared while handling the case.

Be careful to describe the facts rather than evaluate, analyze, characterize, or argue with them. This section only includes facts instead of any conclusions, legal principles, or any discussions of authorities. You can argue and analyze in the section of Discussion.

9.9 Discussion

Up to this point, the memorandum poses the specific legal question, briefly answers that question, and states the facts of your problem. You have been told not to include any analysis, argument, or advocacy in any sections of a memorandum other than the Discussion section. Now it is time for you to analyze, to argue, to advocate. In this section of Discussion, you will analyze the question by applying the relevant legal principles and their policies to the facts of the case. This analysis provides the reasons for your conclusion about the outcome of your problem. The Discussion section is divided into segments according to the issues and sub-issues presented by the problem. Each segment may be headed by a restatement of the question presented, then followed by the applicable rules of law, application of the rules of law to the facts, and a brief conclusion to that question. The process of analyzing is a process of breaking down a subject into its component parts. The purpose of the Discussion section is to reach a conclusion and predict the outcome of the problem.

Again the Discussion must be objective, thorough, and specific. You should consider all the interpretations possible from applying the law to the facts, not just the interpretations that favor your client. You may argue for your client, but do not ignore any other argument that may be made by the opponent against your client. Always remember that your client needs an objective and realistic outcome, not an unrealistic one favoring him. Sometimes you may find that the facts you have known are not sufficient for you to reach the conclusion; in that case, you should explain in the discussion section which facts you need and why they are relevant.

The four main components of the Discussion section are as follows.

First, the restatement of the issue(s) or subissue(s)

A memorandum may discuss more than one issue, which will be reflected in the "Questions Presented" section of the memorandum. In order to discuss the questions in an organized way, the issues (questions) should be analyzed consecutively. For discussion of each issue, you should first restate the issue so that the reader will know what question you are discussing. If one issue contains subissues, you may want to analyze each sub-issue by identifying them one by one. Without first identifying the issue or subissue, the readers may doubt what your discussion is about.

incidentally found herself talented in fashion designing and decided to try something new. She designed two dresses for her friends as Christmas gifts. To her surprise, these dresses had been well received by her friends, and some other friends of her also asked her to design more for them. Believing that she had the ability and talent, and with enough encouragement from her friends and relatives, she was planning to open her fashion design firm "Karen's Dream." Although her talent had been acknowledged in the small community around her neighborhood and among her friends and relatives, she had to convince fashion stores to buy her work products. Well-established fashion stores would surely help her to gain reputation in this area, but they would be reluctant to accept new beginner's products. Karen planned to spend some money for the initial promotion of her new business. When she was finishing up her last landscaping work for one of her customers, she was told that Professor Eric Scott was going to open a fashion store. Several days later, she read on the newspaper that Professor Scott's fashion store had opened. Thinking that all Professor Scott's former students could be the store's customers, and, that if Professor Scott accepted her design, her work products would be promoted among a potentially wide group of young people, Karen wanted to approach Professor Scott regarding her new business.

Eric Scott:

Having taught international relations in a public university for over 25 years, Eric Scott had been tired of talking more about those useless theories to those stupid students who dreamed of being able to control the whole world some day before they died and be written into the history in some way. He decided to change his life style. After completing a 3-month program for small business starters, Eric had made every preparation to open his own fashion store "Eric's Star." However, the competition was very harsh. To be successful, he must find very good fashion designers supporting his business by attracting more potential customers. But famous fashion designers asked for incredibly high price, and, they normally would not look to small and new fashion stores. Eric had talked to three fashion designers, two of whom had rejected his offer, the last one asked for a very strict condition which Eric thought impossible to accept. So far only three of his

3. Apply the rules of law to the facts of the case in an organized and logic way.

4. Explain and support your conclusions with adequate reasons.

5. Analyze all interpretations before coming to an unqualified conclusion.

6. Objectively state your conclusion to each issue or sub-issue of the case in the end of the discussion.

Conclusion

1. Accurately and clearly answer the question presented.

2. Summarize the analysis in the Discussion Section and briefly apply the controlling law to the facts of your problem.

3. Objectively give your prediction about how the court will resolve the issue.

9.12 Drafting Exercise

The following drafting exercise will conclude this Chapter as well as this Book. Read the material reprinted below and draft a legal memorandum according to its requirements. Note that the following office memorandum is intended to assign work task to the junior assistant, therefore it only describes the information and its format is different from a legal memorandum discussed in this Chapter.

OFFICE MEMORANDUM

To: Junior Assistant
From: Senior Partner
Re: Scott *v*. Litchfield (Breach of Contract);
 File No. 05-132
Date: March 10, 2004

Eric Scott is our client and wants us to sue Karen Litchfield. Read the following information and draft a legal memorandum discussing the possible result of the case.

Background Information

Karen Litchfield:
Karen has been working as a landscaping designer in Freeland, CA for twenty years until recently when she

writing a memorandum.

LEGAL MEMORANDUM

To: Name of the person for whom the memorandum is written
From: Name of the writer of the memorandum
Re: Short identification of the matter for which the memo was prepared and the file number of the matter
Date: The date when the memorandum is written

Question Presented

1. Identify the correct and specific issue.
2. If there is more than one issue, organize the issues in a logical order, which you will adhere to through the memo.
3. The question should incorporate the cause of action, the applicable legal rules, and the legally relevant facts that raise the issue, unless the issue is solely a question of law then the facts are not needed.
4. Be objective.

Brief Answer

1. Accurately and clearly answer the question presented.
2. A brief answer should be in the same format as the question presented, but as a statement instead of a question.
3. No discussion of authorities or analysis should be included here.
4. Be objective.

Statement of Facts

1. Provide the background information and the legally relevant facts of the problem.
2. Organize the facts in a way that is easy to understand, such as chronologically, topically, or chronologically within a topical organization.
3. State the facts accurately and objectively and include the facts that are disfavorable to your client.

Discussion

1. Restate the question or questions presented in the beginning of the discussion.
2. Accurately and objectively state the rules of law.

Question Presented section to see what issues are discussed in this memorandum. Then, if they are very busy, they will first read the Brief Answer to get the prediction of the ultimate result; if they have a little more time, they will read the Conclusion section to get a more detailed picture of the analysis. If they have enough time, or if their interests or curiosity has been aroused by the Brief Answer, they will read the entire memorandum. Although the Conclusion section is longer than the Brief Answer, you should not include citations in that section except in rare instances.

Conclusion should be objective because your readers may rely on the memorandum to make significant decisions. To be objective, you must balance adverse interests. On the one hand, you must take a position, make a judgment, and predict the outcome of the case. You must tell your readers how the court will likely decide the issue. On the other hand, you should point out the weaknesses in your client's position. Unless the situation strongly shows that your client will definitely win or lose the case, you should not mislead your reader by using strong and absolute conclusion in your memorandum. Often, however, your analysis will lead you to conclude that your client's chances of success are best measured in degrees of probability, rather than absolutes. Your task then is to frame your conclusion candidly to reflect these degrees of probability.

It is not uncommon that sometimes you find you cannot confidently reach a conclusion because the law is too uncertain or because the facts are not sufficient. In that situation, you should explain briefly why you cannot reach a conclusion at this stage, why your conclusions are <u>tentative</u>, what the alternatives are, or which additional facts you need. If you have a strong conclusion, you can use "most likely" to express it; while you are certain about a conclusion to certain extent, you can use "probably" to put it; while you are not quite certain about your conclusion, you can begin with "on balance," and so forth. No matter what your conclusion is, you must balance competing considerations in your statement and explain your judgment.

tentative 不确定的

9.11 Summary

Below is a checklist that is helpful when you are

Fourth, the conclusion on each issue or subissue

After your analysis is done by applying the rule of law to the specific facts of your case, you need to reach a conclusion by the end of the analysis of each issue or sub-issue, i.e., to predict the probable outcome of each issue or sub-issue. Without a conclusion to each issue or sub-issue, your reader will not get the points you want to make. If there are more than one issue or subissue in your memorandum, you are advised to make a conclusion on each of them and write the conclusion after the application part. State your conclusion on each issue or subissue objectively and candidly. Note that the conclusion here is only the conclusion to each issue or subissue, which is part of the Discussion section of your memorandum. It is different from the Conclusion section described below.

9.10 Conclusion

The purpose of a legal memorandum is to predict how a court will decide the case and then convey this information to your reader so that your reader can make decision accordingly. The prediction is reflected in the section of Conclusion. This section answers the question presented in the memorandum and then summarizes the reasons for that answer from the Discussion section of the memorandum. The Conclusion section is different from the section of Brief Answer. We have discussed the latter knowing that a brief answer normally takes the form similar to the question presented but in a form of statement. Specifically, the brief answer contains the cause of action, the legally relevant facts, and the rule of law to be applied to the facts. The brief answer is thus very "brief." The conclusion, however, is longer than a brief answer because it contains a more thorough description of the reasoning supporting the ultimate conclusion. For each issue, it briefly describes the relevant law and explains how the law does or does not apply to the facts in this case. The conclusion also differs from the brief answer in that it is not segmented by issues. It concludes all of the questions presented in the memorandum in an internally logical way.

You may think that sections of Brief Answer and the Conclusion somehow overlap and wonder why they cannot be combined into one section. Actually, when your readers read the memorandum, they will first read the

Second, the identification of the rule of law

After you restate the issue and before you start your analysis, you should identify the rule of law which is applicable to the issue. When you describe the applicable rule of law, you must describe it accurately and objectively. Objectivity in describing the applicable law is essential to your credibility. Objectivity is different from accuracy. Accuracy may be achieved when you explain one precedent case completely and thoroughly; however, objectivity may not be achieved if you simply analyze one precedent case while ignoring other relevant authorities which may be unfavorable to your client's case. In order to achieve objectivity, you have to do a thorough legal research and cannot afford to omit any relevant authority.

Where to find the rules of law? As we have learned, in common law countries, both the statutes and case law of a jurisdiction are binding on future litigations within that jurisdiction. If there is a statute governing a specific dispute, you should always identify and explain the rules contained in that statute and the cases interpreting that statute. If there is no statute governing the dispute, case law shall be applied. Explain relevant case law first from the highest court of the jurisdiction and then other reported decisions from that jurisdiction's lower courts. Sometimes, however, there is no applicable statute or case law in the jurisdiction; then the rule of precedent requires that the laws from other jurisdictions which are not binding but persuasive be applied. Principles from the secondary sources may also be cited in your discussion.

Third, the application of the rules of law to the facts

After identifying the issues and the applicable rules of law, you should analyze them to see whether the rules of law can be applied to resolve the problems raised in your case. Again, your application of the rule of law must be objective because the weaknesses of your position will be seen sooner or later, and it is better for that to happen sooner. Even if your description of the law is objective, it does not necessarily mean that your analysis is objective. An objective analysis is one that a reasonable attorney, reading dispassionately, would find to be an accurate and fair explanation of the strengths and weaknesses of your position. An objective analysis is also a complete and thorough analysis, with all of the relevant authorities and all the aspects of the case being considered.

former students had promised to visit his store and all the rest were waiting for his failure, since they hated the course he taught. Despite of all these, Professor Scott had made up his mind. With the help of one of the three students who supported him, he located his new store in the Uptown area of the City of Freeland. Although businessmen and professionals of the City mostly lived in the Downtown area, the rent in the Uptown area was much cheaper than the Downtown area. Having been working as a professor for 25 years, Professor Scott had not made enough money at this moment. He thought he could always move to Downtown when his business earned him enough money.

What Happened

Karen published an advertisement on a local newspaper on February 26, 2004:

New Style! New Start!
Karen's Dream is opening on **March 1, 2004**!
The first one who calls the number below will
get two dresses designed by

KAREN LITCHFIELD
FOR FREE!

Karen's Dream
518 Downtown Road
Freeland, CA 37210
Tel: (317) 372-3732

Professor Scott was happy when he read this ad. Although he did not know who Karen Litchfield was, but two free dresses could bring some bright light to his new store. If the free dresses could be sold at a good price, he may be able to get a contract from the fashion designer! Good deal! He woke up very early on March 1 and made the first call to Karen's Dream. Karen's secretary Rosy congratulated him on the phone and said that the two dresses would be delivered to Eric's addresses in two weeks. Eric asked whether he could talk to Ms. Karen Litchfield regarding further business cooperation, Rosy told him that she would pass the passage on to Karen and would call him back.

Karen called Eric that noon. After self-introduction,

the two quickly started discussing about potential business cooperation. Karen said she actually heard of Professor Scott from one of her landscaping customers and would be happy to work with him. Karen would also like to visit Eric's Star to investigate the potential customers so that she could design clothes suitable for them. Both were straightforward and Eric invited Karen to visit his store right away.

At about 2 p.m. that afternoon, Karen drove across the city from Downtown to Uptown to visit Eric's Star, noticing that there were fewer nice buildings around the area. She parked her car in front of the store and Eric came to greet her. Although the neighborhood did not look very nice, the store was decorated quite impressively. When Karen entered the room, the first thing she saw was a huge globe that Professor Scott once used in his class. The store was small but cute. There were scriptures all around the walls, with words and pictures. Eric told Karen that those were all stories about the international relations. Karen was greatly impressed. Eric and Karen sat at a table at the corner of the store and started a discussion. Both were eager to do their new business, so they quickly went to the point.

Eric said he would like to order 5 dresses and 5 sports suits for his store. He asked how much Karen would ask. Karen was excited hearing that Eric was placing an order on her. This would be the first order after her store has opened. For a moment, she had no idea how much she should ask. When she calmed down, she asked when Eric would like them to be delivered. Eric said as soon as possible. Actually Karen had 3 dresses and 4 sports suit on hand, she needed to design and make 2 more dresses and 1 more sports suit. Karen then asked $50 for each.

Eric said the price was surprisingly high, and he could pay this price to buy fashion clothes from other famous designers in this City. Having learned many negotiation skills from the international relations research and study, he decided to use them. He said he would not pay more than $35 each. Karen never negotiated with other people before, now she felt offended because she thought her designs worth that price. However, she did not want to lose this business. After all, this is the first order she would get. So she said: "No less than $45 each, no bargain. I would give you two days to decide. If I do not hear from you within two days, the deal is off." Eric would not give up so easily, he said: "No way! You are robbing me. Give me a call when you change your mind." Then he saw Karen off.

Right after Karen returned back from Eric's Star, she received a phone call from a manager of Empire, the biggest franchising department store in Freeland. Empire had ordered 2,000 pieces of dresses from different fashion designers in the State for the 2004 Freeland Show which would start on March 3, 2004. Unexpectedly, there was a short of 3 dresses and 4 sports suit. They must be delivered by 5 p.m. of March 2, 2004. Empire had contacted all designers they knew, but none of them had stock or could satisfy the order within so short a time. The manager was one of Karen's former landscaping customers and suddenly thought of Karen. The manager told Karen she would get $80 for each dress/suit. Karen did not hesitate at all and agreed to the deal. Karen delivered them to Empire on March 2.

When Karen went to the Empire to execute the contract and to deliver the dresses and suits, Karen's secretary Rosy received a phone call from Eric. Eric asked Rosy to tell Karen that he would like to accept Karen's offer, to order 5 dresses and 5 suits at $45 each, and asked Karen to call him back when she returned.

On March 3, the 2004 Freeland Show started. Karen was invited to attend it. She was excited to see that the clothes she designed were among those designed by famous designers. On her way back from Empire, Karen thought of Eric, she decided to visit his store again telling him that she did not have anything to sell now. When she arrived at the Eric's Star, it was almost 6:30 p.m. and it started to become dark and there were fewer people on the street. It seemed that the store had closed. Seeing the light from Eric's Star, Karen parked her car at the same place she parked last time. When she just came out of the car, two teenagers came from nowhere, hit her on her chest and robbed her purse, a third guy forced to open the car and drove it away. Karen was shocked, everything happened in one second. She ran to Eric's Star, knocked at the door. Eric opened the door, seeing Karen, the first thing he asked was: "How's the deal?" Karen said "the deal is off, but would you please help me ... I was robbed in front of your store ..."

The international relations professor looked at her for a while, said: "Well, if the deal is off, I am going to sue you for breach, you liar! Good luck." And then he closed his door. Karen shouted: "Eric, please, call 911 for me, thanks..." But nothing happened. Karen was so upset and she had to walk a long way to a bus stop. The bus driver was kind enough to let her in without charging her.

Eric now wants to sue Karen for delivering the five dresses and five sports suits, as well as the two free dresses. Please write a memorandum discussing the case.

Review Questions

1. Why is objectivity so important for drafting memos?
2. What is the difference between drafting a case brief and a legal memo?
3. Draft the memo based on the facts printed in section 9.12.

REFERENCES

PART I

ROBERT C. BECKMAN, CASE ANALYSIS AND STATUTORY INTERPRETATION CASES AND MATERIALS (Nat'l Univ. of S'pore 1998).

ZHONGCHENG CHEN, A SELECTION FROM LEGAL LITERATURE IN ENGLISH (Shanghai Translation Publishing Co. 1987).

JOHN C. DERNBACH, RICHARD V. SINGLETON II, CATHLEEN S. WHARTON & JOAN M. RUHTENBERG, A PRACTICAL GUIDE TO LEGAL WRITING & LEGAL METHOD (2d Ed., Rothman & Co. 1994).

DOUGLAS LAYCOCK, MODERN AMERICAN REMEDIES CASES AND MATERIALS (2d Ed., Aspen Publishers, Inc. 1994).

THOMAS A. MAUET, FUNDAMENTALS OF TRIAL TECHNIQUES (Little, Brown & Co. 1992).

JAN MC CORMICK — WATSON, ESSENTIAL ENGLISH LEGAL SYSTEM (2d Ed., Wuhan University Publishing House 2004).

WILLIAM L. REYNOLDS, JUDICIAL PROCESS (3d Ed. Law Press China 2004).

HELENE S. SHAPO, MARILYN R. WALTER & ELIZABETH FAJANS, WRITING AND ANALYSIS IN THE LAW (3d Ed., Foundation Press 1995).

MICHAEL H. WHINCUP, CONTRACT LAW AND PRACTICE, THE ENGLISH SYSTEM AND CONTINENTAL COMPARISONS (3d Ed., Kluwer Law International 1996).

CHRISTOPHER G. WREN & JILL ROBINSON WREN, THE LEGAL RESEARCH MANUAL (Adams & Ambrose Publishing 1986).

STEPHEN C. YEAZELL, CIVIL PROCEDURE (5th Ed. Aspen Law & Business 2000).

PART II

ROBERT C. BECKMAN, CASE ANALYSIS AND STATUTORY INTERPRETATION CASES AND MATERIALS (Nat'l Univ. of S'pore 1998).

DAVID S. CLARK & TUGRUL ANSAY, INTRODUCTION TO THE LAW OF THE UNITED STATES (2d Ed., Citic Publishing House 2003).

JOHN C. DERNBACH, RICHARD V. SINGLETON II, CATHLEEN S. WHARTON & JOAN M. RUHTENBERG, A PRACTICAL GUIDE TO LEGAL WRITING & LEGAL METHOD (2d Ed., Rothman & Co. 1994).

WILLIAM L. REYNOLDS, JUDICIAL PROCESS (3d Ed. Law Press China 2004).

HELENE S. SHAPO, MARILYN R. WALTER & ELIZABETH FAJANS, WRITING AND ANALYSIS IN THE LAW (3d Ed., Foundation Press 1995).

MICHAEL H. WHINCUP, CONTRACT LAW AND PRACTICE, THE ENGLISH SYSTEM AND CONTINENTAL COMPARISONS (3d Ed., Kluwer Law International 1996).

CHRISTOPHER G. WREN & JILL ROBINSON WREN, THE LEGAL RESEARCH MANUAL (Adams & Ambrose Publishing 1986).

PART III

Robert C. Beckman, Case Analysis and Statutory Interpretation Cases and Materials (Nat'l Univ. of S'pore 1998).

John C. Dernbach, Richard V. Singleton II, Cathleen S. Wharton & Joan M. Ruhtenberg, A Practical Guide to Legal Writing & Legal Method (2d Ed., Rothman & Co. 1994).

M. H. Sam Jacobson, Supplemental Materials for Legal Research & Writing (Willamette Uni. College of Law, Fall 1999) (unpublished manuscript, on file with the author).

Helene S. Shapo, Marilyn R. Walter & Elizabeth Fajans, Writing and Analysis in the Law (3d Ed., Foundation Press 1995).

PART IV

John C. Dernbach, Richard V. Singleton II, Cathleen S. Wharton & Joan M. Ruhtenberg, A Practical Guide to Legal Writing & Legal Method (2d Ed., Rothman & Co. 1994).

Helene S. Shapo, Marilyn R. Walter & Elizabeth Fajans, Writing and Analysis in the Law (3d Ed., Foundation Press 1995).

图书在版编目(CIP)数据

英美法判例读写教程:英文/高凌云编著.—上海:复旦大学出版社,2019.7(2021.12重印)
(复旦博学.法学系列)
ISBN 978-7-309-14390-4

Ⅰ.①英… Ⅱ.①高… Ⅲ.①英美法系-高等学校-教材-英文 Ⅳ.①D904.6

中国版本图书馆 CIP 数据核字(2019)第 108405 号

英美法判例读写教程
高凌云 编著
责任编辑/张 炼

复旦大学出版社有限公司出版发行
上海市国权路 579 号 邮编:200433
网址:fupnet@fudanpress.com http://www.fudanpress.com
门市零售:86-21-65102580 团体订购:86-21-65104505
出版部电话:86-21-65642845
上海华业装潢印刷厂有限公司

开本 787×1092 1/16 印张 16.75 字数 447 千
2021 年 12 月第 1 版第 2 次印刷

ISBN 978-7-309-14390-4/D·987
定价:49.00 元

如有印装质量问题,请向复旦大学出版社有限公司出版部调换。
版权所有 侵权必究